ONTRACK
MILITARY EDITION

OnTrack Devotions: Military Edition

Credits
Author: Dwight E. Peterson
Executive Developers: Benjamin J. Wilhite, Timothy R. Morris (SGT, USMC)
Development Team: Chaplain John B. Murdoch, James E. May (COL-R, US
Army), James May (CAPT, US Army), Danielle Wright (SPC, US Army)
Graphic Design: Lance Young (higherrockcreative.com)

READING SCHEDULE

January	Luke
February	1 & 2 Corinthians
March	Galatians to Colossians
April	Matthew
May	Acts
June	Revelation
July	1 Thessalonians to Philemon
August	1 Peter to Jude
September	John
October	Romans
November	Mark
December	Hebrews & James

**This resource was designed so you can begin on any day of the calendar year and work through the entire New Testament over the course of 12 months. The reading schedule rotates through different components of the New Testament to give you variety and a broader sense of context from month to month.

★ ENDORSMENT ★

>>> Why MOTD is so valuable, from a retired chaplain that labored with us to develop it.

I am pleased to recommend Military OnTrack Devotions (OTD) Bible study series as a practical tool to develop a sincere study of God's Word. This month by month study, developed by a former Marine, guides the reader into a thoughtful meditation from selected scriptures. Through provocative questions and stimulating comments the reader is then led through a process of interpretation and application of the text. OnTrack Devotions materials are superb Biblical accompaniments to develop spiritual growth in the committed Christian.

This OTD series is a perfect devotional study that adapts to the high OPTEMPO lives of today's military personnel. The presentations are efficient and to the point. They deal with substantive issues and are always true to the Word. The military experience as a former Marine gives keen insight into what works best for the man or woman in uniform. OTD encourages and requires the same kind of disciplined attention to spiritual duty as the armed services require of their military personnel in order to produce Christian soldiers trained to do battle with the spiritual enemy.

Military OTD was conceived out of a heart of love and passion for the Soldier, Sailor, Airman or Marine who wants to get serious about a routine of daily devotions. I recommend the Military OTD's insightful studies as means to further one's knowledge of the Bible and develop spiritual maturity. Our prayers are asking the Lord to use these Bible study guides to touch the lives of those courageous men and women who wear the uniform of our country in order to protect and defend us. May God bless them and protect them.

James E. May
Chaplain (COL-R, US Army)

★ ACKNOWLEDGEMENTS ★

This OnTrack Military Edition devotional set is the product of countless hours of work by a development team dedicated to investing their gifts and experience to help unlock the Word of God for our military personnel. We cannot repay the debt we owe you for serving this country, but we can thank you with what we are able to produce because we are free. As such, the following are a few of the many that took part in this endevour:

Dwight E. Peterson, Author
Timothy R. Morris (SGT, USMC)
Chaplain John B. Murdoch, Director of Regular Baptist Chaplaincy Ministries
James E. May (COL-R, US Army)
James May - Former Chaplain (CPT, US Army)
Danielle Wright (SPC, US Army)
Lance Young (Graphic Design, Layout)

Like the design and layout? See Lance's portfolio online at
HIGHERROCKCREATIVE.COM..

Some of the hardest periods in my life to be a Christian was the time I spent in the military. Sure I was in Iraq, amongst many other places, but the hardest part was when we were not in combat. It was in the down time and in garrison, the time that gave us the freedom to put our money and our time where WE wanted to. I know there may not be too much of that for you right now, but there is a little, however small it may be.

I also found it to be easy to be a Christian at times in the military. When I made a stand on something, the men around me expected me to keep my word. It would have spoken much more to them if they heard me say one thing and observed me doing another. They wanted to know that if I was saying, "I will have your back," they could count on it.

When I was in the infantry, I thought I was the only one who had this challenge. I have since learned otherwise. It seems that all service members deal with similar situations. I am not the only one who struggled living out their faith in the military. That is a big reason this devotional project is so personal for me. Read it and allow it to guide your interaction with the Word of God. Keep in mind, if you feel at times as if you are the only one left in the military who is a Christian, that you are not alone. You can serve your God and your Country honorably at the same time. Wherever you are, BE SAFE and THANK YOU for continually protecting our freedom. I appreciate it.

Timothy R. Morris (SGT, USMC)
Editing for Military OnTrack Devotions

Timothy R. Morris (front right) with guys from 2/2 Fox at Camp Lejeune the day before deployment.

This devotional guide is designed to both take you on a journey of a book-by-book study through the New Testament and to help you develop your own personal Bible study skills through daily reading in God's Word. Whether you're an Enlisted or Officer rank, whether this is your first time reading the Bible or you have read it for years, whether you are a new Christian or one who has been saved and in the Word for a long time, OnTrack will meet you where you are at.

Here's a quick overview of this resource and how to use it:

Monthly Activities: Each month begins with two activity pages that will help you connect your Bible study to other things God is doing in your life. The first page is the Prayer Sheet which focuses on your relationships and your specific prayer requests. The second is the Commitment Sheet which allows you to set some targets for spiritual growth planning each month. While these are great on their own, they are more powerful in an accountability or small group setting.

Daily Devotional Pages: Each daily devo page walks through the same process of reading and interaction designed to help you build both Bible study skill and discipline your approach to Scripture. Some days have a little more "help" in the question element, while others stretch you to design your own questions from the text.

Step 1: Read the passage of Scripture in the header bar. Always start with what God says, not what the author says!

Step 2: Read the devotional thought on the outside pane of the page. It will help frame your mind toward the interactive questions.

Step 3: Interact with the questions. MOTD uses four questions to help you dig into the Scripture...

Say What? (Observation): Who, what, when, where, why and how are the key questions. The goal is to wrap your mind around what is being said to whom... Context is key!

So What? (Interpretation): This is where you begin to evaluate the main ideas of the passage and sort out the key principles it addresses. God put the passage there for a reason. What do you think it is?

Now What? (Application): Once you sort out key principles, figure out how they apply to your life. What do they look like in your skin? What is happening in your life that those principles speak to?

Then What? (Strategy) This is the kicker. What are you going to do about what you learned from the text? It's commitment time.

Start From Point A: We are all at different points in our walk with God and with our skill in reading His Word. That's a good thing! If you are just starting out or if you still need to stretch to get through all of the questions, that's great. Do as much as you can. Write down or mark the questions that stump you. Ask a friend for some input or march on over to the chaplain and get some insight. Better yet, get involved with a small group that meets regularly to discuss the Bible and bounce your questions around there. Anything worth doing takes a bit of work.

MILITARY
OTD

THE BOOK OF
LUKE

JANUARY
★★★★

★ MONTHLY ★
PRAYER SHEET

I NEED TO REACH OUT TO...	HOW I WILL DO IT...	HOW IT WENT...

OTHER REQUEST	HOW ANSWERED	DATE

MONTHLY
MISSION SHEET

⫸ Share your personal commitments with those who will help keep you accountable to them.

⫸ **NAME:** ....

This sheet is designed to help you make personal commitments each month that will help you grow in your walk with God. Fill it out by determining:

★ What will push you.
★ What you think you can achieve.

⫸ **PERSONAL DEVOTIONS:**
I will commit to read the OnTrack Bible passage and devotional thought .... day(s) each week this month.

⫸ **CHURCH/CHAPEL ATTENDANCE:**
I will attend Church/Chapel .... time(s) this month.
I will attend .... time(s) this month.

⫸ **SCRIPTURE MEMORY:**
I will memorize .... key verse(s) from the daily OnTrack Devotions this month.

⫸ **OUTREACH:**
I will share Christ with .... person/people this month.
I will serve my local church/chapel this month by ....
....
....

⫸ **OTHER ACTIVITIES:**
List any other opportunities such as events, prayer group, etc..., you will participate in this month. ....
....
....
....
....
....

Determine to begin today a journey that will last a lifetime, and will change your life forever.

LEAPED FOR JOY

As you read this passage, was there anything notable which caught your attention? There is so much in this passage that is significant, one could easily miss a few words which hold great importance as we consider issues that face us today. Notice the words found in verse 41. Did you understand their significance? They are in the line, the baby leaped in her womb. From the womb of Elizabeth, a child, John the Baptist, responded to the presence of the baby in the womb of Mary - the Lord Jesus Christ. Why is this important? Because the child in her womb was not just a mass of tissue who had no feelings; he was a living human being that even in the womb could respond to God. In short, he was a baby. This passage clearly supports our position that abortion is wrong because it is the taking of a human life.... a life, though not fully developed, which can respond to what is happening around him and even to who God is. This line of Scripture confirms what we as Christians believe to be true about abortion and one we can use to defend our position to others. Write down this reference and keep it on hand so that you can use it with others in your world.

LUKE 1:41

And when Elizabeth heard the greeting of Mary, the baby leaped in her womb. And Elizabeth was filled with the Holy Spirit,

SAY WHAT?
Observation: What do I see?

SO WHAT?
Interpretation: What does it mean?

NOW WHAT?
Application: How does it apply to me?

THEN WHAT?
Implementation: What do I do?

PREPARATION

SAY WHAT?
Observation: What do I see?

SO WHAT?
Interpretation: What does it mean?

NOW WHAT?
Application: How does it apply to me?

THEN WHAT?
Implementation: What do I do?

Why would God want John the Baptist to live in the desert before he began his public ministry to Israel? Could it be that God knew the ministry for which He had called him was going to be difficult, and God knew he needed that time in the desert to be ready for it? We often dismiss the importance of preparation. We do not seem to realize what it takes to be able to influence people and serve in a public ministry. We do not understand the temptations and pressures that come with being someone who is having a great impact for God. Throughout Scripture, we see that God prepared people for the work He had for them. He knew what their future held, and He knew what was needed to get them ready. Even the Apostle Paul took over two years to prepare before he began his public ministry. What are you doing to prepare yourself for what God might call you to do in your future? If you feel God is calling you to a ministry that will have you in front of people, use these days to prepare yourself for the future. Are you allowing God to mold you as you pursue your activities today for a responsibility He has for your future?

LUKE 1:80
And the child grew and became strong in spirit, and he was in the wilderness until the day of his public appearance to Israel.

THE MIRACULOUS

What do you suppose it was like being a shepherd 2,000 years ago? Think about it - imagine you are one. You are out in the fields tending sheep just like every other night. You and your fellow shepherds are sitting around the fire talking and laughing like you have always done. You are not anticipating anything dramatic to happen in your life. Unexpected terror fills your heart when the sky lights up and you realize an angel is speaking to you. You barely comprehend the news. You hear him say that a Savior has been born in Bethlehem. The sky is instantly filled with a host of angels glorifying God. What would you do? Would you take some time in the next couple of days to write it in your journal? NO WAY! You would run to see the child and tell whomever you saw what happened, just as the shepherds did. We Christians often see God perform the miraculous in our worlds, yet barely respond to it. We don't take the time to share with others what God has done or even praise Him with hearts full of joy. In what ways are you responding to what God is doing in your life? How is that impacting your world?

★★★★

LUKE 2:15

When the angels went away from them into heaven, the shepherds said to one another, "Let us go over to Bethlehem and see this thing that has happened, which the Lord has made known to us."

SAY WHAT?

In the past three months, what significant events have been propelled into your world and into your life?

SO WHAT?

How did you respond to those events?

NOW WHAT?

What does your response tell you about yourself?

THEN WHAT?

What testimony can you give of what God has done in your life lately? To whom can you give it?

COST OF OBEDIENCE

SAY WHAT?
Observation: What do I see?

SO WHAT?
Interpretation: What does it mean?

NOW WHAT?
Application: How does it apply to me?

THEN WHAT?
Implementation: What do I do?

In today's reading, we find one of those phrases that can be overlooked, causing us to miss some very important insights - Insight into the day to day lives of the characters of Scripture. Look in verse 23 and see if you can find it. This verse confirms that the local people thought Jesus' father was Joseph. They knew that Mary had gotten pregnant before she had actually married Joseph. Jesus had been born, and they believed Joseph was the father. Not only did that make Mary look bad, but it also damaged Joseph's reputation. Can you imagine how Joseph felt knowing people believed something about him which was not true? Imagine the kinds of things people said about Joseph to Jesus as He was growing up. We know that Mary and Joseph were examples of great faith. They were people who were willing to follow Christ and to do what was right, even if it meant being ridiculed and insulted. Could you demonstrate such faith in discouraging circumstances? Would you obey if it cost you the same price it cost Mary and Joseph? How can you become someone who is so committed to Christ that what others think does not affect your obedience?

★★★★

LUKE 3:23
Jesus, when he began his ministry, was about thirty years of age, being the son (as was supposed) of Joseph, the son of Heli,

The book of Proverbs was designed to help us in "attaining wisdom and discipline; in understanding words of insight; in acquiring a disciplined and prudent life, doing what is right and just and fair; in giving prudence to the simple, knowledge and discretion to the young." As you read through this chapter, write down the verses that are most significant to you in your present circumstances.

VERSE | WHAT TRUTH IT COMMUNICATES | HOW IT IMPACTS MY LIFE

OPPORTUNE TIME

SAY WHAT?

When do you seem to be most open to Satan's temptation?

SO WHAT?

Why is that an "opportune time?"

NOW WHAT?

How can you prepare yourself to resist Satan's temptations?

THEN WHAT?

What Scripture verses can you arm yourself with?

According to verse thirteen, when did Satan plan to next tempt Christ? Does that information reveal anything to us about Satan which can help us resist temptation? As you read through this account of Christ's temptation, what made it an opportune time? Satan tempted Christ when he thought He was the weakest. Christ had not eaten for 40 days so he tempted him with food. Although the passage reveals Satan had been tempting Him all along, vs 2 tells us that when Jesus became hungry, Satan had the opportunity to attack Him with physical temptation. Satan knows an "opportune time" occurs when we are weary and weak. He then attacks us in an area of greatest weakness. If we feel no one loves or cares about us, he brings a relationship into our lives that seems to fulfill that need, but one that will ultimately harm us. If we are tired, he brings frustrations that end in anger and hurtful words. But Christ, being tired and hungry, did not give in to temptation. He depended upon the Holy Spirit to sustain Him. He was prepared to use the Bible to fight the attacks. What can you do to be ready to resist in your moment of weakness?

★★★★

LUKE 4:13

And when the devil had ended every temptation, he departed from him until an opportune time.

IMPORTANCE OF PRAYER

As you read through this chapter, circle the character qualities of Christ that you observe. Which ones impressed you the most? Consider what we find in verse 16? Jesus was a man who had many demands on His time and emotions. People constantly wanted to talk to Him. Every time He spoke, they hung on each word. He was never alone regardless of the time or occasion. People always followed him, wanting something. That kind of life must have brought Him immense pressure,and keeping up with the demands must have been difficult. In light of the demands, He was careful not to neglect His source of strength. What was it? - withdrawing and spending time in prayer "often." It was vital to His life and He made sure that His priority was to get away alone where He could pray uninterrupted. No matter His schedule or demands,He was never too busy to pray. How do your priorities compare? If Jesus Christ made sure He spent time in prayer, how critical is it then for you? Do not allow your schedule today to keep you from finding time alone for prayer. Prayer needs to be a vital part of every mature believer's life.

LUKE 5:16
But he would withdraw to desolate places and pray.

SAY WHAT?
Observation: What do I see?

SO WHAT?
Interpretation: What does it mean?

NOW WHAT?
Application: How does it apply to me?

THEN WHAT?
Implementation: What do I do?

SAY WHAT?

How can you show love to someone who is mistreating you?

SO WHAT?

How can you do good to someone who hates you?

NOW WHAT?

What positive things can you say about those who curse you?

THEN WHAT?

How can you pray for those who are mistreating you?

What are the four ways we are to respond to the ungrateful and the wicked found verses 27-28? Number them in your Bible. Did you notice that in each case Christ asks us to respond with mercy,the opposite of how we are treated. Some hate us, yet we are to do good to them. Some curse us, yet we are to respond with kind words to them and about them. They mistreat us, yet we pray for them. Christ gives us practical examples of just what He expects of us in verses 29-36. He tells us that it is no credit to us if we love those who treat us with consideration and kindness,but it speaks volumes about us to love those who treat us wrongly. Can you think of someone that you have had situations with due to their mistreating you,one who hates or curses at you that needs you to respond in the way Christ asks in these verses? Try to think of some ways you can demonstrate the godly character required of us which is found in this passage. Ask God to give you the strength today to demonstrate the difference Christ has made in the way you treat others. Be merciful, just as your Father is merciful. The world will notice.

★★★★

LUKE 6:27-28

"But I say to you who hear, Love your enemies,do good to those who hate you,bless those who curse you, pray for those who abuse you.

AMAZING FAITH

According to verse nine, what was it about the Centurion that impressed Jesus? What did he demonstrate to Jesus? A Centurion was a Roman army officer who was in charge of 100 men. This man was a high ranking officer in the Roman army. According to this passage, he really cared about the people around him. His actions, found in verse three, were motivated by love for his servant. Even the Jewish elders encouraged Jesus to heal the servant in spite of the fact that this man was a hated Roman soldier. He treated the Jews with kindness and had even built their synagogue. In spite of his position and all he had done, the truly amazing thing was that the Centurion did not feel worthy to have Christ come to his house. He knew that in the same way his presence was not necessary for his soldiers to follow his orders, Jesus could order the servant to be healed without being there. Jesus needed only to speak the word. So he humbly asked Christ to do just that. Do you have that kind of confidence in God? Do you believe that He needs only to speak the word? Ask God to give you this kind of faith, then trust Him to meet your needs.

LUKE 7:9

When Jesus heard these things, he marveled at him, and turning to the crowd that followed him, said, "I tell you, not even in Israel have I found such faith."

SAY WHAT?
Observation: What do I see?

SO WHAT?
Interpretation: What does it mean?

NOW WHAT?
Application: How does it apply to me?

THEN WHAT?
Implementation: What do I do?

MILITARYDEVOTIONAL.COM
🐦 @MILITARYDEVOS

SEEING WHO GOD IS

SAY WHAT?
Observation: What do I see?

SO WHAT?
Interpretation: What does it mean?

NOW WHAT?
Application: How does it apply to me?

THEN WHAT?
Implementation: What do I do?

How many different miracles did Jesus do in this chapter? Number them in your Bible. Next to each miracle, write what it reveals about Jesus Christ and what conclusion one could come to by observing it. It is beyond comprehension that so many people saw Jesus perform miracles on a daily basis, yet still not receive Him as Lord. He demonstrated His power over nature; He demonstrated His power over the forces of hell. He demonstrated His power over the human body and even power over death. It would sure seem that after witnessing all His power, the only conclusion you could come to is that Jesus is God. Many did not, and unfortunately people today are just as blind. Christians see God do the miraculous all around them, yet still doubt He can meet their immediate needs. The unsaved see the transformed lives of people who have trusted Christ, yet they refuse to humble themselves before Him. Have you witnessed what God has done for others and even in your own life without allowing it to impact your faith? Ask God to open your eyes in a fresh way to what He is doing and who He really is.

LUKE 8:25
He said to them, "Where is your faith?" And they were afraid, and they marveled, saying to one another, "Who then is this, that he commands even winds and water, and they obey him?"

WHAT GOOD IS IT?

Have you ever worked really hard to acquire something, then after you were successful, you felt as if the effort you put into getting it was not worth it? For example, you saved enough money to buy a car you really wanted, and after you bought it you found that you didn't like it as much as you thought you would. Maybe you made sacrifices and worked hard to receive an award and after winning it you realized the effort expended to achieve it was not worth it. If so, you can imagine what it would be like to work your whole life for something that, when you got it, seemed insignificant. That is the point Jesus made to the disciples in verses 23-27. In verse 25, He asked a question to illustrate His point. You can be the richest man in the world and still die with nothing. You can be famous yet have nothing. To pursue what the world is offering will bring sorrow to your life. What good is it to gain emptiness and lose your soul? Christ wants us to make Him our priority. When we do, we may not gain the whole world, but we will surely gain our souls. Underline verse 25 as a reminder to pursue righteousness and not the emptiness that this world has to offer.

LUKE 9:25

For what does it profit a man if he gains the whole world and loses or forfeits himself?

SAY WHAT?

What are most people striving to gain?

SO WHAT?

How can you tell if you are striving to gain the world or righteousness?

NOW WHAT?

How can you insure that what you are striving for is really important?

THEN WHAT?

What can you do to avoid gaining the world, thereby losing your soul?

The book of Proverbs was designed to help us in "attaining wisdom and discipline; in understanding words of insight; in acquiring a disciplined and prudent life, doing what is right and just and fair; in giving prudence to the simple, knowledge and discretion to the young." As you read through this chapter, write down the verses that are most significant to you in your present circumstances.

VERSE | WHAT TRUTH IT COMMUNICATES | HOW IT IMPACTS MY LIFE

BECOMING GREAT!

If you were to compile a list of qualities that make someone great, what would be on your list? How does your list compare to what Christ said in verses 46-48 of this chapter? Christ tells us that one quality that certainly needs to be on our list is "concern for others." In fact, not only is it important that we care for others, it is also important who we are reaching out to. It is not only about what you do, but who you are doing it for. We often care for those who will care back. We do not usually have a problem reaching out to the popular people or to those who will give us recognition or repayment. In this account, Jesus said that if you want to be great in His kingdom, you must demonstrate concern to all people - concern for children, the poor, the drug addict, the girl considering an abortion, your teacher, your little brother, your parents... You get the point. Based on this measuring stick, how great are you? Will you be one of the greatest in the kingdom, or one of the least? How and to whom can you show true greatness today? Strive to be the least among us. There are certainly enough people who already think they are the greatest.

SAY WHAT?
Observation: What do I see?

SO WHAT?
Interpretation: What does it mean?

NOW WHAT?
Application: How does it apply to me?

THEN WHAT?
Implementation: What do I do?

LUKE 9:48

...and said to them, "Whoever receives this child in my name receives me, and whoever receives me receives him who sent me. For he who is least among you all is the one who is great."

SAY WHAT?

What kinds of things can distract you from your walk with Christ?

SO WHAT?

Why is it so easy for them to distract you from your spiritual walk?

NOW WHAT?

How can you prevent those distractions from diverting you?

THEN WHAT?

What personal commitment will you make in light of this passage?

As you read today's passage, what do you see as the differences between Mary and Martha? If you asked both of them to name the most important thing in life, would you receive the same answer? Martha, like so many people, is overly concerned about all the work she has to do. She opened her home to guests, and spent her time getting ready and making them feel welcome. She was so caught up in her work that, although Jesus Christ was in her house, she was too busy to spend time with Him. Mary, on the other hand, was with Jesus the whole time instead of getting caught up in the work that had to be done. She didn't allow busyness to keep her from what she valued the most. Jesus' answer to Martha's concern ought to be a phrase we use when we find ourselves living so fast-paced that we neglect what should be our priority: our time with God. "Martha, Martha.... you are worried and upset about many things, but only one thing is needed." What can you do to remind yourself what is truly important? How can you be sure to not allow your busy schedule to hinder you from spending time with Jesus.

★★★★

LUKE 10:41

But the Lord answered her, "Martha, Martha, you are anxious and troubled about many things,

TEACH US TO PRAY

What question did one of Jesus' disciples ask that resulted in His discussion of prayer? You will find it in verse one. It is interesting to note that the disciple did not ask Jesus to teach them how to pray, but they asked Him to teach them to pray. Jesus' answer then, was not given to be the prayer they were to use, but given as a motivation which would cause them to pray. The story that followed was also intended to motivate us to pray. The point of Jesus' story was if a friend were to give bread because of incessant pounding on his door and not because of real concern, how much more can we expect from God who loves us enough to die for us? This story does not illustrate that God responds to us because we keep pounding on His door, or because He grows tired of our asking. It shows that if this kind of man responded out of frustration, how much more will God respond because He is our Father. We ought to be motivated to pray because of the One to whom we pray. We are not going to a neighbor to wake him up. We are talking to our Father who loves us and wants to meet our needs. Keep that in mind when you pray today.

★★★★

LUKE 11:1

Now Jesus was praying in a certain place, and when he finished, one of his disciples said to him, "Lord, teach us to pray, as John taught his disciples."

SAY WHAT?

Observation: What do I see?

SO WHAT?

Interpretation: What does it mean?

NOW WHAT?

Application: How does it apply to me?

THEN WHAT?

Implementation: What do I do?

MILITARYDEVOTIONAL.COM
🐦 @MILITARYDEVOS

SAY WHAT?

What things are you "worried" about today?

SO WHAT?

What are you concerned the outcome could be?

NOW WHAT?

Write a prayer below expressing to God your desire to trust Him.

THEN WHAT?

What commitment will you make this week based on this passage?

What is the definition of worry? Webster's dictionary says it is "mental distress or agitation resulting from concern for something impending or anticipated." Christ tells His disciples that they are not to worry. They are not to become upset about what appears to be inevitable or what may possibly happen. Philippians 4:6 says the same thing with additional emphasis on the word "anything." "Do not be anxious about anything." Why? Worry demonstrates concern for a future event or circumstance in which we have no idea whether the outcome will be positive or negative. If we assume the outcome is positive, we do not worry. In reality, when we worry, we are doubting God. We demonstrate our lack of confidence in His complete control. We cannot rest in his care. What we know in our heads does not affect our hearts. How much we worry is in direct proportion to how much we trust God. Christ further illustrates this with birds and flowers. If God concerns Himself with them,He is surely able to take care of you. To worry is to tell God you don't trust Him. Don't you think it is time to stop worrying?

LUKE 12:26

If then you are not able to do as small a thing as that, why are you anxious about the rest?

NARROW WAY

How does Jesus describe the way of salvation in verse 24? Why do you think He called it a narrow door? Does He do so because few people will use it, or because it is harder to get through a narrow door than a wide door? Jesus clearly teaches in this chapter and in other places throughout the Gospels that it is not easy to get into heaven. In this passage, Jesus explains that not only is it difficult, but that the day is coming when you will no longer be able to go through the door because it will be shut. What makes salvation hard for most people to accept is that it can't be their way, only God's way. The door is too narrow for their pride to fit through. It's too narrow for their worldly possessions. Sincerity and effort are not ssufficient and will cause God's rejection of them on the doorstep of heaven. It is His way or no way. Our human effort is one of Satan's lies which fools many people into eternal separation from the One who loves them the most. Are you certain you've chosen the narrow gate? Your good works, family background or Bible knowledge won't get you to heaven. Remember the way to heaven is "narrow."

LUKE 13:24

"Strive to enter through the narrow door. For many, I tell you, will seek to enter and will not be able.

SAY WHAT?
Observation: What do I see?

SO WHAT?
Interpretation: What does it mean?

NOW WHAT?
Application: How does it apply to me?

THEN WHAT?
Implementation: What do I do?

HUMILITY IN ACTION

SAY WHAT?

In what ways have you shown the motivations Christ condemns?

SO WHAT?

Who are the "poor," "crippled," "lame," and "blind," in your world?

NOW WHAT?

How can you specifically apply what Christ said in verses 12-14 this week?

THEN WHAT?

What's your action plan to make it happen this week?

In the parable found in verses seven through fourteen, Jesus discussed two groups of people. They are those who exalt themselves and those who humble themselves. The behavior we read about is not uncommon and is likely found in your unit. The exalter-of-himself works hard to manipulate himself into positions of honor. His motivation is not love for others, but promotion of himself. He will take over certain duties or assignments, but only ones that offer recognition, medals or ribbons. Invitations to his party would be limited to those who will reciprocate or are the elite of the unit. Christ rebukes both the attitudes and actions of these people. The humble ones, on the other hand, do not assume anything about themselves. They care about others and put them first. They leave the responsibility of recognition to God. Their attention is on the needs of people and their reward is in heaven. How can you serve God this week in a way that will go unnoticed or unrecognized? Look around and find an insignificant person whom you can "invite to your banquet." He may never repay you, but God certainly will.

LUKE 14:11

For everyone who exalts himself will be humbled, and he who humbles himself will be exalted."

The book of Proverbs was designed to help us in "attaining wisdom and discipline; in understanding words of insight; in acquiring a disciplined and prudent life, doing what is right and just and fair; in giving prudence to the simple, knowledge and discretion to the young." As you read through this chapter, write down the verses that are most significant to you in your present circumstances.

VERSE | WHAT TRUTH IT COMMUNICATES | HOW IT IMPACTS MY LIFE

FINDING WHAT IS LOST

SAY WHAT?
Observation: What do I see?

SO WHAT?
Interpretation: What does it mean?

NOW WHAT?
Application: How does it apply to me?

THEN WHAT?
Implementation: What do I do?

What did the Pharisees say about Jesus that resulted in His giving the three parables we find in this chapter? What do you think He was trying to illustrate by them? Could it be that the Pharisee's accusation of welcoming and eating with sinners was true, and that it should have also been true of the religious leaders of the day? In each story, God was portrayed as caring deeply for something that the Pharisees would never concern themselves with. They looked down upon repentant sinners, a lowly sheep, an insignificant coin or an indulgent father. All of these parables illustrate that God cares about individuals. The shepherd had 99 other sheep, but one of his sheep was lost. The woman had nine other silver coins, but she was concerned about the lost one. The rebellious son got what he deserved, but his father was concerned for him and waited patiently and with open arms for his return. Like the people in each of these stories, Jesus cares very much for each individual. If Jesus cares this much for people, how then should you respond? Do you put forth the same kind of effort to find what is lost (people) as those in these parables did?

★★★★

LUKE 15:32
It was fitting to celebrate and be glad, for this your brother was dead, and is alive; he was lost, and is found.'"

OUR MONEY

Have you ever wondered why some people seem to read their Bibles and have great things revealed to them while others seem to struggle and find nothing? In today's reading Jesus gives an important principle that may explain why this happens in some cases. It is found in verse eleven. Christ told the disciples that they needed to be faithful in the little things before they could expect to receive the bigger things. He then spoke more specifically by saying that if one is not faithful in his handling of worldly wealth, his money, he cannot be trusted with true riches, which are spiritual. How many people do you imagine never really gain spiritual insights because they do not handle their money properly? They use it selfishly to buy what they want. They do not give to the church or see the other needs in God's work which they could give generously to. We must realize that how we handle our money is vitally important to our spiritual growth. Are you demonstrating by the use of your money that you can also be trusted with spiritual wealth? In what ways can you demonstrate that you are trustworthy of the "true riches" of God?

LUKE 16:11

If then you have not been faithful in the unrighteous wealth, who will entrust to you the true riches?

SAY WHAT?
Observation: What do I see?

SO WHAT?
Interpretation: What does it mean?

NOW WHAT?
Application: How does it apply to me?

THEN WHAT?
Implementation: What do I do?

SAYING THANKS

SAY WHAT?
List some of the things that God has done for you in your life.

SO WHAT?
What impact have those things had on your life?

NOW WHAT?
In what ways can you demonstrate to God how thankful you are?

THEN WHAT?
How can you communicate to others what God has done for you?

Think for a moment what it would be like to learn that you had a terminal disease, and until you died, you would have to leave your family and loved ones and live alone. In today's reading we see how ten men reacted when rescued from that very situation. Because of their leprosy, these men were required to stay away from all other people and to announce their presence when anyone came near them. They had to leave their homes and families and would never live a normal life, all the time watching a terrible disease eat away their flesh. You can imagine how they must have felt when Jesus came by. He was their only chance to be healed and He could give them back their lives. It is unbelievable to think that, after what Jesus had done for them, only one returned to say thank you. It sounds incredible, but it happens all the time, even today. You may have even done this. When was the last time you sat down to think about all that God has done for you? When was the last time you stopped to say thank you? Take some time today to thank Him for all He has done and for everything He has given to you by His grace.

★ ★ ★ ★

LUKE 17:18
Was no one found to return and give praise to God except this foreigner?"

PERSISTENCE IN PRAYER

According to verse 1 in today's reading, why did Jesus tell this parable? To whom did He tell it? How does this story accomplish His purpose? In this parable, we find a widow who kept coming to a wicked judge asking for justice. The judge however, refused to give it to her. He ultimately did grant her request, but only to get rid of her and keep her from continually "bugging" him. His motives did not flow out of a heart of love and a commitment to justice, but from a selfish heart. Jesus did not intend to say that God is like this wicked judge, and that He will grant our requests if we just keep "bugging" Him with them. His point was that if an inconsiderate judge who does not fear God would grant a request to a persistent widow, how much more will a loving God respond to the continuing prayers of those He loves? Knowing that God loves us and wants to respond to our needs should be motivation to pray persistently. Is there something that you have prayed for continually and lost hope because an answer hasn't come. Start praying again today with faith in the concern and care of a God who loves you.

SAY WHAT?
Observation: What do I see?

SO WHAT?
Interpretation: What does it mean?

NOW WHAT?
Application: How does it apply to me?

THEN WHAT?
Implementation: What do I do?

LUKE 18:1
And he told them a parable to the effect that they ought always to pray and not lose heart.

MILITARYDEVOTIONAL.COM
 @MILITARYDEVOS

REACHING "SINNERS"

SAY WHAT?

What people in your world are viewed like the tax-collectors were?

SO WHAT?

In what ways are you attempting to reach out to them?

NOW WHAT?

How can you impact these kinds of people for Christ?

THEN WHAT?

In light of this passage, what personal commitment can you make?

Why did people respond with such amazement when Jesus invited Himself to Zacchaeus' house? Apparently, it was Zacchaeus' career choice. Tax-collectors were the most hated of people in the Jewish society. They were often more hated than the Romans who occupied Israel. Their method of collecting taxes was skimming off a generous helping for themselves as they collected the required funds for the government. Tax collectors were considered so untrustworthy that they were not even allowed to testify in Jewish court because of their reputation as liars. They could not worship in the synagogue as such blatant sinners. Imagine Zacchaeus' surprise when Jesus stopped and invited Himself to his house for dinner. Although people reacted negatively to the fact that Jesus went to have dinner with him, Jesus reminded them (verse 10) that it was for people like Zacchaeus that He had come. Are you building a relationship with someone with the express purpose of winning them to Christ? We, like Christ, need to make it our passion to "seek and save what was lost." What step will you take today to impact someone for Christ?

LUKE 19:10

For the Son of Man came to seek and to save the lost."

AVOID OR CORRECT?

Have you ever experienced a time when someone was speaking hypothetically, but you knew that he was really talking directly to you? In today's passage, we see how the teachers of the law and the chief priests responded in that same situation. Jesus gave a parable, and they knew that although He was speaking hypothetically, He was talking about them. They also knew that what He said was true, yet they did nothing about it. Instead of listening and correcting their wrong behavior, they deliberately chose to ignore or justify the issues Jesus addressed. It was easier to get rid of Jesus, which was what they ultimately tried to do. We often do the exact same thing. We hear a sermon, read a passage, or listen to a DVD, and know the Spirit of God is speaking directly to us about an issue in our lives. Instead of seeing it as coming from the mouth of God and finding a way to deal with it, we ignore it. Could that be happening to you today? Could you be suppressing the conviction of God concerning a specific issue in your life? Stop resisting or ignoring what God is talking to you about and respond today to what the Spirit is saying.

LUKE 20:19

The scribes and the chief priests sought to lay hands on him at that very hour, for they perceived that he had told this parable against them, but they feared the people.

SAY WHAT?
Observation: What do I see?

SO WHAT?
Interpretation: What does it mean?

NOW WHAT?
Application: How does it apply to me?

THEN WHAT?
Implementation: What do I do?

The book of Proverbs was designed to help us in "attaining wisdom and discipline; in understanding words of insight; in acquiring a disciplined and prudent life, doing what is right and just and fair; in giving prudence to the simple, knowledge and discretion to the young." As you read through this chapter, write down the verses that are most significant to you in your present circumstances.

VERSE | WHAT TRUTH IT COMMUNICATES | HOW IT IMPACTS MY LIFE

OPPORTUNITY IN DIFFICULTY

Of all the things concerning the end of the age that are listed in this chapter, which ones would be the most difficult for you to endure? It is incredible to realize that in the midst of very difficult circumstances, Christ promises victory (verses 13-15 and 19). Believers will have opportunities to witness for Christ, and their adversaries will not be able to resist or contradict what they say. Even more exciting is that they will also gain life. We often see only the negative in difficult circumstances. We do not see the opportunities these same circumstances bring to be a witness, to have God supernaturally empower us, or to have even greater confidence in our faith. Although our circumstances are difficult, they always produce positive results. How are you viewing the circumstances God has allowed to enter your life? Do you see opportunities, or situations to be changed and eliminated? Remember, that in the midst of the most difficult circumstances come the greatest opportunities for personal growth. They also offer us the ability to demonstrate the difference Jesus Christ makes in our lives. Does anyone notice Him in your life?

★★★★

LUKE 21:17-19

You will be hated by all for my name's sake. But not a hair of your head will perish. By your endurance you will gain your lives.

SAY WHAT?

What difficult circumstances are you now facing?

SO WHAT?

How are you responding to them?

NOW WHAT?

List some positive results that could grow out of your circumstances.

THEN WHAT?

How do you need to respond in order for those things to happen?

SEEING NEEDS

SAY WHAT?
Observation: What do I see?

SO WHAT?
Interpretation: What does it mean?

NOW WHAT?
Application: How does it apply to me?

THEN WHAT?
Implementation: What do I do?

What kinds of emotions or thoughts do you think went through the minds of both Jesus and the disciples during this final meal together? What went through their minds after Jesus informed them that one of the disciples sitting at the table would betray Him? If you had been there, what do you think you would be whispering to the guy sitting next to you? It is amazing to realize that what Luke recorded for us in this chapter took place right in the middle of their time together. According to verse 24, it was a dispute about who would be the greatest. Jesus must have felt tremendously disappointed. This was their last time together before His crucifixion. He had spent three years trying to teach them to be servants. Yet it seemed as though they didn't get it. What an illustration this is to us of Christ's humility and the pride of the disciples. How much similarity is there between the disciples and you? Are there people around you who are hurting? Is important information being given, and you only care about its impact on you? Are you the reason someone else is distracted? How can you be more aware of the needs all around you?

★★★★

LUKE 22:26
But not so with you. Rather, let the greatest among you become as the youngest, and the leader as one who serves.

WHAT DO OTHERS SEE?

As you read Luke's account of the crucifixion, what did you notice about how Jesus responded? In the midst of all the pain He was experiencing, His concern was still with His weeping loved ones. In spite of what He was going through, He comforted them. As He hung between two criminals on the cross, He shared with them the reason He had come. One mocked; the other accepted His words. Jesus was always caring and always reaching out to people. Even in the midst of agony, Jesus still cared and everyone knew it. He always thought of someone else, even when His concern for himself would have appeared to be justified. And as the Centurion looked on and watched these events unfold, he could not help but conclude that Jesus was a righteous man. This chapter ought to cause us to respond in thanksgiving and worship as well as motivate us to follow Jesus Christ's example of putting others before Himself. We must seek to impact our world with the life-changing message of Jesus Christ. What has been the response of those who have been watching you respond to the difficult circumstances in your life?

SAY WHAT?
What difficult circumstances are you facing today?

SO WHAT?
How has your response to them impacted those around you?

NOW WHAT?
In what ways can you become more like Christ in the midst of difficult circumstances?

THEN WHAT?
In light of this passage, what personal commitment can you make?

★★★★

LUKE 23:47

Now when the centurion saw what had taken place, he praised God, saying, "Certainly this man was innocent!"

OVERCOMING DOUBT

SAY WHAT?
Observation: What do I see?

SO WHAT?
Interpretation: What does it mean?

NOW WHAT?
Application: How does it apply to me?

THEN WHAT?
Implementation: What do I do?

What different responses to Jesus Christ's resurrection do you see in this chapter? Number them in your Bible. From Jesus' response to people's reactions, how do you think He felt about them? One response that He didn't appreciate much was surprise. When He appeared to the disciples, at times they acted as if they were shocked to see Him. One could assume from their response that they couldn't believe Jesus would rise from the dead. He had told them on many occasions that He would rise on the third day. On the road to Emmaus, He walked them through the Scriptures again to illustrate this point. Jesus' rebuke was appropriate, "How foolish you are and how slow of heart to believe...." All they needed to do was listen and believe. Could He say that about you? Are you someone who reads what Jesus Christ says and in simple faith, believes it? Or do you find yourself saying too often, "I should have remembered...." It may be time to start believing what Christ said and stop doubting. If you need help, seek out someone who can help you grow in your faith. Your Chaplain is always an option for wisdom and guidance.

★★★★★

LUKE 24:25
And he said to them, "O foolish ones, and slow of heart to believe all that the prophets have spoken!

LUKE REVIEW

As you come to the completion of this book, what have you learned? In what ways are you different because you read it? What have you learned about Jesus Christ? This book is filled with so many lessons. Why not take time to record the impact this book has had in your life. Don't be a hearer of the Word only, but be a doer. What changes do you need to make?

SAY WHAT?
Why do you think this book was written?

SO WHAT?
What key principles can you take with you from this book?

NOW WHAT?
What things about Jesus Christ and His ministry did you learn from reading this book? If this book was not in the Bible, what would you have missed?

THEN WHAT?
Put into one sentence what this book is about.

LUKE 1:4
...that you may have certainty concerning the things you have been taught.

≫ MILITARYDEVOTIONAL.COM

 @MILITARYDEVOS

 FACEBOOK.COM/MILITARYDEVOS

MILITARY
OTD

FEBRUARY
★★★★

★ MONTHLY ★
PRAYER SHEET

"... THE PRAYER OF A RIGHTEOUS PERSON
HAS GREAT POWER AS IT IS WORKING."

JAMES 5:16

I NEED TO REACH OUT TO...	HOW I WILL DO IT...	HOW IT WENT...

OTHER REQUEST	HOW ANSWERED	DATE

★ MONTHLY ★
★ MISSION SHEET ★

⋙ Share your personal commitments with those who will help keep you accountable to them.

⋙ NAME:
....

This sheet is designed to help you make personal commitments each month that will help you grow in your walk with God. Fill it out by determining:

★ What will push you.
★ What you think you can achieve.

⋙ PERSONAL DEVOTIONS:
I will commit to read the OnTrack Bible passage and devotional thought ....
day(s) each week this month.

⋙ CHURCH/CHAPEL ATTENDANCE:
I will attend Church/Chapel .... time(s) this month.
I will attend .... time(s) this month.

⋙ SCRIPTURE MEMORY:
I will memorize .... key verse(s) from the daily OnTrack Devotions this month.

⋙ OUTREACH:
I will share Christ with .... person/people this month.
I will serve my local church/chapel this month by ....
....
....

⋙ OTHER ACTIVITIES:
List any other opportunities such as events, prayer group, etc..., you will participate in this month. ....
....
....
....
....
....

Determine to begin today a journey that will last a lifetime, and will change your life forever.

REQUIREMENTS TO BE USED

What does it take to be someone whom God can use? How smart would you need to be? How popular do you need to be? What kind of talent would be necessary? Paul gives us the answer to those questions in today's reading. According to Paul, it only takes being "foolish," "weak," "lowly," and "despised." I think most of us will find ourselves in at least one of those categories. You see, according to verse 29, God chooses these kinds of people so that when God uses them, they can not boast about themselves. If God used only the "great" people, then the watching world would not see the power of God. They would think the results were because of the abilities of the people involved. God desires to show His great power to the world through you. It is not your ability that determines if God can use you, but your availability He is interested in. Have you allowed Him to use you? He has "enriched you in every way," verse five; therefore, allow Him to use you today. Do not look at your own abilities, but look at God's capabilities to use you in the lives of others. You will be amazed at what He can do through you! Why not allow Him to start today!

★★★★

1 COR 1:28-29

God chose what is low and despised in the world, even things that are not, to bring to nothing things that are, so that no human being might boast in the presence of God.

SAY WHAT?
Observation: What do I see?

SO WHAT?
Interpretation: What does it mean?

NOW WHAT?
Application: How does it apply to me?

THEN WHAT?
Implementation: What do I do?

MILITARYDEVOTIONAL.COM
🐦 @MILITARYDEVOS

SHARING THE GOSPEL

SAY WHAT?
Observation: What do I see?

SO WHAT?
Interpretation: What does it mean?

NOW WHAT?
Application: How does it apply to me?

THEN WHAT?
Implementation: What do I do?

Reread the first four verses of this chapter. At the end of each verse, ask yourself why Paul would not want to use eloquence of speech and superior wisdom when he spoke to people about Christ. One would think that he would want his message to contain wise and persuasive words so the listeners would respond to what he was saying. Why didn't he use them? Because he did not want people to respond to the message of Christ as a result of his abilities or methods. He wanted them to respond because the Spirit of God was moving in their hearts. Paul wanted to be sure people were responding to the message of salvation because of a demonstration of the Spirit's power. It wasn't about him humanly persuading people. If we needed great wisdom, eloquence or persuasive words to bring people to Christ, some of us wouldn't be very effective. But how can God show His power in our lives? In what ways can the Holy Spirit's power be demonstrated by us? One way the world notices is by seeing our transformed lives! We can all demonstrate the difference Christ has made in our lives. Can they see the demonstration of the Spirit's power in your life? How can you take advantage of those opportunities?

★★★★

1 COR 2:5
...that your faith might not rest in the wisdom of men but in the power of God.

MEASURE OF SUCCESS

There is an encouraging phrase in today's reading. Did you notice it? This book was written to a church that had several problems. From this chapter we learn that there was jealousy and quarreling among them. One of the issues was a dispute over Paul and Apollos. Some felt superior because they had been saved through Paul's ministry, while those who had been saved through Apollos' felt they were superior. To counter the jealousy, Paul gave them principles to guide them. One of the principles is found in verse eight, in the phrase, "according to his own labor." This phrase teaches us that the results of someone's ministry, or his impact on others lives, is in God's hands alone. God alone determines the results someone has in the lives of people. We should not be jealous of God's spiritual blessing in another's life. You may have watered the seed, but someone else planted it, and someone else still will harvest it. If you are doing the best you can, trust God with the outcome. We are responsible to be faithful in the areas God has asked us to serve in. We need to trust Him with the results. The only standard you must measure up to is God's.

★★★★

1 COR 3:8

He who plants and he who waters are one, and each will receive his wages according to his labor.

SAY WHAT?

In what ways can God use you to "plant" a seed?

SO WHAT?

In what ways can God use you to "water" a seed?

NOW WHAT?

What are some examples from your life in which you did the planting or watering but God used someone else to make it grow?

THEN WHAT?

In light of this passage, what personal commitment can you make?

SAY WHAT?
Observation: What do I see?

SO WHAT?
Interpretation: What does it mean?

NOW WHAT?
Application: How does it apply to me?

THEN WHAT?
Implementation: What do I do?

If you want to know what made Paul such an effective witness, you need look no further than today's reading. It is what also gave him the ability to confront the Corinthian church with the issues in this book. What is it? You'll find it if you look in verse seventeen. Paul says that he has a life that "agrees with what I teach everywhere in every church." What a statement! No wonder he had such power. He was a person in whom there was no hypocrisy. What he preached and taught to others or confronted others about was what he lived. Otherwise he could not address others' issues knowing his own life had areas that had not been made right. He would avoid saying what needed to be said because his own life did not measure up. In Paul's case, his life was consistent with what he said and taught. When you put the truth of God together with a consistent life, you have incredible power. Could you make this statement? Does your life agree with "everything" you say? Do your friends even know you have a relationship with God? Our world desperately needs to see people living a lives consistent with what they claim to believe. What area do you need to begin to work on so this can be true of you?

★★★★

1 COR 4:17

That is why I sent you Timothy, my beloved and faithful child in the Lord, to remind you of my ways in Christ, as I teach them everywhere in every church.

DEALING WITH SIN

There was sin in the church in Corinth and,not only were they not dealing with it, but they were proud that they were tolerant of people's sin and were not judgmental towards them. They patted themselves on the back as though it was to their credit that the guilty party felt no shame. They felt that ignoring his sin was better than dealing with it out in the open. Paul wrote that this response is wrong. First, the Corinthians response to sin did not help the person come to see his sin as wrong before God. By not confronting it, they led him to believe he was fine and his sin was not a problem. Secondly, their response was wrong because it would allow sin to spread throughout the church. Others would assume that they could engage in this kind of behavior. Sin in our churches cannot be tolerated or ignored. We must lovingly confront it,and,if there is no repentance,we must take a stand for the sake of the one sinning,as well as for the church. It may not be easy,but it must be done. There is too much at stake! Is there sin in your life you have not admitted to God and then confessed? Is there sin in the life of one you care about? How will you respond to this passage of Scripture?

★★★★★

1 COR 5:6

Your boasting is not good. Do you not know that a little leaven leavens the whole lump?

SAY WHAT?

Observation: What do I see?

SO WHAT?

Interpretation: What does it mean?

NOW WHAT?

Application: How does it apply to me?

THEN WHAT?

Implementation: What do I do?

MILITARYDEVOTIONAL.COM
🐦 @MILITARYDEVOS

The book of Proverbs was designed to help us in "attaining wisdom and discipline; in understanding words of insight; in acquiring a disciplined and prudent life, doing what is right and just and fair; in giving prudence to the simple, knowledge and discretion to the young." As you read through this chapter, write down the verses that are most significant to you in your present circumstances.

VERSE | WHAT TRUTH IT COMMUNICATES | HOW IT IMPACTS MY LIFE

MAKING GOOD DECISIONS

When we are confronted with a choice in an area of our lives that Scripture does not directly cover, how do we know what choice to make? How do we know what God would have us do? In today's reading, Paul gives us two principles to consider when confronted with that kind of situation. First, you need to ask yourself if this is something that is beneficial to you spiritually. Will it help you become more like Christ? Will increase your burden for lost people and will it help you reach your mission field? The question to ask is not only "Will this hurt me?" but also, "How will this help me?" A second question to ask yourself is whether it will cause you to become controlled by it. Drugs and alcohol are obvious examples of some things that control people. They are wrong because they become the master and control behavior. But so can TV programs or relationships or sports or even rank. So the next time you are faced with one of these decisions, ask yourself not only if the activity is permissible but if it is beneficial and if it will control. In what areas of your life do you need to be asking these questions? Is there an area in which the Spirit of God is confronting you?

1 COR 6:12

"All things are lawful for me," but not all things are helpful. "All things are lawful for me," but I will not be enslaved by anything.

SAY WHAT?
What kinds of things might not be sin, but would not be "beneficial" to you?

SO WHAT?
What kinds of things might not be sin, but could control you?

NOW WHAT?
What specific area of your life do you need to examine with these two questions in mind?

THEN WHAT?
What personal commitment can you make in light of this passage?

SAY WHAT?
Observation: What do I see?

SO WHAT?
Interpretation: What does it mean?

NOW WHAT?
Application: How does it apply to me?

THEN WHAT?
Implementation: What do I do?

Paul gives a common theme in verses 17,20,24 and 26. Did you pick up on it when you read through these verses? What is it? How does that apply to our lives right now? Often,when we make spiritual decisions,we think it means we need to make major sweeping changes. That may be true at times,but there are some areas that should not change. In the Corinthian church, they thought getting saved meant finding a new wife if you were married to an unbeliever. If a slave trusted Christ, he might think that his decision meant his standing,his position in the culture,needed to change. Paul explained that you can be a Christian and live for God while remaining in your present circumstance. If God called you to be a slave,be the best slave you can possibly be. If married to an unsaved spouse,then seek to honor God in your marriage. Often we are exactly where God wants us to be, but are prone to want to jump ship or bail out. Paul discouraged that kind of attitude. Our spiritual decision might open doors to reach those in our world. In what present circumstance do you need renewed determination to hang on and allow God to work? God has you there for a reason. Do you see it? Can you imagine what God might do through your circumstances?

1 COR 7:26
I think that in view of the present distress it is good for a person to remain as he is.

KNOWLEDGE OR LOVE?

When addressing eating meat sacrificed to idols, why did Paul begin with the statements he did in verses one through three? Why talk about how knowledge puffs people up? Why emphasize how important love is? Paul began here so this church would realize immediately, that it is possible to pursue knowledge and only gain pride. Knowledge alone will not keep you from doing something that may hurt a brother, even though your action may not be wrong. Love, on the other hand, does not lead to pride, but to humility. Its goal is to build others up, not to hurt people. If someone were only interested in knowledge, he wouldn't care if eating meat hurt someone else. All he would care about is whether the behavior was right or wrong, or how he could justify it in his life. He would work to simply gain more knowledge about the matter. Paul wanted the Corinthian church to have their knowledge affected by love. Knowledge should be motivated by what is best for others, not what is best for self. Because Paul was motivated by love, he could say what he did in verse thirteen. Are there things you will not give up even though they may hurt another brother? If you are motivated by love, you will seek to benefit others.

1 COR 9:17

For if I do this of my own will, I have a reward, but if not of my own will, I am still entrusted with a stewardship.

SAY WHAT?

Observation: What do I see?

SO WHAT?

Interpretation: What does it mean?

NOW WHAT?

Application: How does it apply to me?

THEN WHAT?

Implementation: What do I do?

SAY WHAT?

What small,insignificant areas of your life can you glorify God in?

SO WHAT?

How will you go about accomplishing that task?

NOW WHAT?

How can you remind yourself what this passage teaches today?

THEN WHAT?

What personal commitment can you make in light of this passage?

Why does Paul use the illustration of eating and drinking to challenge those at Corinth to glorify God? It would seem that eating and drinking are two of the most insignificant things we do in the course of a day. Surely he could come up with a more significant illustration... like what career we choose or how we use our money might attract our attention better. But, that may just be his point. Paul clearly states that "everything" we do ought to glorify God. Even in the areas of our lives which seem routine and insignificant, we ought to seek to bring Him glory. Paul's point is that we should glorify God not just when our lives are on display in an athletic contest,or at a concert, but also when we clean our weapons,wait in the chow line,or play with our younger brothers and sisters--in "everything." He used an insignificant example to illustrate how important it is to glorify God in every area of our lives. In what "small" area of your life do you need to seek to glorify God? Choose one area and begin today. Circle the words "eating" and "drinking" to remind you of what this passage teaches. You may never realize the difference it will make.

1 COR 10:17

Because there is one bread, we who are many are one body, for we all partake of the one bread.

COMMUNION

How serious is the communion service to God? Are our actions during communion important? Is God even aware that it takes place? When you read this chapter, you will realize communion is very important to God... probably more important than you thought. Paul included this chapter because the Corinthians were struggling with how they conducted communion. They came to the service with great division among themselves. Some did not wait but began eating on their own, some excluded individuals, and others were even getting drunk during the service. Paul made it very clear how significant communion is to God and that it should not be taken lightly. Some of the members of their church were sick and some had even died because they did not respond in a right way to this service of remembrance and examination. Communion is a solemn time to reflect on what Christ did for us at Calvary. It is also a time for us to examine our lives for sin and consider where we stand in our relationship with God. Do you do these things during communion at your church? Next time your church has communion, remember how significant this service really is.

1 COR 11:27

Whoever, therefore, eats the bread or drinks the cup of the Lord in an unworthy manner will be guilty concerning the body and blood of the Lord.

SAY WHAT?
Observation: What do I see?

SO WHAT?
Interpretation: What does it mean?

NOW WHAT?
Application: How does it apply to me?

THEN WHAT?
Implementation: What do I do?

SAY WHAT?

What gifts could make a person feel unimportant to the body?

SO WHAT?

How do we make people feel like they are unimportant to the body?

NOW WHAT?

List ways God can use those gifts to impact the body.

THEN WHAT?

What personal commitment can you make in light of this passage?

What causes dissention in a local church? How can we prevent it? In today's reading, Paul condemns two responses in believers that destroy unity. Could you be guilty of one of these responses? Paul begins this chapter by writing that God has given everyone gifts for the benefit of the body. How do you respond to this information? One way is to look at yourself and determine that you are insignificant because you are not like others and your gifts are not the "important" ones. That response is wrong and hurts the unity of the body. A second response would be to examine others and determine that they are not important because they are not like you or do not have what you consider to be "important" gifts. This response is also wrong and it hurts unity. Imagine either of those attitudes as it relates to your unit. Unity and performance depend on everyone doing their jobs well. We must all realize that God has given to each of us, all members of the body of Christ, gifts to use in the church. If we take ourselves out, or push others out, we hurt the body. We also miss out on what those gifts are designed to give us. Are you using the gifts God has given you? Do you see the role others must play in the body?

★★★★

1 COR 12:11

All these are empowered by one and the same Spirit, who apportions to each one individually as he wills.

GREATEST IS LOVE

Why would Paul follow up a discussion on spiritual gifts with a section on love? One might assume that he would follow the last chapter with a discussion on how to use different spiritual gifts or maybe a discussion on how to determine what spiritual gift you have. Could it be that Paul follows his discussion on gifts with love because love is the most important quality a church could have? We could assume that if a church had a great preacher it would be a great church. But Paul says that without love, it would sound awful. We could assume that if your church had great spiritual power, enough faith to move mountains, it would be a great church. But without love, it would be a church that amounts to nothing. We could assume that if your church made great sacrifices in order to meet the needs of the poor, or was willing to suffer personal harm, it would be a great church. But without love, all these sacrifices are for nothing. Paul followed his discussion of the gifts with love, because it is the most important ingredient for a church. Without love, no matter what spiritual gifts your church might have, it will amount to nothing. Without love, nothing else matters. Why? Love invests those gifts in others.

★★★★

1 COR 13:13

So now faith, hope, and love abide, these three; but the greatest of these is love.

SAY WHAT?

Observation: What do I see?

SO WHAT?

Interpretation: What does it mean?

NOW WHAT?

Application: How does it apply to me?

THEN WHAT?

Implementation: What do I do?

MISSING LOVE

SAY WHAT?
Observation: What do I see?

SO WHAT?
Interpretation: What does it mean?

NOW WHAT?
Application: How does it apply to me?

THEN WHAT?
Implementation: What do I do?

What would happen if the members of a local church body used their gifts but were not motivated by love? In this chapter we see the consequences in a church when that very thing happens. You may even see your own church fitting this description. As the believers in Corinth used their gifts, pride and jealousy developed among them. Pride is the antithesis of love. It serves self. Church members misused their gifts for self-edification rather than for building the body. They concluded that the spiritual gift God gave to an individual determined how spiritual they were. To make matters worse, people at church were using their gifts in a way that was causing confusion and the worship of God was being hindered. Paul gave some very specific and direct guidelines to avoid these problems among the believers. The key was that they were using their gifts in a way that was not pleasing to God. Love was not the motivation of their lives, pride was. Do you see similar characteristics in your church? How are you using the gifts that God has given to you? What can you do to avoid these abuses in your life and in your church? Why not get started today?

1 COR 14:12
So with yourselves, since you are eager for manifestations of the Spirit, strive to excel in building up the church.

IMPACT OF RESURRECTION

In today's reading, we find one of the greatest chapters in the Bible on the Resurrection of Christ. There is so much contained in these verses that we could write many different insights or thoughts. The most important application, however, is what this chapter speaks to you about. The following questions will help you walk through these verses and highlight what you find there. Take the time to read this chapter and respond to the questions to the right. It could change your life forever!

SAY WHAT?

What facts about the Resurrection did you learn from reading this chapter?

SO WHAT?

Why is the Resurrection important to Christians?

NOW WHAT?

What are the implications for our lives if Jesus did not raise from the dead?

THEN WHAT?

According to verse 58, what ought your response be?

1 COR 15:1

Now I would remind you, brothers, of the gospel I preached to you, which you received, in which you stand,

EXPECTATION FOR GIVING

SAY WHAT?
Observation: What do I see?

SO WHAT?
Interpretation: What does it mean?

NOW WHAT?
Application: How does it apply to me?

THEN WHAT?
Implementation: What do I do?

What standard does God have for giving to the church? When does He expect you to give? How can you know if God is pleased with what you are putting in the offering plate? These questions are not only important today, they were issues in the church in Corinth,. Paul closes his letter by addressing them. First, he gave instruction that people were to give every week. Not once a month, not every other week, but they were to give every week. How often do you put money in the offering plate at your church? Second, what was the standard for how much they were to give? According to Paul, it was dependent upon their income. Everyone is expected to give, and the amount they give is determined by their income. God knows how much you make. In reality, He is the one who provides your income regardless of who signs the check. How do you do with these instructions? It is shameful that many believers are not taught that God has expectations for giving for them. When was the last time you took a portion of what you made from your job and put it in the offering plate at church? This week would be a good time to get started honoring God in proportion to the blessings He has poured out on you.

1 COR 16:2
On the first day of every week, each of you is to put something aside and store it up, as he may prosper, so that there will be no collecting when I come.

WHY BAD THINGS?

Why do bad things happen to God's people? If you have ever asked that question, you will find some of the answers in today's reading. In this section of Scripture, Paul gives us two reasons why bad things happen to God's people. The first reason is found in verse four. Bad things happen to God's people so that they will be able to more effectively reach out and comfort those who are going through a similar difficulty. We are able to give them hope by sharing with them how God comforted us in the midst of our trouble. We would have empty words if only the unsaved experienced trouble and God's people never did. A second reason that bad things happen to God's people is so they will learn to rely on God, not themselves. The greater the trial, the greater the need to depend on God. When things are going well, we often forget about God and try to handle everything on our own. In difficult times, remember that God has a purpose. Seek to allow His purpose to be accomplished in your life. What purpose could there be for your present trouble? How should you respond to what God has allowed to come in your life? Is it a problem or an opportunity?

2 COR 1:4

...who comforts us in all our affliction, so that we may be able to comfort those who are in any affliction, with the comfort with which we ourselves are comforted by God.

SAY WHAT?
Observation: What do I see?

SO WHAT?
Interpretation: What does it mean?

NOW WHAT?
Application: How does it apply to me?

THEN WHAT?
Implementation: What do I do?

SAY WHAT?

How do you communicate forgiveness to someone?

SO WHAT?

How can you comfort someone whom you have forgiven?

NOW WHAT?

How can you reaffirm your love to someone you have forgiven?

THEN WHAT?

What will you commit to today based on this passage?

To understand this chapter, you need to remember the instructions Paul gave to the Corinthians concerning the man who was living in sin in 1 Corinthians 5. You may want to go back and read that passage again. Understanding the context will enable you to more fully understand the message of today's text. When the church received the instructions from Paul in chapter five of 1 Corinthians, they followed them. Because they did, the man who was in sin repented. The problem now was that when he did they would not forgive him. Paul gave instructions on what to do after a person repented of their sin. First, the church was supposed to forgive them (2:7). After forgiving them, they needed to comfort them (2:7). True repentance is followed by godly sorrow for sin and sometimes that sorrow is overwhelming. Finally, the church was to reaffirm their love to to the forgiven person (2:8). Those who do not respond to a repentant sinner in this way are themselves committing sin. Circle the words "forgive," "comfort," and "reaffirm," to remind yourself of how you need to respond to those seeking forgiveness. Could there be someone in your life who has sinned and repented, but has not been forgiven, comforted or reaffirmed by you?

2 COR 2:7

...so you should rather turn to forgive and comfort him, or he may be overwhelmed by excessive sorrow.

A PROCESS

What does the verb "being" communicate to you? Does it communicate to you a process, or a moment in time? Why even ask the question? Because Paul uses this verb to illustrate something very important to us in today's reading. It is a crucial factor of the Christian life. Believers often see the Christian life as something that takes place in a moment in time. A decision was made at a church service and the expectation is to be "completely" different immediately. We can become discouraged when change hasn't taken place overnight which can cause us to doubt the sincerity of the decision. In verse eighteen Paul states that we are "being" transformed into the likeness of Christ. He uses this word to illustrate that our growth is a process. Becoming like Christ does not happen in a moment in time. The key is to look for growth. Am I more like Christ this year than last year? The actual decision is needed to begin the process. However, change takes place over time. What steps do you need to take to move forward in your Christian life? Remember it's a process.

SAY WHAT?
Observation: What do I see?

SO WHAT?
Interpretation: What does it mean?

NOW WHAT?
Application: How does it apply to me?

THEN WHAT?
Implementation: What do I do?

2 COR 3:18

And we all, with unveiled face, beholding the glory of the Lord., are being transformed into the same image from one degree of glory to another. For this comes from the Lord who is the Spirit.

MILITARYDEVOTIONAL.COM
🐦 @MILITARYDEVOS

SAY WHAT?

What troubles have you had to face in your life?

SO WHAT?

What positive things have resulted because of these troubles?

NOW WHAT?

How can God use these troubles to help others in your future?

THEN WHAT?

What commitment can you make based on this passage?

What two adjectives did Paul use to describe his troubles in verse seventeen? Circle them in your Bible. Are they the same two words you would use to describe the troubles you are facing right now or have faced in the past? Paul used them because of how he viewed troubles. He knew that even though outwardly he was being "pounded on," inwardly God was doing a great work in his heart. God was renewing him and comforting him in the midst of his trials. Paul knew that the troubles he faced were accomplishing something very important in his life. In light of this perspective, he did not lose heart when trials came his way. When he looked at eternity and what God was accomplishing in his life, his troubles seemed "light" and "momentary." Maybe you need to begin today by fixing your eyes, not on what you can see - your problems, but on what you can't see - God's work in your heart. Maybe you need to focus on what God is accomplishing in your life as Paul does in this passage. To help, make a list of positive things that have resulted from the troubles you have experienced in the past. Use the questions to the left to help you focus on what God is doing in your life.

★★★★

2 COR 4:16

So we do not lose heart. Though our outer self is wasting away, our inner self is being renewed day by day.

LICENSE OR OBLIGATION?

If the Holy Spirit was given to "guarantee" our salvation, does that mean we can live however we want and still go to heaven? Not according to what Paul says in this chapter. Paul tells us what our response ought to be to the truth that the Holy Spirit is a deposit guaranteeing our salvation. First, this truth ought to result in living a life of confidence in our salvation, knowing we have eternal life. We should never doubt our salvation or wonder if a sin we committed would result in losing it. Our salvation is guaranteed. Second, notice what that confidence produces. It produces motivation to please God no matter where we are (2:9). The fact that our salvation is guaranteed does not mean we can do whatever we want; it means we desire to do whatever God wants us to do. Why? Because one day we will all appear before the One who gave us this salvation. You see, eternal security is not a license to do whatever you want and still go to heaven. It is the motivation to serve and please God at all times. If eternal security has not motivated you in this way, maybe you don't understand what it really means. How does this guarantee affect your life and how you live it?

2 COR 5:9
So whether we are at home or away, we make it our aim to please him.

SAY WHAT?
Observation: What do I see?

SO WHAT?
Interpretation: What does it mean?

NOW WHAT?
Application: How does it apply to me?

THEN WHAT?
Implementation: What do I do?

SAY WHAT?
Observation: What do I see?

SO WHAT?
Interpretation: What does it mean?

NOW WHAT?
Application: How does it apply to me?

THEN WHAT?
Implementation: What do I do?

Can a saved person marry an unsaved person and it not be considered sin? From today's reading, we see that the answer is no. But does this passage speak to the issue of dating unsaved people? It does if you understand the principles involved. Look closely at what it says. Paul gives us the reasons why God forbids a believer being yoked together with an unbeliever in marriage and in other relationships. He says it is because we have nothing in common with unbelievers (vs 14). We can't have real fellowship with them (vs 14), we find no harmony (vs 15) and we find no agreement with the unsaved (vs 16). In other words, all the things that are involved in a good dating relationship could not be possible between a saved person and an unsaved person. How can we enjoy dating someone with whom we have nothing in common, can have no real fellowship with,have no harmony and no possibility of agreement. While this passage does not say that dating the unsaved is wrong,it gives solid reasons to discourage it. We need to love, reach out to, and seek to win the unsaved. However, dating the unsaved can at best be confusing and at worst dangerous. Are you willing to do what is best?

★★★★

2 COR 6:14
Do not be unequally yoked with unbelievers. For what partnership has righteousness with lawlessness? Or what fellowship has light with darkness?

TRUE REPENTANCE

How can you tell if someone has true godly sorrow over their sin? How do you know if they are truly repentant or just acting as if they are sorry. Paul lists some defining characteristics of godly sorrow in this chapter. We can use these to examine our own and others' lives in the matter of repentance. Paul heard how this church responded to the correction he wrote about in his first letter to the Corinthians. He knew they had genuine godly sorrow because they had demonstrated seven characteristics which he listed in verses 10-11. You should number them in your Bible. First he saw that they had an earnestness and an eagerness to clear themselves, to make it right. Second, he saw indignation and alarm about what they had done. They felt terrible about their sin. Third, he saw that they had a longing, a concern, and a readiness to see justice done. They were prepared to accept the consequences their sin required. Does your life reflect these characteristics when you sin against God? Have you seen it in the lives of others? If not, ask God to show you the true nature of sin so that godly sorrow might lead you to true repentance and restore the relationship that God desires we have with Him and others.

2 COR 7:10

For godly grief produces a repentance that leads to salvation without regret, whereas worldly grief produces death.

SAY WHAT?

How might someone who has an earnestness and eagerness to clear themself act?

SO WHAT?

How might someone who has indignation and alarm about what they had done act?

NOW WHAT?

How might someone who has a longing, a concern, and a readiness to see justice done in response to their sin act?

THEN WHAT?

What personal commitment can you make in light of what this passage teaches?

GOD'S PREPERATION

SAY WHAT?
Observation: What do I see?

SO WHAT?
Interpretation: What does it mean?

NOW WHAT?
Application: How does it apply to me?

THEN WHAT?
Implementation: What do I do?

If we talked to people in your town and asked them what they knew of your chapel or your church, what would they tell us? Would they describe it the way the church in Macedonia is described in this passage? Wouldn't it be exciting to be part of a church that has such a heart for giving? To be described in this way is a great honor. So many people see Christians as selfish and uncaring. How important is it to be a giving,caring church? While Paul gives five areas this churched excelled in verse seven of chapter eight, Paul also wants them to excel in their giving. Yes they excelled in faith,speech,love,knowledge and complete earnestness. But Paul also wanted giving to be on that list. It is wonderful to be a church that is known for the five qualities that Paul listed. But a church also needs to be a giving body of believers in order to be everything that God wants it to be. What words would you use to describe your church? What words would you use to describe yourself? Do you give out of your poverty with "extreme generosity" and then give even beyond your ability? In what ways can you improve in this area? How can you also help your church to improve in the area of giving? What will you give this Sunday?

★★★★

2 COR 8:7
But as you excel in everything—in faith,in speech,in knowledge, in all earnestness, and in our love for you see that you excel in this act of grace also.

FOOLISH TO COMPARE

When you read verses twelve through eighteen, did they encourage you or concern you? Does this standard reveal that you are doing okay or that you are not where you need to be? For some, it is very encouraging to know that our standard is not based on other people. We can become discouraged by comparing ourselves to others and realize that we can't be what they are or what they think we should be. How comforting to know that God is the only one we need to please. Some however, look at people they know and are comfortable and pleased with where they are in their walks with God. We may not be where we should be spiritually, but compared to some, we are doing well. This passage should concern you if you are someone who determines your spiritual maturity by comparing yourself to those around you. To compare ourselves to any standard but God's is "not wise." Comparisons either discourage you from service and joy or fill you with misplaced confidence in where you stand. Using this as your guide, how do you stand in your walk with God? Determine today to stop comparing yourself to others and use God's standard. He alone is who we must please.

2 COR 10:12

...But when they measure themselves by one another and compare themselves with one another, they are without understanding.

SAY WHAT?

Observation: What do I see?

SO WHAT?

Interpretation: What does it mean?

NOW WHAT?

Application: How does it apply to me?

THEN WHAT?

Implementation: What do I do?

RESISTING TEMPTATION

SAY WHAT?
Observation: What do I see?

SO WHAT?
Interpretation: What does it mean?

NOW WHAT?
Application: How does it apply to me?

THEN WHAT?
Implementation: What do I do?

How did the serpent deceive Eve in the garden? Why not go back to Genesis 3 and read the account again to refresh your memory. If you look closely at Genesis 3, you will see Satan used a method he still employs successfully today. It is also a method Paul was afraid Satan would use on those in the church at Corinth. First, in Genesis 3, you see that Satan tried to get Eve to see God as being restrictive. Instead of Eve looking at all the other trees in the garden she could eat from, her attention was drawn to the "one" tree which God told her not to eat. Then, Satan got her to question God's motives for His instructions and expectations. Satan implied God had given instructions, not for her good or because He loved her, but because He was unkind and selfish. Has Satan tried to convince you that God's ways are restrictive and unfair? Do you focus on what you do not have rather than on all He has given you? Has he tried to convince you that God does not have your best interest at heart and is unkind and selfish? If so, memorize the truth of Scripture so that you can quote it when Satan tries to deceive you. Resist him, and he will flee.

★★★★

2 COR 11:3
But I am afraid that as the serpent deceived Eve by his cunning, your thoughts will be led astray from a sincere and pure devotion to Christ.

RESPONSE TO TROUBLE

How do you know if true conversion has taken place in the life of someone who has made a profession of faith? How can you tell if it is really a work of God or if he is simply responding to the way you have presented the gospel? Paul helps us in today's reading to answer these questions. He begins this book with the realization that this church responded to the power of the Holy Spirit, not to his words. He knows they are truly saved because he saw four characteristics in their lives. First, he saw that they were becoming imitators of Christ and were a people who walked with God. Second, they received the Word of God with joy and excitement. They wanted to attend church to learn what Scripture teaches. Third, their faith had become obvious to others because of the change demonstrated in their lives. Fourth, they had given up their former way of life and began serving the One True God. Paul used their daily lives as a measuring stick to determine whether or not they had turned to the true God. What changes have taken place in your life which demonstrate to others that God has worked? Is there evidence of salvation?

★★★★

2 COR 12:5

On behalf of this man I will boast, but on my own behalf I will not boast, except of my weaknesses.

SAY WHAT?
Observation: What do I see?

SO WHAT?
Interpretation: What does it mean?

NOW WHAT?
Application: How does it apply to me?

THEN WHAT?
Implementation: What do I do?

AIM FOR PERFECTION

SAY WHAT?
Observation: What do I see?

SO WHAT?
Interpretation: What does it mean?

NOW WHAT?
Application: How does it apply to me?

THEN WHAT?
Implementation: What do I do?

Why did Paul close this book by admonishing those in Corinth to aim for perfection? That seems like an impossible goal and one that would ultimately discourage the church. Why not just tell them to do the best they could and remember they are human and God understands when they fail? Most likely, Paul closes with that admonition so they did not become satisfied with the progress they were making in their walks with God and with what was happening in the church. Paul didn't want the changes they were making to stop until they had reached perfection. He wanted them never to be satisfied with where they were personally or where the group was until they became, personally and as a church, perfect. So he gave them this goal to shoot for. What is it that you shoot for? Though you may have experienced great growth in your personal life, don't become satisfied. Aim for perfection. Even though your church is growing and God is at work, don't become satisfied. Aim for perfection. Make it your goal and seek every day to become everything God wants you to be. Why not create some way to remind yourself to never be satisfied in any area and always aim for perfection.

2 COR 13:11

Finally, brothers, rejoice. Aim for restoration, comfort one another, agree with one another, live in peace; and the God of love and peace will be with you.

MILITARY
OTD

MILITARY OTD

THE BOOKS OF
GALATIANS
EPHESIANS
PHILLIPIANS &
COLOSSIANS

MARCH
★★★★

★ MONTHLY ★
PRAYER SHEET

"... THE PRAYER OF A RIGHTEOUS PERSON HAS GREAT POWER AS IT IS WORKING."

JAMES 5:16

I NEED TO REACH OUT TO...	HOW I WILL DO IT...	HOW IT WENT...

OTHER REQUEST	HOW ANSWERED	DATE

>>> Share your personal commitments with those who will help keep you accountable to them.

>>> NAME: ....

This sheet is designed to help you make personal commitments each month that will help you grow in your walk with God. Fill it out by determining:

★ What will push you.
★ What you think you can achieve.

>>> PERSONAL DEVOTIONS:

I will commit to read the OnTrack Bible passage and devotional thought .... day(s) each week this month.

>>> CHURCH/CHAPEL ATTENDANCE:

I will attend Church/Chapel .... time(s) this month.
I will attend .... time(s) this month.

>>> SCRIPTURE MEMORY:

I will memorize .... key verse(s) from the daily OnTrack Devotions this month.

>>> OUTREACH:

I will share Christ with .... person/people this month.
I will serve my local church/chapel this month by ....
....
....

>>> OTHER ACTIVITIES:

List any other opportunities such as events, prayer group, etc..., you will participate in this month. ....
....
....
....
....
....
....

Determine to begin today a journey that will last a lifetime, and will change your life forever.

MOTIVE & MESSAGE

How can you tell if someone is a true servant of Christ? How can you know if you are a true servant of Christ or simply a religious person? The answer is found in today's reading. Paul wrote this letter to refute incorrect teaching the church of Galatia was receiving. After Paul left for another region, someone began teaching wrong doctrine. How could the believers in this church identify who was speaking the truth? First, they should examine the motives of the teachers. Paul's goal was to please God and not men (vs10). Unlike other teachers, his words were not motivated by gaining the approval or acceptance of these people. Second, they should closely examine the message. Paul's message did not come from his personal experiences, his own ideas, or from someone else who taught him. His message came from God. He could, therefore, be trusted and his message could be believed. Likewise today, a true servant of God is characterized by right motives and a right message. What is your motive and message? Is your life about love for others or yourself? Is your message about how people can gain eternal life? Use today's questions to take a closer look.

★★★★

GAL 1:10

For am I now seeking the approval of man, or of God? Or am I trying to please man? If I were still trying to please man, I would not be a servant of Christ.

SAY WHAT?

How can you tell what one's true motivation is?

SO WHAT?

How can you tell if one's message is correct?

NOW WHAT?

In what ways do you demonstrate yourself to be someone who is a servant of God?

THEN WHAT?

In light of this passage, what personal commitment can you make?

SAY WHAT?
Observation: What do I see?

SO WHAT?
Interpretation: What does it mean?

NOW WHAT?
Application: How does it apply to me?

THEN WHAT?
Implementation: What do I do?

We learned yesterday what motivated Paul. What did this chapter reveal to you about the motivation of false teachers? If we look closely, we see they wanted to take away freedom in Christ and make people slaves to them (vs 4). These teachers wanted the believers to depend on them to identify what was right and what was wrong. Paul was different. He wanted these people to know and depend on God's Word and the Holy Spirit to lead and guide them. Paul wanted these believers to develop a relationship with God and learn to be sensitive to the leading of the Holy Spirit. Paul's desire was to help them know God and learn to depend on Him and His Word, not on the Apostle Paul. What kind of believer are you becoming? Do you study the Scriptures for yourself so that you know what it says and can make decisions guided by the Holy Spirit? Or are you dependent on others to tell you what is right and wrong? Are you spending time each day developing your relationship with God and His Word? Commit yourself to developing these skills, and allowing the godly leadership in your life to help you along the way.

★★★★

GAL 2:4
Yet because of false brothers secretly brought in—who slipped in to spy out our freedom that we have in Christ Jesus, so that they might bring us into slavery—

OUR SALVATION

Throughout his letter, Paul gave proof to the Galatians that earning salvation and growing spiritually by following the law was wrong. In today's reading, he gave them another example of how faulty the information from some of their leaders was. Did you notice it as you read these verses? Paul asked each of them to examine their lives in order to determine what to believe. Paul had clearly communicated the message of the gospel to them. They knew that Jesus had died to pay for their sins. They knew that the only requirement was trusting Christ, accepting the salvation He offered by faith. They were justified by faith because they believed what they heard. Paul's example of Abraham further illustrated this truth. Take a look at your own life. Has your life changed since you trusted Christ? Did it change because you followed a religious system of good works? No! It changed when you trusted Christ. This is the message we must take to the world. We need to let people know that salvation and change comes not from good works, but by the work of Christ. Are you telling them? Does your life support your message?

GAL 3:3

Are you so foolish? Having begun by the Spirit, are you now being perfected by the flesh?

SAY WHAT?

Observation: What do I see?

SO WHAT?

Interpretation: What does it mean?

NOW WHAT?

Application: How does it apply to me?

THEN WHAT?

Implementation: What do I do?

THE LAW

SAY WHAT?
Observation: What do I see?

SO WHAT?
Interpretation: What does it mean?

NOW WHAT?
Application: How does it apply to me?

THEN WHAT?
Implementation: What do I do?

If the Law, or works, does not bring about transformation or a right relationship with God, what was the purpose of the Law that God gave to Moses? According to verse 24, it was given to bring us to Christ. Christ is our only means of becoming righteous. The Law cannot make us righteous. The purpose of the Law was to reveal one's need of a Savior. It shows us that it is not possible to earn one's way to heaven through good works. It is a standard that is too high for any human to achieve. The Law shows us our need for another way to gain access to God. It demonstrates our sinfulness and ultimately leads us to the Savior. The law enables us to see that the only way we can gain access to God is through faith in Jesus Christ. Through Him we become sons of God. We are not slaves who follow a system in order to gain favor. We are sons who have gained our sonship through our new birth into the family of God. Without a standard, we would not know how short we have fallen or how much help we need. There are so many people who are trying to earn their way to God and don't realize that Jesus Christ has already done the work. Are you letting them know?

★★★★

GAL 3:17
This is what I mean: the law, which came 430 years afterward, does not annul a covenant previously ratified by God, so as to make the promise void.

WASTED?

Think of an individual or two who have invested time and effort in your life to help you grow in your walk with God. As they evaluate your spiritual journey to this point, how do you think they feel about the time and effort they have devoted to your life? Paul, in verse 11 of today's reading, makes a statement that ought to cause us to think about this very question. He invested a lot of time in the lives of the believers in the church of Galatia. Most of his time was devoted to studying the Word, teaching it carefully and trying to build relationships with them to help them grow spiritually. If they began to fall away and believe the false teachers, he feared his effort would have been in vain. Had the Galatians ignored the truth and lived as though they had never heard it, Paul's many hours of patient teaching would have been for nothing. It is discouraging to work to ensure that one knows the truth and how to apply it only to see them disregard it by word or deed. It must break the hearts of parents, pastors, and friends who try diligently to help us, only to see the truth rejected. As they examine your life, how do you think they feel about where you are now?

GAL 4:11
I am afraid I may have labored over you in vain.

SAY WHAT?
Name people who have invested time and energy into your life?

SO WHAT?
In what ways have they impacted your life?

NOW WHAT?
How can you demonstrate to them that their efforts are not in vain?

THEN WHAT?
In light of this passage, what personal commitment can you make?

MILITARYDEVOTIONAL.COM
🐦 @MILITARYDEVOS

The book of Proverbs was designed to help us in "attaining wisdom and discipline; in understanding words of insight; in acquiring a disciplined and prudent life, doing what is right and just and fair; in giving prudence to the simple, knowledge and discretion to the young." As you read through this chapter, write down the verses that are most significant to you in your present circumstances.

VERSE | WHAT TRUTH IT COMMUNICATES | HOW IT IMPACTS MY LIFE

BY THE SPIRIT

If our actions cannot gain us favor with God, and we are not to live according to lists of right and wrong, can we then do whatever we want once we are saved? Not according to Paul. Paul writes that we are not to live by lists, but by the Spirit. He realizes that it could be possible for some to interpret his statements as a license to do wrong. They could use their freedom in Christ to do what their sinful nature wants to do, and then justify their behavior because as believers, they are free from restrictive laws. Paul wrote to correct that reasoning which some were living by. Instead, they were to fulfill the principle of Scripture: "love your neighbor as yourself," while being guided by the Holy Spirit. We need to learn what the principles of Scripture are and then allow the Holy Spirit to lead us to live accordingly. We, as believers, live by Biblical principles, implemented by the guidance of the Holy Spirit, not by a list of rules from men. How are you doing in this area? Are you successfully living by the Holy Spirit? Use today's questions to help you determine the steps you need to take to increase your dependence on the Holy Spirit.

★★★★

GAL 5:16

But I say, walk by the Spirit, and you will not gratify the desires of the flesh.

SAY WHAT?

How are the acts of the sinful nature demonstrated in my life? (5:19-21)

SO WHAT?

In what ways do I see the fruit of the Spirit in my life? (5:22-26)

NOW WHAT?

What can I do to diminish the acts of the sinful nature and increase the fruit of the spirit in my life?

THEN WHAT?

What personal commitment can I make in light of today's reading?

ESPECIALLY...

SAY WHAT?
Observation: What do I see?

SO WHAT?
Interpretation: What does it mean?

NOW WHAT?
Application: How does it apply to me?

THEN WHAT?
Implementation: What do I do?

How important are fellow Christians to you? Are they a high priority in your life? Is your commitment and care for your saved friends greater than your commitment to your unsaved friends? In today's reading Paul finishes with an interesting phrase that we could easily overlook. It is found in verse 10. His closing admonitions to the Galatians were to be careful of the false teachers, be careful what is sown, and not to become weary in doing good. He further closed his letter encouraging them to take every opportunity available to do good to all people. Then he added the phrase, "especially to those who belong to the family of believers." In other words, it is more important for us to take advantage of every opportunity to do good to our brothers and sisters in Christ than it is to those who are not saved. Other believers ought to be the priority of our lives. That's a tough one because we tend to expect more out of them... but maybe that's why we need the humility Paul talks about early in the chapter. We ought to care for each other and seek always to meet each other's needs because of our relationship to each other through Christ. Does your life reflect this priority? In what ways have you demonstrated love to the family of believers recently? How can you get started today?

★★★★

GAL 6:10
So then, as we have opportunity, let us do good to everyone, and especially to those who are of the household of faith.

EVERYTHING

What if my present situation does not work out? What if it just gets worse and never gets better? Have you ever been haunted by those thoughts? Maybe today you are in the midst of a situation that looks tough, and there seems to be no way out. All you see ahead is more pain and difficulty. It looks like it will never change and you have concluded that there is no hope. If that describes you,then you must have found today's reading motivating. Why? Because Paul tells us that we have been chosen by the one who works out "everything" in conformity to His will. Think about that for a moment. What in our life is not included in "everything?" Is your present situation included? God knows exactly what is going on in your life and He wants you to know that it will work out exactly as He has planned. You must trust Him and realize "everything" includes what you are presently facing. Ultimately,God's will is going to be accomplished even if right now it might not seem like that is possible. Trust Him and be amazed at what He does.

EPH 1:11

In him we have obtained an inheritance, having been predestined according to the purpose of him who works all things according to the counsel of his will,

SAY WHAT?
Observation: What do I see?

SO WHAT?
Interpretation: What does it mean?

NOW WHAT?
Application: How does it apply to me?

THEN WHAT?
Implementation: What do I do?

MILITARYDEVOTIONAL.COM
@MILITARYDEVOS

SAY WHAT?
Observation: What do I see?

SO WHAT?
Interpretation: What does it mean?

NOW WHAT?
Application: How does it apply to me?

THEN WHAT?
Implementation: What do I do?

What kinds of things do you pray for? If God answered your prayers, what would happen in your life, in your unit, in your church or in your family as a result of your requests? If you ask for the kind of things Paul asked for in today's reading, your life would never be the same. Look at some of the things Paul asks God to do in people's lives here in today's reading. In verse 18, he prays that their eyes would be opened so they could see three things. He knew that if the Ephesians could see these as clearly as God intended, they would never be the same. First, Paul wanted God to open their eyes to the hope they had. Second, he asked that they see the riches of the inheritance God had given to them. Third, he wanted God to open their eyes to the power that was available to them. Think what would happen in your life or in your church or in your family if you and others really began to see these three things the way God sees them. Start today asking God to open your eyes to all you have in Him. Ask Him to do the same for others. Ask Him to do what will really change lives. You and your family and your church will never be the same.

★★★★

EPH 1:18
...having the eyes of your hearts enlightened, that you may know what is the hope to which he has called you, what are the riches of his glorious inheritance in the saints,

DEAD MEN WALKING

What does it mean to be 'dead in your sins?" In today's reading, Paul gives four characteristics of someone who is not saved. Knowing them will help us have a greater burden for the unsaved and a greater appreciation for our salvation. First, he says that those who are dead in their sins follow the ways of the world (vs2). They live by its value system and it sets their goals. Second, they follow Satan (vs2). They live according to his goals and can't resist his temptations. They have no power over sin. In fact, they are his slaves. Third, they gratify the cravings of their sinful nature (vs3). They do whatever makes them feel good and is comfortable. They are controlled by their desires. They have no self control. Fourth, they follow the desires and thoughts of their sinful nature. This characteristic literally means they willfully choose to go against the will of God and follow the world. Thankfully, God saw us in this condition and made us alive through faith in Jesus Christ. Why? That He might show the incomparable riches of His grace. Who in your world is living as one who is dead in his sin and needs to be made alive?

★★★★

EPH 2:3

...among whom we all once lived in the passions of our flesh, carrying out the desires of the body and the mind, and were by nature children of wrath, like the rest of mankind.

SAY WHAT?

Observation: What do I see?

SO WHAT?

Interpretation: What does it mean?

NOW WHAT?

Application: How does it apply to me?

THEN WHAT?

Implementation: What do I do?

PREJUDICE CONDEMNED

SAY WHAT?
Observation: What do I see?

SO WHAT?
Interpretation: What does it mean?

NOW WHAT?
Application: How does it apply to me?

THEN WHAT?
Implementation: What do I do?

Racism and prejudice are despicable. Nobody who truly understands and follows Biblical teaching will engage in prejudice of any kind. This passage shows us why. Paul explained to this church, made up of mostly Gentiles, that, at one time, they were outside of God. They were Gentiles and not part of God's promise. Jesus Christ came and abolished what divided the Jew and the Gentile. He made it possible for all people to become part of the body of Christ. There are no longer foreigners or aliens. The power of the gospel goes beyond race or nationality and makes believers of all races and nationalities one in Christ. We are all members of one body. We should not need black churches, white churches, Hispanic churches and Oriental churches. Our churches ought to be an example to the world that the gospel of Jesus Christ breaks the walls that divide us and we are all one in Him. Does your life demonstrate you believe this? Is your church an example of this to your community? Jesus Christ broke down the walls that divided the races. Look at your friends and evaluate your life.

★★★★

EPH 2:21
...in whom the whole structure, being joined together, grows into a holy temple in the Lord.

The book of Proverbs was designed to help us in "attaining wisdom and discipline; in understanding words of insight; in acquiring a disciplined and prudent life, doing what is right and just and fair; in giving prudence to the simple, knowledge and discretion to the young." As you read through this chapter, write down the verses that are most significant to you in your present circumstances.

VERSE | WHAT TRUTH IT COMMUNICATES | HOW IT IMPACTS MY LIFE

WALK WORTHY

SAY WHAT?
Observation: What do I see?

SO WHAT?
Interpretation: What does it mean?

NOW WHAT?
Application: How does it apply to me?

THEN WHAT?
Implementation: What do I do?

What does it mean to live a life "worthy" of your calling? Christians today have lost credibility in the eyes of the world because we do not understand what this word means and fail to follow what it teaches. We as Christians talk a big talk, but it seldom matches our walk. The word Paul uses here, translated worthy, addresses that very issue. The word worthy is a term which originally had to do with scales. If one wanted the scale to balance, he would place an equal weight on the other side. When it was balanced, it was "worthy." Paul wrote in previous three chapters about what we have since we've trusted Christ. For the rest of the book, he will tell us how we ought to act in light of this truth. On one side of our scale is what Paul described in chapters 1-3. Paul now says the other side, our behavior, must balance or be "worthy" of what is true of us. Do you walk "worthy" of who you are in Christ? Does your conduct balance with what Christ has done in you? Does your walk match your talk? What changes do you need to make to walk a "worthy" one?

★★★★

EPH 4:1
I therefore, a prisoner for the Lord, urge you to walk in a manner worthy of the calling to which you have been called,

REPLACEMENT PRINCIPLE

In today's reading, we find one of the most important sections of Scripture on how to become mature and godly in our faith. It contains the pattern for putting into practice all Paul has discussed in chapters 1-3. It is called the replacement principle. Paul teaches us that growing spiritually is more than just stopping wrong behavior. For those who struggle with lying, just stopping is not enough. Maturing involves replacing the wrong behavior with the right behavior. A liar must not only stop lying, but start telling the truth. A person who steals should not just stop stealing; he must start to do something positive with his hands. If we struggle with our thought life, we cannot just stop thinking bad thoughts; we replace those thoughts with good, pure thoughts. Often we make decisions to "put off" wrong behavior or thoughts but never follow through in "putting on" the right behavior and thoughts. When we determine what to "put off," we must then "put on" what Scripture tells us is the right behavior. In what area of your life do you need to replace the wrong with what's right? Use today's sheet to help you get started "putting on."

★★★★

EPH 4:22

...to put off your old self, which belongs to your former manner of life and is corrupt through deceitful desires,

SAY WHAT?

What specific issues of attitude and/or behavior do you need to "put off?"

SO WHAT?

What specific behavior and/or attitudes do you need to "put on" in order to replace the wrong?

NOW WHAT?

What plan can you develope to make sure you "put off" sin and "put on" what's right?

THEN WHAT?

What personal commitment can you make in light of today's reading?

MILITARYDEVOTIONAL.COM
@MILITARYDEVOS

SAY WHAT?

Observation: What do I see?

SO WHAT?

Interpretation: What does it mean?

NOW WHAT?

Application: How does it apply to me?

THEN WHAT?

Implementation: What do I do?

After spending time with you, would an acquaintance know whose child you are? Have you ever had someone who did not know you ask you if you were your parents' child just by observing how you act? Would someone know you belong to Jesus Christ after watching you for a while? They would if you are successful in doing what Paul asks us to do in today's reading. He explains that we need to be imitators of God. We see kids everywhere who imitate someone. At basketball games, some players wear sweat bands exactly like their favorite NBA player does. They're imitating those individuals. People imitate their favorite musicians in dress and hair styles. Paul stresses that we, as Christians, need to be imitating God. We need to act, wherever we are, like He would. While doing our job, we need to do it as He would. When people see us, they need to see Jesus Christ. Who are you imitating? Do your actions, attitudes, dress, etc, demonstrate that you are striving to be like Him? Can people see Him in all you do? If not, concentrate your efforts on imitating Him and let the people in your world see Christ.

EPH 5:1

Therefore be imitators of God, as beloved children.

OUR SWORD

When He was on earth, did Jesus use the armor of God to stand against Satan's schemes? What examples can you think of? In one example, Luke tells how Jesus used a piece of the armor we find here and demonstrated how we can use that piece of armor too. In verse 17, Paul tells us to take up the "sword of the Spirit." The word for "sword" here is not a large sword pulled out of the belt, but a small dagger-like sword used in hand-to-hand combat. It had a very specific purpose and target. He then says that for us, this sword is the Word of God. Paul wasn't referring to the Bible in general, but "specific" passages of the Bible which deal with particular situations. Our sword, in hand-to-hand combat against Satan's schemes, is "specific" verses of Scripture which attack "specific" schemes of Satan. When Satan strikes us with fear, we strike back with verses like Philippians 4:6-7. That is what Christ did in Luke 4:1-13. We need to arm ourselves with "specific" verses that address the scheme Satan is using against us. Remember, the best defense is a good offense. What verses should you memorize to help stand against Satan?

EPH 6:17

...and take the helmet of salvation, and the sword of the Spirit, which is the word of God,

SAY WHAT?

In what way is Satan currently attacking you?

SO WHAT?

What specific verses can you memorize to help you fight these attacks?

NOW WHAT?

Write some of them here to begin the process of memorizing them?

THEN WHAT?

What personal commitment can you make in light of today's reading?

SAY WHAT?
Observation: What do I see?

SO WHAT?
Interpretation: What does it mean?

NOW WHAT?
Application: How does it apply to me?

THEN WHAT?
Implementation: What do I do?

If you had to make a choice between something that is good, better or best, which one would you choose? Of course most would say that they would want the best, but often they are willing to settle for better or good. We live in a world that seems to be very satisfied with just getting by or just being "good." We are satisfied with "good" grades, a "good" game, or having a "good" job. Is that what God intended for Christians? NO! If God never intended us to settle for good, then how do we make sure we have "best?" We find the answer in Paul's prayer. He didn't want those in Philippi to settle for "good," so he asked God to grant these two requests. The first is that their love would abound more and more in knowledge, one of learning new Biblical truth. Second, he asks for depth of insight, which is a deep understanding of something being right or wrong. We too will choose what is best if we are gaining more Biblical knowledge and as a result growing in our Spirit-led sense of what is right. Ask God to enable your love to abound in these two ways today when you pray. You will never be the same!

★★★★

PHIL 1:10
...so that you may approve what is excellent, and so be pure and blameless for the day of Christ,

ATTITUDE

With what words would you describe your attitude most of the time? Are you known for having a humble attitude or a prideful attitude? According to today's passage, your attitude towards every circumstance should be just like Jesus Christ's. Paul tells us that Jesus Christ was in every way God, but He didn't demand or fight for the advantages or rights of being God. If He had He would not have left the throne room of heaven to become a man. Instead, He was able to make Himself nothing and become a servant. He not only became a man, but a servant and was obedient to death. It was not just any death however, He became obedient to death on a cross, the most humiliating way to die in that culture. Why? Because He cared about your needs above His own. That's what it took to redeem you. Do you demand preferential treatment from those of lower rank or are you willing to put aside your position in order to serve others? "I deserve better" is not something a person with Christ's attitude would say. Is God speaking to an area in which your attitude is not like Christ's?

SAY WHAT?

In what areas do you find it difficult to have an attitude like Christ's?

SO WHAT?

Why is it hard for you to have Christ's attitude in this area?

NOW WHAT?

What can you do to begin to demonstrate an attitude like Christ's?

THEN WHAT?

What personal commitment can you make in light of this passage?

PHIL 2:5

Have this mind among yourselves, which is yours in Christ Jesus,

The book of Proverbs was designed to help us in "attaining wisdom and discipline; in understanding words of insight; in acquiring a disciplined and prudent life, doing what is right and just and fair; in giving prudence to the simple, knowledge and discretion to the young." As you read through this chapter, write down the verses that are most significant to you in your present circumstances.

VERSE | WHAT TRUTH IT COMMUNICATES | HOW IT IMPACTS MY LIFE

PURSUING GROWTH

What does "to work out your salvation" mean in this passage? We know that it certainly does not mean that you can earn your way to heaven because that would contradict what Paul taught in the book of Romans and several other places in his writings. A close look at verse 13 explains Paul's meaning and gives us one of the greatest promises in all of Scripture. Paul tells the Philippians to work out in their lives the results of their salvation. That is, to make sure that their lives were demonstrating fruit from their salvation. Why could he expect them to be able to see the results in their lives? Because, according to verse 13, "it is God who works in you to will," the want to, "and to act," the ability to carry it out, "according to His good pleasure." In other words, it is God who gives you the desire to do what is right and the ability to carry it out. Success in the Christian life is possible for everyone who is saved. If you want to be more faithful in your devotions or in sharing Christ, ask God to give you the will and the ability to. In what area of your life right now do you need the will to do what is right? Start by asking God to give it to you.

PHIL 2:13

...for it is God who works in you, both to will and to work for his good pleasure.

SAY WHAT?

Observation: What do I see?

SO WHAT?

Interpretation: What does it mean?

NOW WHAT?

Application: How does it apply to me?

THEN WHAT?

Implementation: What do I do?

MILITARYDEVOTIONAL.COM
🐦 @MILITARYDEVOS

SAY WHAT?

What things do people look at to determine if they are saved?

SO WHAT?

What do you look at as evidence that you are saved?

NOW WHAT?

What does Scripture identify as confirmation of your salvation?

THEN WHAT?

What personal commitment can you make in light of this passage?

Why would Paul, at one time in his life, feel he was right with God even though he was not? Can we learn from his example how to avoid doing it in our own lives? The answer? He put confidence in the wrong things. At one time he thought he was righteous because of his heritage. He had been born into a Jewish family and had followed all the Jewish regulations and laws. He was a Hebrew of Hebrews which meant he had come from a family that avoided all assimilation into the popular culture of the day. They remained true to the law. He became a Pharisee. He kept the law and lived according to strict standards. He had so much zeal for God. He even persecuted the church. According to Jewish standards, he was faultless. But he wasn't saved. He felt he was righteous because of the "spiritual things" he had done and the family into which he had been born. Could you be making the same mistake? Do you feel all is well because you come from a Christian family and do the "Christian" things? Do you really know God? Have you ever trusted Christ?

★★★★

PHIL 3:3

For we are the circumcision, who worship by the Spirit of God and glory in Christ Jesus and put no confidence in the flesh—

ONE THING

Could you squeeze everything you do into "one thing?" Or is your life filled with so many things that to describe what you do that you would have to use the number five or ten. What an amazing statement the Apostle Paul makes in today's reading! He says in verse 13, "one thing I do." The one thing he did was to press on toward the goal to which God had called him. No matter what he did in his life, it could all be boiled down into "one thing." How did he do it? He did it by forgetting the past and straining toward the future. Why is it important to forget the past? First, the past can cripple you with guilt over past sin or past failures. Second, the past can make you proud. You can look back and become satisfied with what you have done and no longer strive for what is ahead. So if Paul wanted to achieve his "one" goal, he had to forget the past and strive for the future. Remember that Paul's past included high achievement... and murder. Guilt and pride will keep you from moving forward. What is your "one" goal? Is it to win the prize God has for you? Forget the past, its failures and its successes, and strive for what is ahead. The past can be a dangerous place, so leave it there!

PHIL 3:13

Brothers, I do not consider that I have made it my own. But one thing I do: forgetting what lies behind and straining forward to what lies ahead,

SAY WHAT?
Observation: What do I see?

SO WHAT?
Interpretation: What does it mean?

NOW WHAT?
Application: How does it apply to me?

THEN WHAT?
Implementation: What do I do?

SAY WHAT?
Observation: What do I see?

SO WHAT?
Interpretation: What does it mean?

NOW WHAT?
Application: How does it apply to me?

THEN WHAT?
Implementation: What do I do?

One of the beautiful things about Scripture is how God's choice of words make it perfectly clear what He expects of us. Today we find a verse that does exactly that. Did you notice it? Paul tells the church in Philippi not to be anxious about "anything," and in "everything," present their requests to God. That is all-inclusive. God does not want us to worry about one thing, no matter what it is. We should not fret or worry about "anything." Instead, when we face something that could make us anxious, we are to take it to God in prayer. We must not only take it to God, but take it with a thankful heart. We must be thankful for the certainty that He will always provide and always meet our needs. He will either take care of what concerns us or He will give us grace to allow it to strengthen us. Therefore, in "everything," take your concerns to God. What are you anxious about today? What are you concerned might take place? Whatever the circumstances, do not be anxious. Instead, give it to God in prayer. Ask Him to take care of it. Then His peace will guard your heart. Why not take it to Him right now!

★★★★

PHIL 4:6
...do not be anxious about anything, but in everything by prayer and supplication with thanksgiving let your requests be made known to God.

RESULTS OF PRAYER

When you pray, what do you pray for? As you have read through these four books known as the Prison Epistles, hopefully you have learned a great deal from observing the way Paul prayed. In today's reading, we have another one of his prayers to more closely observe. It gives us an example of how to pray. It also shows the results of our prayers in the lives of those we have prayed for. Paul prayed that God would fill the people in the church of Colosse with the knowledge of His will through spiritual wisdom and understanding. We find that there are six results from this prayer. Number them in your Bible. "They will live a life worthy of the Lord (vs. 10); they will please God in every way (vs. 10); they will bear fruit in every good work (vs. 10); they will grow in the knowledge of God (vs. 10); they will strengthen with all power (vs. 11); and they will joyfully give thanks to God (vs. 11)." Who would not want these items to characterize his spiritual life? Imagine what would happen in your church when these six results begin to show themselves in people's lives. Ask God to give you what Paul prayed for in this chapter.

SAY WHAT?
Observation: What do I see?

SO WHAT?
Interpretation: What does it mean?

NOW WHAT?
Application: How does it apply to me?

THEN WHAT?
Implementation: What do I do?

COL 1:9

And so, from the day we heard, we have not ceased to pray for you, asking that you may be filled with the knowledge of his will in all spiritual wisdom and understanding.

SAY WHAT?

Observation: What do I see?

SO WHAT?

Interpretation: What does it mean?

NOW WHAT?

Application: How does it apply to me?

THEN WHAT?

Implementation: What do I do?

Have you noticed as you read your Bible how important certain words are? Change one seemingly insignificant word and the whole meaning of a verse or passage changes. One of these words is in today's reading. It could be easily overlooked or missed. If God had chosen a different word, the whole meaning and its significance would change. Look at the pronoun Paul uses in verse 29 of chapter one. He talks about how he is striving to admonish and teach them with all wisdom that he might present them in every way perfect to God. It sounds like hard,tiring work,doesn't it? How can he do that? He tells us by the pronoun he uses. Circle in your Bible whose energy he was using. If we are going to accomplish what God wants for us, we must also learn to operate with HIS energy. Paul operated in God's power, not in his own strength. You may be struggling because you are trying to accomplish things in your energy,not HIS. Allow God's unlimited energy to strengthen you today. Stop trying to live the Christian life on your own. Take time today to surrender your will and let God have complete control.

COL 1:29

For this I toil, struggling with all his energy that he powerfully works within me.

The book of Proverbs was designed to help us in "attaining wisdom and discipline; in understanding words of insight; in acquiring a disciplined and prudent life, doing what is right and just and fair; in giving prudence to the simple, knowledge and discretion to the young." As you read through this chapter, write down the verses that are most significant to you in your present circumstances.

VERSE | WHAT TRUTH IT COMMUNICATES | HOW IT IMPACTS MY LIFE

SAY WHAT?
Observation: What do I see?

SO WHAT?
Interpretation: What does it mean?

NOW WHAT?
Application: How does it apply to me?

THEN WHAT?
Implementation: What do I do?

As you read this chapter,can you feel the emotion Paul had as he wrote? He was very concerned about what was happening in this church. There were some who came into the church and taught that the people needed to live according to a set of human established lists in order to be really spiritual. In other words,they were being legalistic. According to verse 22,they had made up rules not found in Scripture, but based on man's wisdom and teaching. Paul's concern was that,while they had an appearance of wisdom,living by those standards gave them no power over sin. Paul was concerned that they were living according to those standards. Although they appeared to be spiritual outwardly, they were powerless over sin. Examine your life. Do you have power over sexual temptation both mentally and physically? When people wrong you,do you have the power to forgive and go on? If not,it could be that you are living according to human standards that give no power. How can you tell? Spend some time today honestly examining your life. Tomorrow's reading will tell you how to change what you find.

★★★★

COL 2:23
These have indeed an appearance of wisdom in promoting self-made religion and asceticism and severity to the body, but they are of no value in stopping the indulgence of the flesh.

PUT TO DEATH

We arrive at today's reading eager to learn how to put into practice yesterday's text. Paul tells us that since human standards and regulations do not give us any power over sin, we are to set our hearts on Christ. How? He explains in this chapter the process to be able to accomplish this task. First, we must make sure we have our hearts set on things above. Our ambition needs to be to please God alone. Second, we need to think about those things. When we think about them, we will desire them and then we will seek to "put to death" greed, evil desires, anger, rage, malice, filthy language, etc. We will not only stop doing them but will replace them with the items he lists in verses 12-15. He then closes with three keys to success in this area. Put numbers next to them in your Bible. First, we accomplish this by letting the peace of Christ RULE in our hearts (vs15). Second, we let the Word of Christ, which is the Bible, DWELL in us (vs16). We finish by DOING everything in the name of God (vs17). How are you doing in this process? Use the questions to the right to help you create ways to begin changing these areas in your life.

SAY WHAT?

In what ways can I begin to allow the peace of Christ to rule in my heart?

SO WHAT?

In what ways can I begin to allow the Word of God to dwell in me richly?

NOW WHAT?

How can I begin to do everything in the name of God?

THEN WHAT?

What personal commitment can you make in light of what this passage teaches?

COL 3:5

Put to death therefore what is earthly in you: sexual immorality, impurity, passion, evil desire, and covetousness, which is idolatry.

MAKE THE MOST OF

SAY WHAT?
Observation: What do I see?

SO WHAT?
Interpretation: What does it mean?

NOW WHAT?
Application: How does it apply to me?

THEN WHAT?
Implementation: What do I do?

How many opportunities in a typical day do you have to impact others? How many opportunities do you have to give a word of encouragement to someone who is discouraged? How many people will you see who are ready to give up, even though they may not appear so? How many opportunities do you have to plant a seed that will help someone make an important decision in their future? How many opportunities do you have to share something about your faith that will encourage an unsaved friend to think about his relationship to Christ? How many opportunities do you have to demonstrate to someone who is watching the difference that Jesus Christ makes in your life? If you are honest, you would have to answer all of those questions with the word "many." With that knowledge in mind, Paul closes this letter with an important admonition. He tells the Colossians to make the most of "every" opportunity. What a great prayer it is for you each day. "Today, God, help me to see the many opportunities I have to influence my world and to make the most of every opportunity to impact others."

★★★★

COL 4:5
Walk in wisdom toward outsiders, making the best use of the time.

The book of Proverbs was designed to help us in "attaining wisdom and discipline; in understanding words of insight; in acquiring a disciplined and prudent life, doing what is right and just and fair; in giving prudence to the simple, knowledge and discretion to the young." As you read through this chapter, write down the verses that are most significant to you in your present circumstances.

VERSE | WHAT TRUTH IT COMMUNICATES | HOW IT IMPACTS MY LIFE

» MILITARYDEVOTIONAL.COM

 @MILITARYDEVOS

 FACEBOOK.COM/MILITARYDEVOS

MILITARY OTD

NAV 2

APRIL
★★★★

MONTHLY
PRAYER SHEET

"... THE PRAYER OF A RIGHTEOUS PERSON HAS GREAT POWER AS IT IS WORKING."

JAMES 5:16

I NEED TO
REACH OUT TO...

HOW
I WILL DO IT...

HOW
IT WENT...

OTHER
REQUEST

HOW
ANSWERED

DATE

★ MONTHLY ★
★ MISSION SHEET ★

⟫ Share your personal commitments with those who will help keep you accountable to them.

⟫ **NAME:** ....

This sheet is designed to help you make personal commitments each month that will help you grow in your walk with God. Fill it out by determining:

★ What will push you.
★ What you think you can achieve.

⟫ **PERSONAL DEVOTIONS:**
I will commit to read the OnTrack Bible passage and devotional thought .... day(s) each week this month.

⟫ **CHURCH/CHAPEL ATTENDANCE:**
I will attend Church/Chapel .... time(s) this month.
I will attend .... time(s) this month.

⟫ **SCRIPTURE MEMORY:**
I will memorize .... key verse(s) from the daily OnTrack Devotions this month.

⟫ **OUTREACH:**
I will share Christ with .... person/people this month.
I will serve my local church/chapel this month by ....
....
....

⟫ **OTHER ACTIVITIES:**
List any other opportunities such as events, prayer group, etc..., you will participate in this month. ....
....
....
....
....
....

Determine to begin today a journey that will last a lifetime, and will change your life forever.

GOD'S WOMEN

How many women are mentioned in the genealogy of Christ? Circle them in your Bible. In what way are these women different from each other? Why do you think,in the genealogy of Christ recorded here in Matthew, that God mentions these particular women? It seems obvious that God is trying to specifically identify these women. If you examine Scripture, you find that they are all so very different. Maybe from their examples God is trying to show that He chooses to use all kinds of people. You may identify with: Tamar - a victim of lies and disappointment, Rahab - a background of sexual sin, Ruth - a different culture and background than those you are around, Bathsheba - a victim of violation and pain, Mary - an example of purity and quiet spirit. Whatever your background, God will use you. God loves you and wants to use you no matter who you are. In what way have you allowed Satan to convince you that God cannot use you? Concentrate today on God's ability to transform, rather than focucsing on your limitations. Allow the examples of these women to encourage your heart.

SAY WHAT?
What do you or others see as things that limit your ability to be used by God?

SO WHAT?
How might God want to use those limitations?

NOW WHAT?
What would it take for you to be convinced He could transform them?

THEN WHAT?
In light of this passage,what personal commitment can you make?

★★★★

MATTHEW 1:1
The book of the genealogy of Jesus Christ, the son of David, the son of Abraham.

WITHOUT HESITATION

SAY WHAT?
Observation: What do I see?

SO WHAT?
Interpretation: What does it mean?

NOW WHAT?
Application: How does it apply to me?

THEN WHAT?
Implementation: What do I do?

What thoughts do you think went through Joseph's mind when the angel told him to leave home? How many different times was he asked to move? Number them in your Bible. What do you think was involved for Joseph and his family to get up and leave each time? It is amazing, with all Joseph had to do, that he would so quickly obey. The angel said go and he "got up." Leaving family, friends, a job, and moving to a foreign land must have been tough. However, you read nothing of any hesitation. He seemed to be concerned about only what God wanted for his life and he was willing to go anywhere and make any sacrifice necessary to do what God wanted. Joseph sure was a great man of faith in his world. How much would you be willing to give up if God asked you? Would you give up friends, sports, a boyfriend or girlfriend, your job, your rank? Might there be something right now that you know God would have you do, but you have resisted? Ask God to make you more like Joseph. He commands and you obey without hesitation. Start today to obey right away.

MATTHEW 2:14
And he rose and took the child and his mother by night and departed to Egypt...

IT IS WRITTEN

What response do you think Satan expected from Christ when He was being tempted? What can you learn from Jesus' response to His temptations? In this account we see demonstrated the most important weapon we have in resisting temptation. What is it? Scripture. Because He was God, Jesus could have just commanded Satan to leave Him alone. Instead, He responded to temptation with Scripture. Christ gives to us a wonderful example to follow in resisting the temptations of Satan in our lives today. We need to arm ourselves with specific passages of Scripture to quote whenever we are faced with temptation. If God Himself used Scripture, how important it must be for us to memorize Scripture so we can use it to resist the temptations of Satan. In what way is Satan tempting you? What Scripture passage can you memorize that will enable you to resist and not sin? If you need help, ask someone to help you find some specific verses. Start now hiding God's Word in your heart that you might not sin against Him.

SAY WHAT?

Make a list of the temptations you face most often.

SO WHAT?

What Scripture verses address those kinds of temptations?

NOW WHAT?

Pick one of the verses above and write it out below to begin memorizing it.

THEN WHAT?

In light of this passage, what personal commitment can you make?

MATTHEW 4:6

...and said to him, "If you are the Son of God, throw yourself down, for it is written,"'He will command his angels concerning you,'

SAY WHAT?

Observation: What do I see?

SO WHAT?

Interpretation: What does it mean?

NOW WHAT?

Application: How does it apply to me?

THEN WHAT?

Implementation: What do I do?

What verbs does Christ use in verse thirteen that He also uses in verse fourteen to describe salt and light? Circle the verb in your Bible. How would verses thirteen and fourteen be different if, instead of the verb, are, it was, could be? It would change the whole meaning of what Christ was saying. He is not saying that it is possible, or that we "could be," or even that we "should be" the salt of the earth and the light of the world. He is, in fact, saying we "are." Therefore, it should be natural for us in our worlds to do what salt and light does. If we are not salt and light, it is because we have chosen in some way to hinder what we already are. Maybe we say things so we don't stick out or we laugh at things so people won't know who we are. What a tragedy to have people not see our good deeds and praise our Father in heaven. How are you hindering yourself from being salt and light? Have you covered up your light so that it barely shines or doesn't shine at all? Plan now to begin to let what you "are" show forth in your daily living. How can you begin to show to others who you are?

★★★★

MATTHEW 5:13

"You are the salt of the earth, but if salt has lost its taste, how shall its saltiness be restored? It is no longer good for anything except to be thrown out and trampled under people's feet.

WHERE'S YOUR TREASURE?

What do people view as treasures here on earth? What are examples of treasures that would be in heaven? How do we store them up? How can you tell where you are storing yours? It seems that one way to tell would be to look at where you spend most of your time. There are those who claim to have their treasure in heaven yet spend no time in personal devotions, or don't take time to reach out to someone who is hurting, etc. They probably don't miss weight training or a TV show. Can they say their treasure is in heaven? People who choose weights over time with God or attending church would seem to be more interested in laying up treasures on earth than treasures in heaven. How tragic to store up all kinds of treasures here on earth that will only waste away and not store up treasures where they will last forever. Be honest,. Where is your treasure? Do the things of God take priority over friends, gaining rank, family, music, etc.? Make time with God your priority and lay up for yourself treasures in heaven. Your heart will be where it should be.

SAY WHAT?
Observation: What do I see?

SO WHAT?
Interpretation: What does it mean?

NOW WHAT?
Application: How does it apply to me?

THEN WHAT?
Implementation: What do I do?

★★★★

MATTHEW 6:21
For where your treasure is, there your heart will be also.

MILITARYDEVOTIONAL.COM
@MILITARYDEVOS

SAY WHAT?

What fruit in your life identifies you as being saved?

SO WHAT?

In what areas have you seen growth this past year?

NOW WHAT?

Where are you spiritually? What do you need to move forward?

THEN WHAT?

In light of this passage, what personal commitment can you make?

Are verses 21-23 an encouragement to you, or do they scare you? How awful to be someone who thinks they are saved when, in fact, they are not. This section of chapter 7, verses 21-23, is sobering. It is amazing to realize that there are people who actually believe that they have eternal life when, in fact, they do not. They will even give to God examples of things that they have done which they think illustrate that they are saved. How shocked they will be when they hear the words, "I never knew you." Could you be one of those people? Have you ever taken the time to examine your life and honestly determine if you are saved? What "fruit" is there in your life that clearly identifies you as being saved? Are you gaining more victory over sin than you were this time last year? Can you say no to peer pressure more than last year? A true believer will show it by his fruit. What does your fruit tell you? If you have concerns, ask God to show you the true condition of your heart. Use the sheet to the left to help you. Make sure you have the courage to respond to what it reveals. Is there sin in the life of one you care about? How will you respond to this passage of Scripture?

MATTHEW 7:23

And then will I declare to them, 'I never knew you; depart from me, you workers of lawlessness.'

The book of Proverbs was designed to help us in "attaining wisdom and discipline; in understanding words of insight; in acquiring a disciplined and prudent life, doing what is right and just and fair; in giving prudence to the simple, knowledge and discretion to the young." As you read through this chapter, write down the verses that are most significant to you in your present circumstances.

VERSE | WHAT TRUTH IT COMMUNICATES | HOW IT IMPACTS MY LIFE

PEOPLE OR STUFF?

SAY WHAT?
Observation: What do I see?

SO WHAT?
Interpretation: What does it mean?

NOW WHAT?
Application: How does it apply to me?

THEN WHAT?
Implementation: What do I do?

How do you think the townspeople felt about the two men who were demon-possessed? Do you think they felt sorry for them or did they make fun of them? Did they pray for them? Avoid them? As you observe their responses in today's reading, you get a glimpse of how they really felt and learn something about yourself. Jesus freed the demon-possessed men and the townspeople respond by asking Him to leave. Why? It would seem that they would have been thrilled by what they had seen. Had they been concerned about the men, you would think they would have gone crazy with excitement. Could it be that they were more concerned over the loss of their property than they were over the men who were healed? Why did they not rejoice with them in their deliverance? Do your possessions mean more to you than people? What item of yours would you submit to damage or even ruin if it meant that someone would be helped? Your car, stereo or clothes? Ask God to help you become a person who sees the people in your life as more valuable than your "stuff."

MATTHEW 8:34
And behold, all the city came out to meet Jesus, and when they saw him, they begged him to leave their region.

SHARE YOUR STORY

What different responses do people have just after they become a Christian? What did you do after you first trusted Christ? Did you tell someone, or keep it to yourself? How long after Matthew became a disciple did it take before he had all his friends into his house to meet Jesus? Isn't it cool to read how quickly Matthew wanted to share with his friends what had happened to him? One thing you see all through Scripture is that people whose lives were touched by Christ want to share their story so others could have the same joy. They wanted so desperately to see the people they loved find all they themselves had found in Jesus Christ. What a thrill it must have been for Matthew to be able to see Jesus reach out to people in his world, those people whom the religious leaders would have nothing to do with. How often do you bring people from your world to hear about Christ? Do you look for opportunities to tell what He has done for you? Who can you share your story with this week? How are you going to share it with them? Their life may never be the same.

SAY WHAT?
Observation: What do I see?

SO WHAT?
Interpretation: What does it mean?

NOW WHAT?
Application: How does it apply to me?

THEN WHAT?
Implementation: What do I do?

MATTHEW 9:13

Go and learn what this means, 'I desire mercy, and not sacrifice.' For I came not to call the righteous, but sinners."

NOTHING INSIGNIFICANT!

SAY WHAT?

What are some of the details of your life that seem insignificant?

SO WHAT?

How can you begin to use this truth in your daily walk with Christ?

NOW WHAT?

How can you begin to show others in your world this kind of love?

THEN WHAT?

In light of this passage, what personal commitment can you make?

What one detail about you does verse 30 tell us that God keeps in His mind? How often in the course of a day does God have to change the number? Why does God have the hairs on our head numbered? That seems to be a very unimportant thing. It is also a piece of information that He must continually update. Seems like a lot of effort for information that makes no difference. However, if you ever watch a mother with her new baby, you begin to understand. She seems to study the baby for hours wanting to know every detail about the child. If she could, she might even count the hairs on his head. God cares about every detail of your life - even how many hairs you have. If He cares about your hair, how much more does He care about things like being singled out for your faith or being the only Christian in your unit? In what ways have you felt forgotten and alone? Underline verses 30 and 31 in your Bible to remind you of this great truth. Remember, God cares about every detail in your life. He will never forget you.

★★★★

MATTHEW 10:30

But even the hairs of your head are all numbered.

WHO IS CHRIST?

What question did John send his disciples to ask Christ in verse two? Did John doubt who Christ was? In today's reading we learn some encouraging things to help us in our own walks with God. John was obviously wondering if all this were really true. It is encouraging to know that even the greatest men of God sometimes have questions. What was Christ's answer? He simply told them to tell John what He was doing. Could it be that all John needed to hear was what Christ was doing and that would be enough for him to have faith? Jesus' answer must have been enough because we do not read that he asked it again. What would it take for you to really believe? What has Christ already done in your life that proves who He is? We can learn from John that when we doubt, we need to examine what God has already done to prove to us who He is. That should be all we need to have our faith restored. Take some time to list the ways God has demonstrated who He is in your life and in the lives of others. As you look at your list, allow it to fill you with confidence and to remove any doubt.

MATTHEW 11:4

And Jesus answered them, "Go and tell John what you hear and see..."

SAY WHAT?
Observation: What do I see?

SO WHAT?
Interpretation: What does it mean?

NOW WHAT?
Application: How does it apply to me?

THEN WHAT?
Implementation: What do I do?

CARELESS WORD?

SAY WHAT?
Observation: What do I see?

SO WHAT?
Interpretation: What does it mean?

NOW WHAT?
Application: How does it apply to me?

THEN WHAT?
Implementation: What do I do?

What does a "careless word" mean? How many of them will we give an account for? They are words that you say when you do not really think about what you are saying or how they might be received. How many of them do you speak in a day - words in haste or anger when you have lost control? Are they words about others when you are hanging out with after work? Are they responses to those you live with when they have borrowed something without asking? Think about them and then imagine what it is going to be like for you to give an account for every one of them. Can you ever say,"oh,it doesn't matter?" Too often we excuse our words because we say we didn't really mean it or because we were not thinking. This passage says that those excuses will not fly with God. Maybe it is time for you to think a bit more before you speak. How is Judgment Day going to be for you? Try to create a plan to begin to gain more control over your words. Circle "careless word" in verse 36 to remind you.

★★★★

MATTHEW 12:36
I tell you, on the day of judgment people will give account for every careless word they speak,

TYPES OF SOIL

How many different soils does Christ mention in the parable of the sower? Number them in your Bible. Since three of the four responses seem positive at first, how can you tell who really does believe and therefore is saved? What this passage shows is that it is possible to have what looks like a positive response to the Gospel and even show temporary signs of being saved, but not really be saved. Many people get really excited and tell everyone about it, like the second person, only to die out when the tough times come. Another doesn't get excited at all, but still seems to show signs of being saved. However, after a while, he begins to choose the world's temptations over God's plan for his life. Too often, a person believes he is saved based on a past decision and an illusion of temporary fruit when, in fact, he is not saved. He is really like the seed that fell on rocky places or thorns. Who do you know like that? You? Or a friend? Ask God to give you an opportunity to talk with him about how he stands before God. Use the sheet below to prepare yourself.

SAY WHAT?

What are some specific characteristics of someone who is like soil #1?

SO WHAT?

What are some specific characteristics of someone who is like soil #2?

NOW WHAT?

How can you share your concerns with them?

THEN WHAT?

In light of this passage, what personal commitment can you make?

MATTHEW 13:9

He who has ears, let him hear."

The book of Proverbs was designed to help us in "attaining wisdom and discipline; in understanding words of insight; in acquiring a disciplined and prudent life, doing what is right and just and fair; in giving prudence to the simple, knowledge and discretion to the young." As you read through this chapter, write down the verses that are most significant to you in your present circumstances.

VERSE | WHAT TRUTH IT COMMUNICATES | HOW IT IMPACTS MY LIFE

WATER WALKER?

How do you think the disciples responded when Peter started to get out of the boat? How did Peter get back to the boat? Could it be that when Christ reached down and picked him up, that the two of them walked back together? What an incredible lesson it must have been to all of them about being willing to step out in faith for God. To see firsthand that as long as we keep our eyes on Him, and not the problems around us, we can walk on water. Too often people miss walking on water because they keep looking around at the problems, not believing that God can overcome any obstacles. So they stay in the safety of their boat and watch others walk on water. What keeps you from getting out of the safety of your "boat?" Peer pressure? Fear of failing? Waiting for everyone else to move? Not willing to pay the price? Although Peter did not make it all the way, he did step out, and he did, with God's help, make it back. In what area is God calling out to you to step out by faith? Highlight a phrase that will remind you to get out of your boat.

SAY WHAT?
Observation: What do I see?

SO WHAT?
Interpretation: What does it mean?

NOW WHAT?
Application: How does it apply to me?

THEN WHAT?
Implementation: What do I do?

MATTHEW 14:29

He said, "Come." So Peter got out of the boat and walked on the water and came to Jesus.

IMPACT OF A MEMORY

SAY WHAT?
Observation: What do I see?

SO WHAT?
Interpretation: What does it mean?

NOW WHAT?
Application: How does it apply to me?

THEN WHAT?
Implementation: What do I do?

In what ways is the feeding of the 4,000 here in chapter 15 similar to the feeding of the 5,000 in chapter 14? Does the story in verses 29-39 sound familiar? In both cases you have a large group of people needing to be fed. In both cases, Jesus asks the disciples how they think they can feed the crowd. In both cases they respond the same way. "Where could we get enough bread in this remote place to feed such a crowd?" How could the disciples forget that Christ fed the 5,000? Hello, remember the 5,000? But before we get too critical of the disciples, how often do we do the same thing? God has proven Himself faithful in your life. He has even done the miraculous for you. Yet when you face a situation similar to one you faced in the past, you panic. Just like the disciples, you forget what God has already done and that causes you doubt. What are you doubting right now that God has already proven He can accomplish? Ask God to give you a better memory that you will trust more and doubt less. In what way can you help yourself remember better?

MATTHEW 15:34

And Jesus said to them, "How many loaves do you have?" They said, "Seven, and a few small fish."

WAITING FOR LIGHTNING?

What did the Pharisees and Sadducees ask Christ for in verse one? Why didn't Jesus give them a sign? Had He given them any up to that point? It would be interesting to go back over the chapters you have already read in Matthew and list all the signs Jesus had given them to indicate that He was the Messiah. It would appear that the problem with the Pharisees and Sadducees was not that they had no sign, but their own hard hearts that refused to believe in spite of the signs that were all around them. Unfortunately,people use excuses like this all the time to try to justify their rebellion. You know, "if God would just show me who He is," "if He gave me a sign that He really wanted me to witness to my friend," "I need a sign that I should break up with him/her." Could you be one of these people? What sign are you waiting for? Maybe it is time to do what you already know is right and stop, as a song says, "waiting for lightning." Spend time today reflecting on the signs you already see that indicate what God wants you to do,and respond to them! Are you ready?

★★★★

MATTHEW 16:4

An evil and adulterous generation seeks for a sign, but no sign will be given to it except the sign of Jonah." So he left them and departed.

SAY WHAT?
Observation: What do I see?

SO WHAT?
Interpretation: What does it mean?

NOW WHAT?
Application: How does it apply to me?

THEN WHAT?
Implementation: What do I do?

WHOSE STRENGTH?

SAY WHAT?
Observation: What do I see?

SO WHAT?
Interpretation: What does it mean?

NOW WHAT?
Application: How does it apply to me?

THEN WHAT?
Implementation: What do I do?

How do you think Peter, James and John felt when they were coming down the mountain? What daydreams do you think they had about what they could accomplish after an experience like that? How do you think they felt when they got back and saw the other disciples' failure? How do you think the disciples not being able to cast out the demon affected Christ? What a discouragement it must have been for Him to watch the disciples try to do something in their own strength and fail - fail because they had such little faith. In Mark's account we find that Jesus also told them that they failed because they did not pray. They had a problem and decided to just go ahead in their own strength and try to solve it without taking the time to pray and get God's counsel and strength. How often do you try to do things in your own strength? What situation are you presently facing that you are fighting and losing because you have not given it to God, but are trying to solve it in your own power? Like the disciples, learn to give everything to God in prayer and allow Him to work in your life.

★★★★

MATTHEW 17:20
He said to them,, "Because of your little faith. For truly, I say to you, if you have faith like a grain of mustard seed, you will say to this mountain, 'Move from here to there,' and it will move...

TRUTH ABOUT FORGIVENESS

When you hear the word forgive, what goes through your mind? What thoughts went through Peter's mind as Christ was telling the story of the "Unmerciful Servant"? It was he who asked the question about forgiveness that resulted in Christ's telling this story. Maybe he had someone in his mind that he had failed to forgive and was hoping Christ's answer would give him a reason for not forgiving him. Christ's response was not what he had expected. What a powerful passage on forgiveness this is - to realize that we are the unmerciful servant who has been forgiven "zillions." Our debt was wiped clean when we trusted Christ. How can we face those whose debt to us is small, $18, in comparison to our debt to God, and not forgive? It saddens the heart of God to know what He has forgiven us and to see us refuse to forgive others. Who are you refusing to forgive? Though their debt may seem large to you, it is very small compared to the debt Christ forgave you. Highlight verse 35 again and ask God to use it to motivate you to forgive. It will free your soul.

SAY WHAT?
What kinds of things has God forgiven you for in your past?

SO WHAT?
What are some things you have a hard time forgiving?

NOW WHAT?
How does the list in #1 compare to what you wrote in #2?

THEN WHAT?
Who is God asking you to forgive? What are you going to do about it?

MATTHEW 18:35

So also my heavenly Father will do to every one of you, if you do not forgive your brother from your heart."

PERSPECTIVE ON RICHES

SAY WHAT?
Observation: What do I see?

SO WHAT?
Interpretation: What does it mean?

NOW WHAT?
Application: How does it apply to me?

THEN WHAT?
Implementation: What do I do?

What kind of person does Christ say in verse 24 has a very hard time getting to heaven? What about riches is so attractive? Why do you think it is so hard for rich people to get to heaven? Scripture is so very clear in telling us that riches are one of the most dangerous things we can face in our spiritual growth. If riches are so dangerous to our spiritual life, why do we pursue them so hard? It is interesting to watch everyone, including Christians, always trying to make more money. They get part time jobs, they seek raises, or they choose which career to pursue based on its pay scale. Yet Scripture is clear that it is much harder to walk with God as a rich man than one who is not. If that is so, then why do we want more money? Maybe we out to choose the path that allows us to walk in the riches of the Kingdom, regardless of whether it involves worldly wealth. In what ways do people around you pursue riches? What are you pursuing? How are you deciding what you want to do with your life? Ask God to help you to see riches as He does and to avoid pursuing them over Him. Read verses 29-30 again to remind you of the perspective God wants you to have about riches.

★★★★

MATTHEW 19:29
And everyone who has left houses or brothers or sisters or father or mother or children or lands, for my name's sake, will receive a hundred-fold and will inherit eternal life.

The book of Proverbs was designed to help us in "attaining wisdom and discipline; in understanding words of insight; in acquiring a disciplined and prudent life, doing what is right and just and fair; in giving prudence to the simple, knowledge and discretion to the young." As you read through this chapter, write down the verses that are most significant to you in your present circumstances.

VERSE | WHAT TRUTH IT COMMUNICATES | HOW IT IMPACTS MY LIFE

TRUE SERVANTHOOD

SAY WHAT?

Make a list of the things you are presently doing to serve people.

SO WHAT?

Do you do those things for recognition or to serve people?

NOW WHAT?

What needs to change for you to be more of a servant of people?

THEN WHAT?

In light of this passage, what personal commitment can you make?

What request did James and John's mother make to Christ in verse 21? Was it wrong to ask for those positions? By her question, she is stating that she wants her two boys to have the most important positions in Christ's kingdom. Why do you think the other disciples got angry when they heard what James and John had requested? It may be because James and John beat them to the punch. They wanted the important positions for themselves. If James and John got to sit on the left and right, then the other disciples would have lesser positions. Have you ever noticed how hard it is to find people to do things which get little or no recognition or honor? How much of what you do in your unit is based on an attitude of simply serving people? Christ communicated that it is wrong to always selfishly seek positions of honor and to desire to be first while being unwilling to serve others and go last. In what ways have you put others first? What can you do in your unit or circle of influence that requires being a servant? Begin now seeking to serve others and not promote yourself above them.

MATTHEW 20:28

...even as the Son of Man came not to be served but to serve, and to give his life as a ransom for many."

HYPOCRACY

When Jesus saw that the fig tree had no fruit, what did He do to it? Why did He curse the fig tree? Could it be that He was trying to illustrate to the disciples an important spiritual truth? From a distance, the fig tree looked great. In fact, they had walked up to it to get some fruit. But, when they got up close to it, they realized that it didn't have fruit on it. It was similar to what was true of the temple in the first part of this chapter. The temple was beautiful on the outside, but inside the worship wasn't worthy by God's definition. God hates hypocrisy, which occurs when something looks one way on the outside, or from a distance, but the inside is very different. Are you like the fig tree or the Temple? What would a close examination of your life reveal? Is there an area of your life in which you are a hypocrite? Make a list of those areas in your life that may look good on the outside, but you know you need to change. Make a commitment today to change the inside to match what appears to please God from the outside. Begin working on those changes right away.

SAY WHAT?
Observation: What do I see?

SO WHAT?
Interpretation: What does it mean?

NOW WHAT?
Application: How does it apply to me?

THEN WHAT?
Implementation: What do I do?

MATTHEW 21:13

He said to them, "It is written, 'My house shall be called a house of prayer,' but you make it a den of robbers."

SAY WHAT?

What evidences that you love God with all your heart, soul and mind?

SO WHAT?

What evidences that you love your neighbor as yourself?

NOW WHAT?

What can you do to grow in your love for God and people?

THEN WHAT?

In light of this passage, what personal commitment can you make?

Why did the Pharisees ask Jesus the question you find in verse 35? Did they really want to know the answer? Regardless of their motives, Jesus' answer gives a significant truth of Scripture. It reveals to us the two most important expectations God has for our lives. Jesus says that the greatest command in the Bible is to love the Lord our God with all our heart, soul and mind. He then says that the second command is like it. This means that it is just as important as the first one. It is to love others as ourselves. Why is this true? According to verse 40, it's because all of the law hangs on these two principles. In other words, if you violate any command in Scripture, you reveal that you do not love God or your neighbor properly. All of God's expectations are built on these two commands. Are you doing well in these two areas? Is the motivation of your heart, soul and mind, your love for God? Is your love for others demonstrated in your daily living? What have your done this week to demonstrate your love in these two areas? Use the sheet to the left to help examine yourself.

★★★★

MATTHEW 22:40

On these two commandments depend all the Law and the Prophets."

SIGNS OF A HYPOCRITE

How many times does Jesus use the word hypocrites in this chapter? Circle them in your Bible and write your definition of a hypocrite. Do the Pharisees fit your definition? You could summarize hypocrisy from this chapter in two ways. One, it occurs when the motivation for your religious actions is not done out of love for God, but is done in order to be noticed by men. You may be doing good things, but you do them to fit in, or get noticed by others, or so that they think you are acceptable. It is not because you love God. Second, it occurs when your appearance is not a true reflection of what is inside. These two would be good definitions for a hypocrite - someone who does things for the wrong reason or whose talk is different from his walk. Would either of these categories be true of your life? What is your motivation for the religious things you do? Is what people think about you really true on the inside? Examine your life and determine what areas may be hypocritical. Begin now to correct them. If you need help, talk to your chaplain or another believer in your unit.

SAY WHAT?
Observation: What do I see?

SO WHAT?
Interpretation: What does it mean?

NOW WHAT?
Application: How does it apply to me?

THEN WHAT?
Implementation: What do I do?

MATTHEW 23:3
...so practice and observe whatever they tell you— but not what they do. For they preach, but do not practice.

SO BE READY

SAY WHAT?
Observation: What do I see?

SO WHAT?
Interpretation: What does it mean?

NOW WHAT?
Application: How does it apply to me?

THEN WHAT?
Implementation: What do I do?

What question did the disciples ask in verse three? List some of the signs that Jesus gave to answer their question. How do you think Jesus' answer made the disciples feel? From reading verses 42-51, how do you think Jesus wanted them to respond? It seems that Jesus wanted the disciples to understand the signs and as a result be motivated to be ready for His return. The signs would demonstrate that He could return at any time. It seems that knowing that Jesus was going to be coming back soon should have motivated them to be ready. They knew what the signs were, but not when He would come, so they had to be ready at any time. What if Jesus came back as soon as you finished reading this paragraph? Would you be ready? Would you be ready to go to heaven? Would you be ready to hear Him say, "well done?" Ask God to enable you to live each day as if it were the day He was returning. Commit to work at getting all areas of your life in order so you will be ready. Highlight the phrase in your Bible, "So you also must be ready," to remind you of your commitment.

MATTHEW 24:44
Therefore you also must be ready, for the Son of Man is coming at an hour you do not expect.

USE WHAT YOU HAVE

What was the quantity of talents that was given out in verse fifteen? What are the different numbers of talents? The essence of this section is not how many talents each man got, but how the master responded to what they did with the talents. His response was not based on how many they had in the end, but how they used what they had. The one who began with two talents got the same response as the one who began with five because he used what he had to their fullest. In fact, the response is exactly the same. The man who had one was condemned, not because he ended up with less, but because he did nothing with what he had. God does not respond to us based on how much talent we have, but on what we do with it. It is comforting to know that God only looks at how I use my talents and does not compare me with everyone else. How are you using your talents? Are you using your talents in a way that would please God? How can you begin today using the talents God has given you? Answer the questions below to help you begin your evaluation of your gifts and abilities.

SAY WHAT?
What talents or abilities do you feel God has given you?

SO WHAT?
What talents do others feel God has given you? (You may need to ask.)

NOW WHAT?
How are you using them more effectively for God in your world?

THEN WHAT?
In light of this passage, what personal commitment can you make?

★★★★

MATTHEW 25:29
For to everyone who has will more be given, and he will have an abundance. But from the one who has not, even what he has will be taken away.

JOY OR SORROW

SAY WHAT?
Observation: What do I see?

SO WHAT?
Interpretation: What does it mean?

NOW WHAT?
Application: How does it apply to me?

THEN WHAT?
Implementation: What do I do?

Who are the people in this chapter who brought Jesus real joy by their actions? Place a + sign next to their names. Who are the people in this chapter who hurt Jesus by their actions? Put a - sign next to their names. Which person hurt Him the most? Was it Judas who was so selfish and greedy that he would sell out for money, steal from his friends and get angry when someone did something nice for Christ? Or how about Peter? He not only denied Christ, but when Christ was hurting and needed Peter to pray with Him, he couldn't stay awake. Or maybe the other disciples who when Jesus was arrested forsook Him and fled, even though they had told Him they never would? Clearly this chapter is filled with examples of people who brought Jesus great joy. But there are also examples of those who brought Him great emotional pain which he endured for you and me. Looking back on this past week, how have you brought Him joy? What have you done to bring Him sorrow? What is something you can do today simply to bring Christ joy and show Him how much you love Him?

MATTHEW 26:13
"Truly, I say to you, wherever this gospel is proclaimed in the whole world, what she has done will also be told in memory of her."

FOR YOU!

How many different things did they do to Christ to physically hurt Him? Circle them in your Bible. Which of them do you think would be the most painful? How does it make you feel to know that Jesus Christ went through all that for you? From getting slapped in the face, to nails in His hands and feet, to a spear in His side, He did it all for you. After all the beating, He then carried the cross to where He would be crucified. How do you respond knowing He did it all for you? How do you respond to such love? Does it bore you to read such details? Do you half-heartedly live your Christian life? Does it cause you to keep it to yourself and avoid talking to someone about what He did for you? How tragic to have someone demonstrate such amazing love and to respond with apathy. Since Christ has done all that for you, what are you doing for Him? Since He took the blows that were meant for you, shouldn't you be willing to take some blows that are meant for Him? How can you show God today how thankful you are for this kind of love? Don't act like it doesn't matter!

SAY WHAT?

How would you tell if you truly understood and appreciated what Christ has done for you?

SO WHAT?

What would it take for you to more fully appreciate what Christ endured for you?

NOW WHAT?

What can you do today to demonstrate to Him how thankful you are for what He has done for you?

THEN WHAT?

In light of this passage, what personal commitment can you make?

MATTHEW 27:54

When the centurion and those who were with him, keeping watch over Jesus, saw the earthquake and what took place, they were filled with awe and said, "Truly this was the Son of God!"

MILITARYDEVOTIONAL.COM
@MILITARYDEVOS

MAKE DISCIPLES

SAY WHAT?
Observation: What do I see?

SO WHAT?
Interpretation: What does it mean?

NOW WHAT?
Application: How does it apply to me?

THEN WHAT?
Implementation: What do I do?

What did Jesus want the disciples to do in verses 16-20? Circle in your Bible the different things they were to do. How do these instructions differ from what He told them in Matthew 10:5-7? In one case He told them to make disciples. In the other case, He told them to tell people the kingdom of heaven was at hand. What is the difference between making disciples and telling people the Kingdom of Heaven is at hand? One involves what we would call evangelism; while the second one involves much more. To fulfill the first charge, they would have only to be involved in evangelism. That is, share the gospel and lead people to Christ. To make disciples, we not only lead them to Christ, but we help them to become like Christ. This charge, in verse 16-20, includes what He said in chapter 10, but goes so much further. It involves becoming a part of their lives to help them grow. How are you doing with making disciples? Who are some people that are more like Jesus Christ because of your influence on their lives? How can you begin today, "making disciples?"

MATTHEW 28:19
Go therefore and make disciples of all nations, baptizing them in the name of the Father and of the Son and of the Holy Spirit,

» **MILITARYDEVOTIONAL.COM**

MILITARY OTD

MAY
★★★★

MONTHLY
PRAYER SHEET

I NEED TO REACH OUT TO...	HOW I WILL DO IT...	HOW IT WENT...

OTHER REQUEST	HOW ANSWERED	DATE

MONTHLY
MISSION SHEET

⏵⏵ NAME: ....

This sheet is designed to help you make personal commitments each month that will help you grow in your walk with God. Fill it out by determining:

★ What will push you.
★ What you think you can achieve.

⏵⏵ PERSONAL DEVOTIONS:

I will commit to read the OnTrack Bible passage and devotional thought .... day(s) each week this month.

⏵⏵ CHURCH/CHAPEL ATTENDANCE:

I will attend Church/Chapel .... time(s) this month.
I will attend .... time(s) this month.

⏵⏵ SCRIPTURE MEMORY:

I will memorize .... key verse(s) from the daily OnTrack Devotions this month.

⏵⏵ OUTREACH:

I will share Christ with .... person/people this month.
I will serve my local church/chapel this month by ....
....
....

⏵⏵ OTHER ACTIVITIES:

List any other opportunities such as events, prayer group, etc..., you will participate in this month. ....
....
....
....
....
....

Determine to begin today a journey that will last a lifetime,and will change your life forever.

AN UNLOCKED DOOR?

How, in this chapter, did the disciples demonstrate they were growing in their faith? One example is found by what has been omitted in this chapter, not what is written. Their growth was depicted by what they did not do. In John chapter twenty, we read that when the disciples gathered in the room, they locked the door for fear of the Jews. Even though they had seen Jesus after His resurrection, they still locked the doors in fear. However, here in this chapter, they gathered again, but now the doors were not locked. They had gathered together to pray and to select a new man as an apostle to replace Judas. This time they were not so afraid of the Jews that they felt it necessary to lock the door. It is very encouraging to see specific ways in which we are growing. We should never be satisfied with where we are spiritually, but we can be encouraged to see how far we have come. In what ways can you see growth in your life over this past year? What issues have come up? Use the questions below to gauge how far you have grown in your walk with God. You should see specific ways of how God has worked in your life.

ACTS 1:14

All these with one accord were devoting themselves to prayer, together with the women and Mary the mother of Jesus, and his brothers.

SAY WHAT?
Observation: What do I see?

SO WHAT?
Interpretation: What does it mean?

NOW WHAT?
Application: How does it apply to me?

THEN WHAT?
Implementation: What do I do?

SAY WHAT?
Observation: What do I see?

SO WHAT?
Interpretation: What does it mean?

NOW WHAT?
Application: How does it apply to me?

THEN WHAT?
Implementation: What do I do?

Of all the wonderful things that took place in this chapter, which ones amazed you the most? Put an * in your Bible next to those examples. Was it the change in Peter's behavior that amazed you? Remember, it was Peter who, in fear, denied even knowing Christ. Yet in verses 14-36 of today's passage, he stood before a crowd and clearly proclaimed the gospel message to them. Or, was it that the disciples spoke to the crowd, and they understood them, not only in their own language, but in their own dialect? Maybe the most awesome thing may be what we find in verse 44. It is that "all" the believers had "everything" in common. This was complete unity. We must understand that they were unified because of what had happened in their lives. They were devoted to prayer, the Apostle's teaching, and to fellowship with each other. When a group of people sell out to Christ, making their highest priority reaching the world with the gospel, unity results. If you desire unity in your church, each individual must make his spiritual walk a priority. How about you? Is your walk helping unity?

★★★★

ACTS 2:40
And with many other words he bore witness and continued to exhort them, saying, ("Save yourselves from this crooked generation."

USING WHAT YOU HAVE

What gifts and abilities has God given to you? In what ways do you influence the lives of people using those gifts and abilities? Do you encourage them? Listen to them? Give good advice? In this chapter, we find an example we need to follow in order to use our God-given gifts and abilities to influence the lives of people. A man came to Peter and John. All he asked for was money. The problem was that Peter and John had no money to give him. But, they did have the gifts and abilities which God had given to them. They knew they could use them to touch the life of this poor man in such a wonderful way. So, instead of feeling guilty or embarrassed because of what they didn't have, they used what they had to touch his life. We sometimes feel that only those with particular gifts or abilities can effectively touch the lives of people. We forget that God has given all of us something special that enables us to influence the lives of others. God brings people into our lives that need our influence with our specific abilities. Look for ways to touch a life with what God has given you. Someone needs what you have to offer. Ask God to reveal him/her to you.

ACTS 3:6

But Peter said, "I have no silver and gold, but what I do have I give to you. In the name of Jesus Christ of Nazareth, rise up and walk!"

SAY WHAT?

What gifts or abilities has God given you?

SO WHAT?

How would the people closest to you answer that question? What feedback have you gotten concerning the impact you have had on their lives?

NOW WHAT?

How can you use your gifts and abilities to encourage someone today?

THEN WHAT?

In what specific ways can you use those abilities in your church?

MILITARYDEVOTIONAL.COM
🐦 @MILITARYDEVOS

DEVELOPING COURAGE

SAY WHAT?
Observation: What do I see?

SO WHAT?
Interpretation: What does it mean?

NOW WHAT?
Application: How does it apply to me?

THEN WHAT?
Implementation: What do I do?

How would the people who heard Peter deny Christ in the courtyard describe him? Would the word "courageous" come to mind? Notice in this chapter how differently Peter's response was than when he denied Christ. He not only refused to deny knowing Him, but blamed the crowd for crucifying Him! He used the opportunity to clearly state that in Jesus Christ alone is salvation. He boldly spoke these words to the people he once feared the most. He was so different that those who saw and heard him were amazed at his courage (vs13). The difference? - The Holy Spirit. The Holy Spirit was residing in him, strengthening and guiding him. His confidence and obvious growth was evidence of the fact that the Holy Spirit now lived within him. We also can see that same kind of change in our lives, to the point that others are amazed and take note that we have been with Christ. When we trusted Christ, the Holy Spirit came to dwell in us. He desires to change us just as He did Peter. He will replace our fear with boldness and confidence. He is the power of God that transforms us to accomplish what He desires. Is He at work in your life?

★★★★

ACTS 4:13
Now when they saw the boldness of Peter and John, and perceived that they were uneducated, common men, they were astonished. And they recognized that they had been with Jesus.

A SECOND CHANCE

Have you ever been in a situation when, out of the blue, you recall an experience from your past and suddenly your present experience takes on a whole new meaning? You view your circumstance with a new perspective? We see today in chapter five that the Apostles were taken before the Sanhedrin. They were told never to speak in the name of Jesus Christ again. When they refused, verse fourty tells us that they were flogged. What do you imagine went through Peter's mind as he was led to be flogged? Could it be that he vividly recalled his denial in the courtyard? Do you suppose he felt that he had been given another chance to take a stand for Christ, and he determined he was not going to blow it this time? No wonder he left rejoicing to be counted worthy to suffer for Him. Not only was he worthy to suffer disgrace for Christ's name, as verse 41 says, but he also made the most of his second chance. Could God be giving you a second chance? When God does give you an opportunity, allow your past to motivate you to do the right thing, not repeat your mistakes. Like Peter, you will rejoice when you make the most of your opportunities.

ACTS 5:41

Then they left the presence of the council, rejoicing that they were counted worthy to suffer dishonor for the name.

SAY WHAT?
Observation: What do I see?

SO WHAT?
Interpretation: What does it mean?

NOW WHAT?
Application: How does it apply to me?

THEN WHAT?
Implementation: What do I do?

SOMEONE IS WATCHING

SAY WHAT?

Can you think of someone whose life affected yours as you observed him/her walking through difficult times? How did it affect you?

SO WHAT?

What was it about his/her response that impressed you?

NOW WHAT?

How can your response to your present circumstances influence those around you?

THEN WHAT?

How can you prepare yourself to respond to difficulty in a way that positively affects those around you?

Why did Saul step up his persecution of the church? Could it be that the images of Stephen's stoning were burned into his memory, and they haunted him? Think about it. He stood and listened to what Stephen said to the crowd. He watched the crowd's reaction and saw them drag Stephen away and stone him. Then,to his amazement, Stephen prayed in the midst of being executed,and asked God to forgive them,not to hold that sin against them. That sight must have troubled him immensely. His mind must have replayed it over and over. To see such courage and love in Stephen's behavior must have overwhelmed Saul. Stephen could not have had any idea the impact his life and death would have on all of history. His commitment to Christ was used, not only to impact the Apostle Paul,but to scatter the church all over the world, and thereby spread the message of the Gospel. What impact is your life having on those who observe or cause your suffering? Does your response to your circumstances point them to Christ? Could God want to use your present circumstances to impact your world as Stephen impacted his?

ACTS 8:1

And Saul approved of his execution.

The book of Proverbs was designed to help us in "attaining wisdom and discipline; in understanding words of insight; in acquiring a disciplined and prudent life, doing what is right and just and fair; in giving prudence to the simple, knowledge and discretion to the young." As you read through this chapter, write down the verses that are most significant to you in your present circumstances.

VERSE | WHAT TRUTH IT COMMUNICATES | HOW IT IMPACTS MY LIFE

RESPONDING TO GOD

SAY WHAT?
Observation: What do I see?

SO WHAT?
Interpretation: What does it mean?

NOW WHAT?
Application: How does it apply to me?

THEN WHAT?
Implementation: What do I do?

Why did Philip have such a great opportunity to share the gospel with the Ethiopian man? The answer is found in verse 26. In fact, the answer ought to be an encouragement and motivation to us. Do you ever sense the Spirit of God move your heart about sharing your faith? When God prompts you to speak to someone in your life or unit, do you immediately take action and talk to the individual He has pointed out? Philip's example can teach us valuable lessons. In this example, we find a pattern to follow. First, he made himself available. His heart was open to God's leading. Second, Philip responded to the prompting of God. When God moved his heart about going over to the Ethiopian, Philip obeyed. And last, he began right where the Ethiopian was. Philip helped him understand what he was reading and didn't answer questions the Ethiopian hadn't asked. Could there be someone God has been prompting you to reach out to? How can you make yourself available to help with his questions? When he is ready to ask, are you ready to answer? If not, there are steps you can take to prepare yourself for these questions. Ask for help.

ACTS 8:26
Now an angel of the Lord said to Philip, "Rise and go toward the south to the road that goes down from Jerusalem to Gaza." This is a desert place.

BEING WILLING TO SUPPORT

Think of someone you know who does not behave at all like a Christian. How would you respond if he came to you unexpectedly and told you he had gotten saved? How would you react to someone who had been a terrible gossip but had recommitted his life to Christ and no longer wanted to be known as one? What if he had gossiped about you? Much too often, we as Christians are slow to accept the changes people attempt to make. In this passage, we see that Paul's life had changed, and those he needed most were skeptical and afraid. They did not trust his words and were unwilling to give Paul the support he needed to be able to grow. It was remarkable to read in verse seventeen that Ananias greeted Paul by calling him, "brother." It was remarkable also that Barnabas stepped forward as a witness that God had truly changed Paul's life. Are you guilty of treating someone with doubt and suspicion who has recently made a commitment? What can you do today to show love and acceptance toward them? It would be an encouragement and may be just what he needs. Be open to the work of God in other people's lives.

SAY WHAT?
Observation: What do I see?

SO WHAT?
Interpretation: What does it mean?

NOW WHAT?
Application: How does it apply to me?

THEN WHAT?
Implementation: What do I do?

ACTS 9:17

...And laying his hands on him he said, "Brother Saul, the Lord Jesus who appeared to you on the road by which you came has sent me so that you may regain your sight and be filled with the Holy Spirit."

MILITARYDEVOTIONAL.COM
@MILITARYDEVOS

SAY WHAT?

How do people today show favoritism in sharing the gospel?

SO WHAT?

Why do you think people show favoritism in other areas or ways?

NOW WHAT?

How do you show favoritism?

THEN WHAT?

What are some specific ways you can avoid showing favoritism?

Why was it so difficult for Peter to go to Cornelius' house? Why had God sent him there? While it may have been difficult for Peter a Jew, to go into the house of a Gentile, it is clear that God wanted him to go. God wanted this household to hear the message of the gospel and gain eternal life. Although they feared God and sought to know Him, they had not yet heard the message of the gospel in order to receive eternal life. Although they were God fearing, they were not saved. When Peter arrived, he shared with them the message of salvation and all who heard were saved. Further, it was significant that Peter was the one that led Cornelius' household to Christ. This was an important event in the life of the early church. God wanted the Apostles to realize that the message of the gospel was for all people, not just Jews. Although God had already told Peter, he had missed it. Everyone needs to hear about Christ. "God does not show favoritism." Do you believe that all people in your world need to hear what Jesus Christ has done? Are you willing to share it with them? Choose today, someone to share it with.

★★★★

ACTS 10:47

"Can anyone withhold water for baptizing these people, who have received the Holy Spirit just as we have?"

SHARING WITH EVERYONE

As you read the beginning of this chapter, did a verse you read earlier in Acts come to mind? What about Acts 1:8? In this verse, Jesus told the Apostles how and to whom He wanted the gospel message to be proclaimed. He told them that after they received the Holy Spirit, they were to go to all people. They were to go to the ends of the earth with the message of Christ. They were to begin in Jerusalem, but it was not to stop there. In light of this verse and the events recorded in chapter ten, how could the apostles and brothers in Christ have missed the obvious and criticized Peter when Gentiles became believers? God wants all men everywhere to hear that Jesus Christ has died for them. God clearly illustrated this to the early church so that they would understand what He meant in Acts 1:8. He continues to clearly demonstrate it to us today. Are there some in your school or town with whom you would be unwilling to share the salvation message because of their race or appearance? Write the reference Acts 1:8 in the margin of your Bible to remind you to reach out to all people. It's not too late to begin sharing the message. Why not today?

ACTS 11:17

"If then God gave the same gift to them as he gave to us when we believed in the Lord Jesus Christ, who was I that I could stand in God's way?"

SAY WHAT?
Observation: What do I see?

SO WHAT?
Interpretation: What does it mean?

NOW WHAT?
Application: How does it apply to me?

THEN WHAT?
Implementation: What do I do?

CHARACTERISTICS OF A WEAK MAN

SAY WHAT?

In what areas do you care more about what pleases others than about what pleases God?

SO WHAT?

Do you hear the truth but refuse to listen to it because it may make you look bad?

NOW WHAT?

Are you taking credit for something someone else is doing?

THEN WHAT?

How can you begin to turn those areas into strengths and not feed your weaknesses?

As you read this chapter, what did you notice about those mentioned? Was it the lack of faith which was demonstrated by the disbelief that Peter could possibly be at the door? Or was it the courage of Peter in the midst of certain death? Or how about the spineless leadership of Herod? After reading the record of Herod's actions, it makes one wonder how he ever got into a position of leadership. He had Peter arrested, not because he had done anything wrong, but only because it would please the Jews. Herod could not accept the fact that Peter had escaped, and so in frustration, he executed the guards. But, his mistakes did not stop there. His final mistake was accepting praise for himself which should have been given to God. Herod's life illustrates that weak people's actions are based upon the opinions of others; they refuse to accept responsibility for their actions and accept credit for what others have done. Are you like Herod, motivated by what pleases God or by pleasing men? Do you give credit where it belongs or take it for yourself? Do either of these characteristics describe your life? If so, ask God to remove them from your life.

ACTS 12:23

Immediately an angel of the Lord struck him down, because he did not give God the glory, and he was eaten by worms and breathed his last.

THE POWER OF THE WORD OF GOD

What is it that brings people to the point of realizing the gospel message is true? Is it seeing or hearing about something spectacular? Would witnessing some great miracle do it? In today's reading, we see an example of what often causes people to respond to the gospel. Did you notice it? In this chapter, Paul and Barnabas were sharing the gospel with the Proconsul but were being opposed by Elymas. Paul performed a miracle causing blindness to come over him. As Paul expected, the Proconsul was amazed, and the passage tells us that he believed. What convinced him? The miracle? No! According to verse twelve, it was their "teaching", not the miracle. Often, we think it takes great and dazzling demonstrations of the supernatural to convince people of their need of Christ. "If only we could do miracles like they did in the early church," we might think. It should encourage us to know that it is the Word of God that transforms lives. Underline the last part of verse twelve to remind you to just share it and allow the power of the Word of God to transform lives! While we can't perform miracles, we have God's Word.

SAY WHAT?
Observation: What do I see?

SO WHAT?
Interpretation: What does it mean?

NOW WHAT?
Application: How does it apply to me?

THEN WHAT?
Implementation: What do I do?

ACTS 13:12

Then the proconsul believed, when he saw what had occurred, for he was astonished at the teaching of the Lord.

The book of Proverbs was designed to help us in "attaining wisdom and discipline; in understanding words of insight; in acquiring a disciplined and prudent life, doing what is right and just and fair; in giving prudence to the simple, knowledge and discretion to the young." As you read through this chapter, write down the verses that are most significant to you in your present circumstances.

VERSE | WHAT TRUTH IT COMMUNICATES | HOW IT IMPACTS MY LIFE

STAYING FOCUSED

Why were Paul and Barnabas so committed to sharing the message of Christ? They continued to face great opposition, yet in spite of the circumstances confronting them, they kept on sharing Christ. Of all the things they went through in this chapter, which do you think would be the most difficult for you to endure? Which ones might cause you to give up? Could it be the verbal abuse, physical abuse, or the personal gain and pride when the crowd tried to make them gods? But through it all, they stayed true to their mission, sharing Christ. God had called them to a task, and they were committed to it no matter what the cost might be. They had seen the gospel transform their lives personally and had seen countless other lives transformed. Regardless of the price, they wanted everyone to know what Christ had done. What does it take to make you stop sharing your faith with others? A little kidding? Some mocking? A "religious freak" reputation? The task of sharing what Jesus Christ has done is too important to be sidetracked by any discouragement. Allow this example to motivate you to persevere.

SAY WHAT?
When was the last time you were mocked for your faith?

SO WHAT?
How did you respond? Why?

NOW WHAT?
What can you change in order to help you respond like the example in today's reading?

THEN WHAT?
In light of this passage, what personal commitment can you make?

★★★★

ACTS 14:27
And when they arrived and gathered the church together, they declared all that God had done with them, and how he had opened a door of faith to the Gentiles.

OUR FINAL AUTHORITY

SAY WHAT?
Observation: What do I see?

SO WHAT?
Interpretation: What does it mean?

NOW WHAT?
Application: How does it apply to me?

THEN WHAT?
Implementation: What do I do?

If you had been sitting in the meeting in which Paul described what was happening in his ministry, how would you have reacted. In the response of one of the men, James, we see a principle that must be carefully followed when evaluating what direction to take or decision to make. That principle is found in what James' said beginning in verse thirteen. Paul and Barnabas reported what God had been doing in their ministry among the Gentiles. These men however needed confirmation that what they were doing was God's plan, not their own. It was critical to the ministry to be able to back up what they were doing with the Word of God. James referred them to Amos 9:11-12 to give Scriptural support for what they saw taking place among the Gentiles. He knew that everything believers do must be in agreement with God's Word. In the same way, we must never allow our experiences to determine what we believe. They can never be the final authority for what we do or what we believe. Scripture is our standard, not someone's opinion, circumstances, and not even his experiences. We must find our support in the Word.

ACTS 15:13
After they finished speaking, James replied, "Brothers, listen to me."

RESPONDING TO DIFFICULTY

How would you react if you were imprisoned for something you did not do? A false accusation can be extremely discouraging. In today's reading we read of Paul and Silas being imprisoned wrongly after being beaten and placed in stocks. What was their response? What were the next things to take place in the prison in verse 25 and following? How would you have responded? Would you have started to sing? Which is more challenging to you, the fact that they were singing after being beaten or that after they were free they did not run? Their response to the circumstances they found themselves in resulted in the jailer and his whole family being saved and baptized. Could your reactions be influencing others to walk toward or away from God? The most difficult time in our lives show our heart of hearts. What do they tell you about you? What are they telling others about you?

SAY WHAT?
What difficult circumstances are you facing right now?

SO WHAT?
What is your response communicating to others?

NOW WHAT?
Is your response helping or hindering what God might want to accomplish? How?

THEN WHAT?
Write a commitment outlining your response to those circumstances from now on.

ACTS 16:25
About midnight Paul and Silas were praying and singing hymns to God, and the prisoners were listening to them.

SAY WHAT?

Observation: What do I see?

SO WHAT?

Interpretation: What does it mean?

NOW WHAT?

Application: How does it apply to me?

THEN WHAT?

Implementation: What do I do?

Did Paul succeed in reaching people with the gospel? How did they respond? Amazingly, every town had people come to Christ for salvation as a result of Paul's witness. How incredible it would have been to be with him when so many acknowledged Christ as Savior. This chapter also reveals what can happen when we speak out for God and He begins to move in the hearts of people. There were many who responded to the message and trusted Christ, but there was another group who opposed Paul and his message. It seemed as if every time God began to move, a group of Jews worked to counter what Paul was doing. His response was to faithfully preach the message and use his opportunities to the best of his ability. Although he must have felt discouraged at times, he knew he must faithfully continue his ministry. Any time God moves, we must expect opposition. When God begins to move in your unit or family or church, opposition will come. When it does, you need to stay focused on God and allow Him to comfort you (1 Peter 4:12). Do you need to change your perspective on opposition that may be facing you right now?

ACTS 17:34

But some men joined him and believed, among whom also were Dionysius the Areopagite and a woman named Damaris and others with them.

THE NEED TO REFOCUS

In this chapter, there is a bit of information that can help us a great deal in determining how to reach out to our individual mission fields. Do you know where it is found? Look at the example of the Apostle Paul in verse six. Paul tried diligently to reach the Jews and share the message of Christ with them. They resisted no matter what he tried. He did not appear to have made any progress with the Jews. He decided to find people who were interested and spend time with them. He was not going to continue investing his time with those who had no interest in spiritual things. He was wasting his time. God directed him to begin building relationships with Gentiles who responded to the gospel message overwhelmingly. We can sometimes do the same thing and focus on those who have no real desire for our message and miss people surrounding us who would be open to Christ. It is good, at times, to examine our outreach and maybe refocus on those who are open. The Bible makes it clear that there will be some who do not want to hear about Christ, and others who are searching. Can you name someone you know who is open to the message of Christ?

★★★★

ACTS 18:6

And when they opposed and reviled him, he shook out his garments and said to them, "Your blood be on your own heads! I am innocent. From now on I will go to the Gentiles."

SAY WHAT?

Make a list of people you have been trying to reach out to.

SO WHAT?

How have they responded?

NOW WHAT?

List some people you know who might be open to the gospel?

THEN WHAT?

How can you begin to share it with them?

STAYING FOCUSED

SAY WHAT?
Observation: What do I see?

SO WHAT?
Interpretation: What does it mean?

NOW WHAT?
Application: How does it apply to me?

THEN WHAT?
Implementation: What do I do?

What is the greatest opposition you have ever faced because you are a Christian? How did you respond to it? What were the results of your response? In today's reading, we read one of the most spectacular responses to the gospel in Scripture. The chapter begins with God doing miracles in the midst of this church. People were getting saved which resulted in burning their sorcery scrolls publicly. The chapter ends with an out-of-control riot incited by Demetrius whose business had been affected by the salvation of those in Ephesus. Can you imagine having people yell for two hours in opposition to you and your message? Why did they react so violently? When God changes the lives of many people,there is opposition. Satan will not sit idly by and do nothing while God is at work changing lives. He will do whatever he can to disrupt the movement of God. We must prepare for it and not allow it to discourage us. God has a plan and will strengthen us to walk forward. When opposition is great,God's ability to deliver is greater. Does your life reflect confidence in God's ability? Are you boldly proclaiming your faith?

★★★★

ACTS 19:11
And God was doing extraordinary miracles by the hands of Paul.

The book of Proverbs was designed to help us in "attaining wisdom and discipline; in understanding words of insight; in acquiring a disciplined and prudent life, doing what is right and just and fair; in giving prudence to the simple, knowledge and discretion to the young." As you read through this chapter, write down the verses that are most significant to you in your present circumstances.

VERSE | WHAT TRUTH IT COMMUNICATES | HOW IT IMPACTS MY LIFE

OUR GREATEST MOTIVATION

SAY WHAT?
Make a list of all the activities you are involved in.

SO WHAT?
Of those, which ones are the most important to you?

NOW WHAT?
Which ones will be important when you stand before God?

THEN WHAT?
What needs to change in order to have the task God called you to become the most important thing in your life?

What is the one thing that motivates you more than anything else? What is it that occupies your time, your money and your thoughts? Sports? Music? Military Career? Video games? The computer? How would the Apostle Paul answer that question? He did so in today's reading. This was an emotional time for Paul and these believers as they began to understand what was ahead. In his final talk to the Ephesian elders, he shared that the Holy Spirit had warned him many times about what he had to face in future days. His response was to continue with his ministry. The reason for his commitment is stated in verse 24. He wanted to finish the task that God had given him. If that meant imprisonment, so be it. He wanted to be able to stand before God and know that he had accomplished God's will for his life. What responsibility has God given to you? Are you working to complete it or only occasionally thinking about it? Is fulfilling your responsibility your primary motivation of life? Sadly, other things often motivate us more than fulfilling God's purpose for our lives. Is something more important to you than that?

★★★★

ACTS 20:24
But I do not account my life of any value nor as precious to myself, if only I may finish my course and the ministry that I received from the Lord Jesus, to testify to the gospel of the grace of God.

SENDING OUT RIGHTS

What character traits did Paul demonstrate in this chapter? Write some of them in the margin of your Bible. An obvious one is courage. Paul knew that hardship was ahead, yet he was willing to die for the name of Christ if that was what it would take. There is another trait that is not as obvious without careful reading. It is found in verse 26. In this verse, we see Paul submitting himself to Jewish customs even though he was not obligated to do so. Why? Because he wanted to put their fears concerning his obedience to the law to rest and prove that he still observed the law. The rumors going around about him were not true, and he was willing to submit to these customs so that he might have an opportunity to minister to them. His rights and preferences were not important enough to him to sacrifice his ministry in someone's life. Do you need this same trait in your relationship with someone? Others in your unit? A family member? Some friends? Do you miss opportunities to minister to someone because you are unwilling to give up your rights? Your rights are not worth missing opportunities to impact someone's life.

SAY WHAT?
Observation: What do I see?

SO WHAT?
Interpretation: What does it mean?

NOW WHAT?
Application: How does it apply to me?

THEN WHAT?
Implementation: What do I do?

ACTS 21:26

Then Paul took the men, and the next day he purified himself along with them and went into the temple, giving notice when the days of purification would be fulfilled and the offering presented for each one of them.

GOD'S PREPERATION

SAY WHAT?

List some of the significant events that have taken place in your life.

SO WHAT?

What talents or abilities do you have or have you acquired?

NOW WHAT?

What kinds of ministries could God be preparing you for?

THEN WHAT?

In light of this passage, what personal commitment can you make?

In what way did God prepare Paul for what he would be facing as recorded in this chapter? It is awesome to see both the big and small areas that God used in preparation for the difficult events ahead. Think about it. He was arrested and received an opportunity to speak to the crowd because he asked the commander for permission in Greek. Was it a coincidence that he knew Greek? The crowd listened to him because he spoke Aramaic to them. How fortunate he knew Aramaic! As they listened, they heard the names of men who had impacted his life who were renowned among the Jews. What a coincidence that he was trained by them. The point? God had been preparing Paul for his new opportunities of ministry. These examples are not coincidence or luck but the sovereign plan of God. It was with this ministry opportunity in mind that God organized the events of Paul's life. It should encourage you to know that He is doing the same with your life now. As you evaluate the events and circumstances in your life, what could God be preparing you for? Are you willing to trust Him with your future? He will prepare you for His plan.

ACTS 22:21

And he said to me, 'Go, for I will send you far away to the Gentiles.'

GOD'S WATCH CARE

Why did God say to Paul what He did in verse eleven? How do you think Paul was feeling up until that point? What thoughts do you think went through his mind when he heard God say it? Although you probably have not faced the same kinds of circumstances Paul did, you may have wondered if God knew what was going on in your life or if He even cared. In this case, God demonstrated His watch-care to Paul in a remarkable way. The Jews plotted to kill Paul and "fortunately" their plot was overheard by Paul's nephew. What a coincidence that was! He told Paul about the plot, and then, at the instruction of Paul, told the commander. As a result, Paul's life was spared. Did you stop to think how amazing it was that God had the boy in that location at the exact moment the plot was discussed? Could you be facing a situation which may cause doubt about God's ability to understand and care? Allow Paul's example to give you comfort that He is already making a way for you. Circle the words "Take courage" in your Bible to remind you that God knows where you are and He will respond when the time is right.

ACTS 23:11

The following night the Lord stood by him and said, "Take courage, for as you have testified to the facts about me in Jerusalem, so you must testify also in Rome."

SAY WHAT?

Observation: What do I see?

SO WHAT?

Interpretation: What does it mean?

NOW WHAT?

Application: How does it apply to me?

THEN WHAT?

Implementation: What do I do?

MILITARYDEVOTIONAL.COM
@MILITARYDEVOS

PROVIDING OPPORTUNITIES

SAY WHAT?

What circumstances are you facing right now that could open up new ministry doors?

SO WHAT?

What will you need to do to be able to take advantage of these new opportunities?

NOW WHAT?

What could keep you from taking advantage of these new opportunities?

THEN WHAT?

In light of this passage, what personal commitment can you make?

Do you think Paul ever got discouraged by the fact that he was once a great missionary but now found himself a prisoner with seemingly few opportunities to continue his preaching ministry? Why would God take a man who was doing a great work leading Gentiles to Christ and put him in prison? We find a reason for that unfolding in this chapter. Did you notice it? God wanted Paul to have opportunities to share the gospel with people with whom he would not otherwise have had a chance. He had to be in prison to accomplish God's task for him. In this chapter he got a chance to share with Felix publicly and, according to verse 26, he shared privately with Felix and his wife on several occasions. The Scriptures tell us that Felix sent for Paul "regularly". How exciting it must have been for Paul to see the plan of God unfold in his life! What opportunities has God brought into your life recently? Could He want you to share your faith with doctors and nurses through an illness? Could He want you to share with athletes on your team? Could He be organizing the events of your life to provide you opportunities to witness?

★★★★

ACTS 24:24

After some days Felix came with his wife Drusilla, who was Jewish, and he sent for Paul and heard him speak about faith in Christ Jesus.

THOUGHTS ON CAPITAL PUNISHMENT

Is it ever right to take a life under certain circumstances? What about capital punishment? Is there a crime that would warrant the death penalty? This is a debate that has gone on for years, and one that Paul gives us some insight into in today's reading. Did you notice it? Paul makes a comment in verse eleven that helps us understand his views on the issue of capital punishment. We know from reading the Old Testament that there were crimes that were punishable by death. Read through the Old Testament and you will discover them. We however,we are not under Old Testament law. Does that mean that capital punishment should no longer be enforced? Paul was accused of a crime that was punishable by death under the law of that day. He did not argue against the death penalty but, submitted himself to it in verse eleven. He said that if he had done something which deserved death,he would not fight the penalty. He,a New Testament saint, seemed to support the death penalty. We can assume by this that,if he felt it were wrong in all cases, he would have said so. This is an example of how Scripture addresses all issues that are relevant today.

★★★★

ACTS 25:11

If then I am a wrongdoer and have committed anything for which I deserve to die, I do not seek to escape death. But if there is nothing to their charges against me,no one can give me up to them. I appeal to Caesar.

SAY WHAT?

Observation: What do I see?

SO WHAT?

Interpretation: What does it mean?

NOW WHAT?

Application: How does it apply to me?

THEN WHAT?

Implementation: What do I do?

SHARING YOUR FAITH

SAY WHAT?

What was your life like before you met Christ, or what would it have been like if you were not saved?

SO WHAT?

Record the story of your salvation.

NOW WHAT?

How has your salvation changed your life?

THEN WHAT?

In light of this passage, what personal commitment can you make?

If you had an opportunity to share your faith with a group of people who do not know Jesus Christ, what would you say? How would you begin? What would you make sure you included? In today's reading we receive (from the Apostle Paul) an excellent pattern to follow when sharing our faith. God again had given him an opportunity that few men would have, to share with King Agrippa. He began by being polite and kind (26:2-3). He set a positive tone right away. Next, he shared with him what his life had been like before his encounter with Jesus Christ (26:4-11). Then, he shared with the king how he had met Jesus Christ (26:12-18), and how he had gotten saved. He concluded by letting him know how his life had changed as a result of what God had done (26:19-27). This structure can be used by anyone who has an opportunity to share his faith with others. Use the sheet below to put together your story so you can share it with others. Think of someone you can share it with when you are finished. Pray for an opportunity to do so.

★★★★

ACTS 26:29

And Paul said, "Whether short or long, I would to God that not only you but also all who hear me this day might become such as I am—except for these chains."

GIVING THANKS AT MEALS

You are sitting in a crowded chow hall and, before you begin to eat, what do you do? You find yourself at a restaurant with some unsaved friends. The food is placed before you and they begin to eat. What do you do? A better question might be, what do these examples have to do with the story of Paul's shipwreck found here in chapter 27? Look at verse 35, and you will find an interesting phrase. The ship's crew and passengers found themselves in the midst of a storm that was destroying the ship. They had a small amount of food left and prepared for one last meal. It is recorded that before they ate, Paul prayed and gave thanks for the food, in front of them all. Why would God direct Luke to record what seems like an insignificant fact? Maybe because it is not insignificant. Even in the midst of a crisis situation, Paul stopped to demonstrate to those around him that he knew where his food came from and that he was thankful for it. Are you this kind of example as well? What a simple way to let people in your world know how you feel about your faith. Don't allow an opportunity like this to pass because you are too ashamed.

★★★★

ACTS 27:35

And when he had said these things, he took bread, and giving thanks to God in the presence of all he broke it and began to eat.

SAY WHAT?

Observation: What do I see?

SO WHAT?

Interpretation: What does it mean?

NOW WHAT?

Application: How does it apply to me?

THEN WHAT?

Implementation: What do I do?

MILITARYDEVOTIONAL.COM
@MILITARYDEVOS

A FOCUSSED LIFE

SAY WHAT?

Observation: What do I see?

SO WHAT?

Interpretation: What does it mean?

NOW WHAT?

Application: How does it apply to me?

THEN WHAT?

Implementation: What do I do?

What one word could you use to describe the Apostle Paul? How about the word focused? No matter what circumstances Paul faced, it seemed that he always viewed them as opportunities to share his faith with others. It seems as though he saw everything in his life as an opportunity to influence. He was shipwrecked, so he began a ministry on the island of Malta. He arrived in Rome and began to share with those around him what God had done in his life. While under house arrest, he spent from "morning till evening" sharing with people from the Scriptures. Why? He was focused! The book of Acts ends with a verse that sums up his life. What a great ending to a great book! Underline it in your Bible. Could the words of verse 31 be said of you? Do you boldly and without hindrance share the gospel? How about the word focused? Could it be used to describe your life? What would need to change in your life for someone to be able to use these words about you? What keeps distracting you from serving Christ with your whole heart? Today would be a great day to begin living a "focused" life. Are you ready?

ACTS 28:31

Proclaiming the kingdom of God and teaching about the Lord Jesus Christ with all boldness and without hindrance.

The book of Proverbs was designed to help us in "attaining wisdom and discipline; in understanding words of insight; in acquiring a disciplined and prudent life, doing what is right and just and fair; in giving prudence to the simple, knowledge and discretion to the young." As you read through this chapter, write down the verses that are most significant to you in your present circumstances.

VERSE | WHAT TRUTH IT COMMUNICATES | HOW IT IMPACTS MY LIFE

WHEN YOUR SERVICE IS DONE, WHAT'S YOUR NEXT STEP?

Pilgrimage offers a unique opportunity to earn a master's degree in **ORGANIZATIONAL LEADERSHIP from an accredited Christian college or university,** while working in your professional field of choice... even while you continue to serve in the military.

Our **experience-based distance learning model** uses your current leadership context as the classroom for learning... and applies essential organizational leadership skills that convert to any role or environment.

Put your GI Bill benefits to work for your future!

Need an undergraduate degree? Ask about our undergrad programs or the accelerated graduate degree program.

LEARN MORE OR APPLY ONLINE AT:

ORG-LEADERSHIP.COM

 PILGRIMAGE

PILGRIMAGE EDUCATIONAL RESOURCES / CLARKS SUMMIT, PA
P: 570.504.1463 / E: INFO@SIMPLYAPILGRIM.COM / SIMPLYAPILGRIM.COM

MILITARY

OTD

» **MILITARYDEVOTIONAL.COM**

 @MILITARYDEVOS

 FACEBOOK.COM/MILITARYDEVOS

THE BOOK OF
REVELATION

JUNE
★★★★

MONTHLY
PRAYER SHEET

I NEED TO REACH OUT TO...	HOW I WILL DO IT...	HOW IT WENT...

OTHER REQUEST	HOW ANSWERED	DATE

★ MONTHLY
★ MISSION SHEET ★

⟫⟫ Share your personal commitments with those who will help keep you accountable to them.

⟫ NAME: ....

This sheet is designed to help you make personal commitments each month that will help you grow in your walk with God. Fill it out by determining:

★ What will push you.
★ What you think you can achieve.

⟫ PERSONAL DEVOTIONS:
I will commit to read the OnTrack Bible passage and devotional thought .... day(s) each week this month.

⟫ CHURCH/CHAPEL ATTENDANCE:
I will attend Church/Chapel .... time(s) this month.
I will attend .... time(s) this month.

⟫ SCRIPTURE MEMORY:
I will memorize .... key verse(s) from the daily OnTrack Devotions this month.

⟫ OUTREACH:
I will share Christ with .... person/people this month.
I will serve my local church/chapel this month by ....
....
....

⟫ OTHER ACTIVITIES:
List any other opportunities such as events, prayer group, etc..., you will participate in this month. ....
....
....
....
....
....

Determine to begin today a journey that will last a lifetime, and will change your life forever.

WHAT MUST TAKE PLACE

Today you begin a journey that might be brand new for you,but one that you can be excited about. You begin your journey through the book of Revelation. It is a book that everyone seems to be interested in, but a book which few have read through completely. It is important to keep in mind statements that John made to begin this book. The first is that this book is the revelation of Jesus Christ, which God gave to John. It is not John's opinion or his own personal perceptions about the future. What you will be reading came directly to John from God,and he simply wrote down what he saw (vs11). Second, it is important to know the reason God gave John this book. God wanted us to be able to know what will imminently take place (vs1). This book is our preview of what is coming in the future. Third,it comes with a promise from God. John tells us that we will be blessed if we read it,hear it,and take to heart what it says. Although you may not catch everything your first time through,you will learn much that will excite you and be a challenge to you. Be faithful to your reading. Also, be faithful to apply to your life what you have read.

SAY WHAT?
What do you hope to gain from reading Revelation?

SO WHAT?
What do you think reading this book will do for your faith?

NOW WHAT?
What will you need to do to achieve the goal in question #1?

THEN WHAT?
In light of your reading in Revelation 1,what personal commitment will you make?

★★★★

REV 1:3
Blessed is the one who reads aloud the words of this prophecy, and blessed are those who hear, and who keep what is written in it for the time is near.

MILITARYDEVOTIONAL.COM
@MILITARYDEVOS

SAY WHAT?
Observation: What do I see?

SO WHAT?
Interpretation: What does it mean?

NOW WHAT?
Application: How does it apply to me?

THEN WHAT?
Implementation: What do I do?

Over the next seven days we will be reading God's personal message to the seven churches. These were actual local bodies of believers to whom this book was written. In most cases, the letters contain positive characteristics and then God revealed what was wrong with each of them. Today we read about the church in Ephesus. This was a church that had much to be proud of. A positive characteristic God gave to these believers was that they had persevered in the midst of hardship. It was not a church which had given in when the pressure was on. It was also a church that did not tolerate wickedness. It was, however, a church who had lost it's first love. The joy and excitement they once had about their faith was gone. The fire that once burned bright was out, and they were just going through the motions. God called them to remember where they once had been, repent and come back to the place they had previously held. Could this be true of you or your church? Have you or has your church lost the fire and passion of earlier days? If so, remember, repent, and do what you once did. Losing your first love is serious.

★★★★

REV 2:4
But I have this against you, that you have abandoned the love you had at first.

BE FAITHFUL

Imagine that someone came to you at work and told you that when you left the building, you were going to be beaten because of the stand you had taken for Christ. What thoughts would run through your mind? That is exactly what happened to this church. The church in Smyrna had two characteristics that they were known for. They were afflicted and were poor. Yet in spite of that, God said that they were rich. They did not allow their afflictions or their poverty to cause bitterness or discouragement. God informed them that Satan would attack them. He would put some of the believers in prison and they would suffer for ten days. Their challenge? - To remain faithful to God and He would give them the crown of life. It would have been a comfort to them to know that God was watching and knew exactly what was going on in their lives. He would help and reward them for their faithfulness. Are you experiencing opposition in your life in which you need this encouragement? Underline verse ten to remind you to remain faithful.

★★★★

REV 2:10

Do not fear what you are about to suffer .... Be faithful unto death, and I will give you the crown of life.

SAY WHAT?

What opposition do you face or could you be facing these next few months?

SO WHAT?

What could God desire to accomplish in your life through it?

NOW WHAT?

How can today's reading help you be faithful in the midst of opposition?

THEN WHAT?

In light of this passage, what personal commitment will you make?

MILITARYDEVOTIONAL.COM
🐦 @MILITARYDEVOS

I HAVE A FEW THINGS

SAY WHAT?
What doctrinal issues are you aware of with other believers or churches?

SO WHAT?
What could wrong views of those doctrines lead to?

NOW WHAT?
How can you keep yourself from doctrinal error?

THEN WHAT?
In light of this passage, what personal commitment can you make?

How important is it to keep wrong doctrines and wrong teachings out of the local church? According to today's reading, it's crucial. God tells the church in Pergamum that there are some things He is pleased with among them. The letter states that He knows that they have remained true to Him. Even when one of their leaders was put to death, they did not renounce their faith but stayed true to what they believed. There was, however, something about this church that He did not approve of. In spite of all the positive things about them, there were those in their church who held to teachings which were contradictory to God's law. One group specifically mentioned was the Nicolaitans. They taught that a Christian has liberty, like free love, once he was saved. Although these believers had not yet denounced Christ in the midst of suffering, purity of doctrine was not a priority. God warned them that if they allowed this teaching to continue, it could cause others to fall into great sin. We often think that doctrine is not something we should be concerned about. Each person can believe what he wants. God tells us that that is not true.

REV 2:14
But I have a few things against you: you have some there who hold the teaching of Balaam, who taught Balak to put a stumbling block before the sons of Israel...

YOU TOLERATE

When John referred to a woman named Jezebel in this passage, was he referring to an actual woman in the church at Thyatira? Possibly, but that name most likely referred to a specific woman whose actions resembled those of Jezebel in the Old Testament. God saw this church and knew that they had some good things going for them. They had a church of love and faith that resulted in service to others and perseverance in suffering. God told them that in the areas of service and perseverance they had grown and increased. However, as in the case of the church of Pergamum, they tolerated a woman who, by her teaching, led believers into committing sexual immorality and eating meat sacrificed to idols. She may have even taught that homosexuality was permissible or that engaging in sex before marriage was fine if the couple were in love. Whatever she taught, it misled people into committing sin. We must never permit teaching that contradicts what the Bible says, or is not found in Scripture. If it is not in your Bible, it must be rejected, even if someone claims it is true. If you can't defend it with Scripture, forget it.

REV 2:20

But I have this against you, that you tolerate that woman Jezebel, who calls herself a prophetess and is teaching and seducing my servants to practice sexual immorality and to eat food sacrificed to idols.

SAY WHAT?
Observation: What do I see?

SO WHAT?
Interpretation: What does it mean?

NOW WHAT?
Application: How does it apply to me?

THEN WHAT?
Implementation: What do I do?

The book of Proverbs was designed to help us in "attaining wisdom and discipline; in understanding words of insight; in acquiring a disciplined and prudent life, doing what is right and just and fair; in giving prudence to the simple, knowledge and discretion to the young." As you read through this chapter, write down the verses that are most significant to you in your present circumstances.

VERSE | WHAT TRUTH IT COMMUNICATES | HOW IT IMPACTS MY LIFE

I KNOW YOUR DEEDS

Can you imagine being in the church at Sardis when this letter was read? Everyone gathered together after having been told that a letter had arrived from God. The church sat quietly, waiting to hear what God had to say about what was right and what was wrong with them. God began by reminding them that He knew their deeds and was aware of their reputation for being spiritually alive. When people evaluated this church, it was obvious that God was at work and that it was filled with spiritual life and power. The obvious conclusion was that God was pleased and proud, but the reality was "I know you are dead." Although their reputation was that they were alive, they weren't. They fooled even themselves. His challenge - "wake up!" He warned that what life remained was about to die. Think about how true this is for us. Our churches are not doing all they could or should. Could God say this about your life or your church? Our response? - To remember obedience and repentance. Do people think you are alive, but inside you know you are dead? As you take an honest look at your own life and your church, what do you see?

SAY WHAT?

What signs of spiritual life and power do you see in your life and your church?

SO WHAT?

What signs indicate that you or your church could be close to dying?

NOW WHAT?

What needs to happen in order to change it?

THEN WHAT?

In light of this passage, what personal commitment will you make?

★★★★

REV 3:1

And to the angel of the church in Sardis write: 'The words of him who has the seven spirits of God and the seven stars.'

HOLD ON

SAY WHAT?
Observation: What do I see?

SO WHAT?
Interpretation: What does it mean?

NOW WHAT?
Application: How does it apply to me?

THEN WHAT?
Implementation: What do I do?

What is the difference between this and the other letters we have read so far? Look at it again and see if you notice the difference. It is that God did not make a negative statement about this church. They were surely astonished to hear that God approved of what they were doing and had no criticisms of them. He said that He had given them an open door that no one would be able to shut. Although they had little strength, they still keep His Word and stayed true to His Name. It must have thrilled them to hear God say that those who opposed and criticized the church would one day publicly admit that God did love them. They had not only endured, but they had done so patiently. God's response was to keep them from the hour of trial - to take them away so they wouldn't have to face it. How would God evaluate you and your church? This passage should encourage us to see that it is possible to have a church about which God only makes positive statements. Could He describe your church this same way? Could He describe your life like this? What changes can you make in order for this to be said of you? What role can you play to begin the process?

★★★★

REV 3:11
I am coming soon. Hold fast what you have, so that no one may seize your crown.

YOU DO NOT REALIZE

On a scale of 1-10, how would you rate your spiritual life? A 1 being the worst and a 10 being the best. Write a number right now somewhere on this page. How does God feel about the number you just wrote down? If we consider God's opinion of the number we recorded, most of us should be concerned because our numbers are in the middle. Many people evaluate their spiritual lives, and although they are not where they should be, they convince themselves that God is pleased that they are not on the lowest levels of spiritual immaturity. That is not how God responds, however. In this letter to the Laodiceans, God says that lukewarm or average is worse than cold. How do you think the Laodiceans felt when they realized what God's position on average is? Why is it so wrong? - Because it leads to wrong conclusions about the true condition of one's heart. The average Christian is convinced that he is okay. In fact, he thinks that he is rich and needs nothing. In reality, he is wretched, pitiful, poor, blind and naked. God's counsel is for him to repent of his sin and come back to Him. What is God's opinion of where you currently are in your walk with Him? What can you do about it?

REV 3:17

For you say, I am rich, I have prospered, and I need nothing, not realizing that you are wretched, pitiable, poor, blind, and naked.

SAY WHAT?

How would you rate your spiritual life today on a scale of 1-10 (do not use 5)? Why?

SO WHAT?

How does God feel about where you are in your walk with Him?

NOW WHAT?

What needs to change in order for you to move to a higher number?

THEN WHAT?

In light of this passage, what personal commitment will you make?

SAY WHAT?
Observation: What do I see?

SO WHAT?
Interpretation: What does it mean?

NOW WHAT?
Application: How does it apply to me?

THEN WHAT?
Implementation: What do I do?

Why is the message the four creatures gave different from what the twenty four elders said to Christ? Could it be that the four creatures viewed God differently than the elders? The creatures who had not experienced redemption saw the holiness of God. All creation can recognize His purity, His majesty, and His holiness. But to those of us who have been redeemed, He is far more than just holy, He is worthy. Their song does not have the joy that the song of the redeemed has. The elders had once been dead in their sins and slaves to sin. They had no ability to please God or know a way to be cleansed from sin. The provision for salvation through faith in Jesus Christ was revealed to them and they accepted God's gift. When they stood before the throne of God, they laid down their crowns and said,"You are worthy..." How one responds to God reveals his view of God and the value he places on the gift God has given him. How do you respond to God? Why not take some time today in private to express to God how you feel about all He has done for you. Whether or not you live what you say, will reveal your heart's condition.

REV 4:11
"Worthy are you, our Lord and God, to receive glory and honor and power, for you created all things, and by your will they existed and were created."

FELL DOWN AND WORSHIPED

Who is the "Lion of the tribe of Judah, the Root of David?" How did He triumph? The answer to both these questions is found by looking closely at this chapter. The Lion of the tribe of Judah and the Root of David was the One who was slain and, with His shed blood, purchased men for God. By His sacrifice, He made people of all nations to be a kingdom and priests of God. He was the Lamb who was slain. Who is the One who did all this? - Jesus Christ. Because of what He did on the cross, He is worthy to not only open the scroll, but worthy to receive everything that belongs to God. He is worthy to receive power, wealth, strength, honor, glory, and praise. Jesus Christ did what no man could ever do. He did for you what you could never do for yourself. He purchased you for God that you might become a kingdom and a priest and might serve Him. How have you responded to this truth? Hopefully, not only by worshiping and praising Him, but also by serving Him with your whole heart. After all He has done for us, is there a sacrifice too great or task too menial to demonstrate our thankfulness and love? Is this how you live your life?

SAY WHAT?
Observation: What do I see?

SO WHAT?
Interpretation: What does it mean?

NOW WHAT?
Application: How does it apply to me?

THEN WHAT?
Implementation: What do I do?

★★★★

REV 5:14
And the four living creatures said, "Amen!" and the elders fell down and worshiped.

SAY WHAT?
Observation: What do I see?

SO WHAT?
Interpretation: What does it mean?

NOW WHAT?
Application: How does it apply to me?

THEN WHAT?
Implementation: What do I do?

In this chapter,we begin reading about how God is going to judge the world for their sinfulness. We,as Christians,will not be on the earth at this time because the rapture will have taken us to heaven. What takes place on earth at this time ought to motivate us to be more diligent in our witness. In this chapter, John reveals six of the seven seal judgments. They involve peace being removed from the earth and men beginning open war with each other. Famine befalls the earth so severely that what had been staples of life,become luxuries. One-fourth of the population of the earth is killed by the sword, hunger, natural death, and wild beasts. There will be major physical changes to the earth. The great earthquake will occur; the sun will be darkened like sackcloth. The moon will be reddened as blood; a meteor shower will pound the earth. Mountains and islands will be moved. It is hard to even imagine such devastation. What effect should these facts have on our lives? First, thankfulness towards God who saved us from this,and second,a renewed motivation to share Christ so that others will not have to experience this disaster.

★★★★

REV 6:17
For the great day of their wrath has come, and who can stand?

The book of Proverbs was designed to help us in "attaining wisdom and discipline; in understanding words of insight; in acquiring a disciplined and prudent life, doing what is right and just and fair; in giving prudence to the simple, knowledge and discretion to the young." As you read through this chapter, write down the verses that are most significant to you in your present circumstances.

VERSE | WHAT TRUTH IT COMMUNICATES | HOW IT IMPACTS MY LIFE

SAY WHAT?

Write down the names of people you care about whom you would love to see come to Christ.

SO WHAT?

What obstacles could keep you from sharing Christ with them?

NOW WHAT?

How will you go about sharing Christ with them?

THEN WHAT?

In light of this passage, what personal commitment can you make?

Why did God insert the account of the redemption of the 144,000 sealed Jews before finishing the record of the seven seals, describing the seventh one? It could be easy for one to assume after reading about the seal judgements that no one could get saved during such devastation. It is as if God stopped the account to let us know that in spite of what will occur on the earth, He will still save people. The activity of grace and men trusting in the Son of God for salvation will continue. John tells us that 144,000 Jews will be saved as well as "a great multitude that no one could count." This group will be made up of all kinds of people. What a comfort to know that no matter how awful the circumstances may seem to us, or how wicked this world may yet get, God is still able to reach out and save people. In spite of what might be happening in their lives, there will be people who see their need to trust Christ. Who in your world needs to hear what Christ has done for them? Do not assume you know what response will be given or if their environment will negatively affect their decisions. Do not allow assumptions to hinder sharing.

★★★★

REV 7:4

And I heard the number of the sealed, 144,000, sealed from every tribe of the sons of Israel.

THERE WAS SILENCE

Why was there silence in heaven after the seventh seal was opened? As you read this chapter, you realize silence is about the only reaction one could have in response to what will be taking place. How would you respond to such news? Can you imagine what it is going to be like to live on the earth during the Tribulation? Think about this seventh seal judgment. One third of the earth will be burned up, a third of the sea will be turned to blood, and, as a result, a third of the creatures in the sea will die. Can you imagine the smell that is going to create? Also, a third of the rivers become bitter and even more people will die. The fourth trumpet results in a third of all light from the sun and moon turned dark. A third of each day will be totally black. How horrible it will be for those left trying to survive the judgment of God during these days. We need to be more diligent in sharing the message of Christ with those who are headed for these judgments because they are not saved. Do you love your unsaved friends enough to share Christ with them? How can you reach out to them this week? What should you say to him?

REV 8:1

When the Lamb opened the seventh seal, there was silence in heaven for about half an hour.

SAY WHAT?
Observation: What do I see?

SO WHAT?
Interpretation: What does it mean?

NOW WHAT?
Application: How does it apply to me?

THEN WHAT?
Implementation: What do I do?

SAY WHAT?

Observation: What do I see?

SO WHAT?

Interpretation: What does it mean?

NOW WHAT?

Application: How does it apply to me?

THEN WHAT?

Implementation: What do I do?

How do you imagine you would respond if you were living on the earth during the Tribulation period? Imagine experiencing what you have read in Revelation up to this point. God's judgment, however, is not finished. Today we read about more of God's judgment. John reveals that there will be demonic forces coming up out of hell that will torture people for five months. People will be in such agony that they will want to die but will not be able to. According to verse six, death will elude them. Four angels will be released, and they will kill a third of all mankind. Keep in mind that these two events follow the events found in chapter eight. One would assume that people would flock to God in repentance, seeking His mercy. One would think that by now, they would be getting the message that God hates sin, and they need to repent and seek His forgiveness. Do they? - Not according to verse twnety. They still do not stop worshiping demons and idols, or repent. Often, we do the same thing. God convicts us about sin in our lives, yet we refuse to repent. Is God dealing with you right now about an area in which you need to repent and seek forgiveness?

★★★★

REV 9:20

The rest of mankind, who were not killed by these plagues, did not repent of the works of their hands nor give up worshiping demons and idols...

MY STOMACH TURNED

What is God trying to communicate to us from this interlude between the trumpet judgments? As He did before, John apparently stops his description of the judgments to encourage us. In this chapter, John saw a book that contained the events that are yet to come. John was told not to reveal them. He was then asked to do something that must have seemed bizarre. The voice of heaven told him to get the scroll and eat it. The angel said that it would taste sweet in his mouth, but then grow sour in his stomach. What reason could there be for doing that? Could God want us to know that His Word must be inside of us before we communicate it? Could He be illustrating the truth of this entire book? - That prophecy compels us to read and study. The events of the future are exciting. When the reality of the future is comprehended, it sours in your stomach. This book, while exciting and interesting, ought to grieve the heart of every believer. What happened to John when he ate the scroll should happen to each of us as the Word really gets inside us. What does your response to this book tell you about yourself?

★★★★

REV 10:10

And I took the little scroll from the hand of the angel and ate it. It was sweet as honey in my mouth, but when I had eaten it my stomach was made bitter.

SAY WHAT?

What are the most interesting things you have learned in Revelation so far this month?

SO WHAT?

What are the most difficult things you have learned about the future?

NOW WHAT?

What should your response be to what you are learning?

THEN WHAT?

In light of this passage, what personal commitment can you make?

SAY WHAT?
Observation: What do I see?

SO WHAT?
Interpretation: What does it mean?

NOW WHAT?
Application: How does it apply to me?

THEN WHAT?
Implementation: What do I do?

With all that has gone on thus far in the tribulation, one would think that the hearts of people would be softening. One would think that the survivors would be open to seeking God's forgiveness. In today's reading we see that their hearts are, in fact, growing harder. We read that there will be two witnesses on the earth at this time. They will be a testimony to who God is and what He expects their response to Him should be. The world will not respond well. For 1,260 days the witnesses will preach, and no one will be able to harm them. After the appointed days are up, they will be killed. The world will celebrate. Their mockery towards God is demonstrated by the desecration of the witnesses bodies. The world will turn their deaths into a holiday of gift giving and celebration. What contempt! But God will intervene and will raise them from the dead and call them to heaven. A major earthquake will occur and 7,000 more lives will be lost. You can almost sense the calm before the greatest storm ever known. God desires that we allow His judgment to soften us and bring us to repentance, not to harden our hearts against Him.

★★★★

REV 11:14
The second woe has passed; behold, the third woe is soon to come.

NOW HAS COME

What does this chapter mean? Did you wonder what the answer to that question was as you read? Let's examine the passage closely and see if we can understand what John wrote. First, the woman in this chapter refers to the Nation of Israel. It is from them that Christ was born. The child is obviously Christ. The dragon is Satan. Satan tried, at the time of Christ's birth, to destroy Him yet was unable to. Christ died for our sins and rose again the third day, accomplishing His purpose. Since Satan was unable to defeat the child, he turned his attention to the woman, the Nation of Israel. We also learn that there will be a battle between Michael and God's army and Satan and his army. Satan will be defeated, probably in the middle of the tribulation, and then cast out of Heaven. He will not be permitted there again. Satan will intensify his attack on the Nation of Israel. God will provide refuge so they will not be totally defeated. This is the beginning of the end for Satan and his army. God will be victorious against Satan and He will provide deliverance for His people. Does your life illustrate that God is already victorious?

REV 12:10

"Now the salvation and the power and the kingdom of our God and the authority of his Christ have come, for the accuser of our brothers has been thrown down, who accuses them day and night before our God.

SAY WHAT?
Observation: What do I see?

SO WHAT?
Interpretation: What does it mean?

NOW WHAT?
Application: How does it apply to me?

THEN WHAT?
Implementation: What do I do?

The book of Proverbs was designed to help us in "attaining wisdom and discipline; in understanding words of insight; in acquiring a disciplined and prudent life, doing what is right and just and fair; in giving prudence to the simple, knowledge and discretion to the young." As you read through this chapter, write down the verses that are most significant to you in your present circumstances.

VERSE | WHAT TRUTH IT COMMUNICATES | HOW IT IMPACTS MY LIFE

THIS CALLS FOR...

Who is the first beast in this chapter, and who is the second beast? The first beast is commonly known as the Antichrist. He is a man who will rule on the earth during the tribulation and will be given his power and his throne by Satan himself. The second beast is known as the false prophet. His job will be to promote the Antichrist and convince the world to worship him. Satan is attempting to counterfeit the trinity of God with these two evil ones. He will set himself up as God and the Antichrist as Jesus. Satan will even deceive people into believing that the Antichrist has died of a head wound and is then raised back to life. All this is designed to counterfeit what God has done. It would seem hopeless if we did not know that God was in total control. While Satan may think he is in control, he is just accomplishing what God has designed. God is in control, and the saints are given great encouragement in verse ten when they are told to have patient endurance and faithfulness. Likewise, when we face what appear to be hopeless situations, we need faithfulness and endurance as we wait for God's solution.

★★★★

REV 13:10

If anyone is to be taken captive, to captivity he goes; if anyone is to be slain with the sword, with the sword must he be slain.

SAY WHAT?

What circumstances are you facing that seem to be hopeless?

SO WHAT?

Can you think of a situation from your past in which God delivered you?

NOW WHAT?

How can you find comfort in your present circumstances after reading this passage?

THEN WHAT?

In light of this passage, what personal commitment can you make?

MILITARYDEVOTIONAL.COM
🐦 @MILITARYDEVOS

JUDGEMENT HAS COME

SAY WHAT?
Observation: What do I see?

SO WHAT?
Interpretation: What does it mean?

NOW WHAT?
Application: How does it apply to me?

THEN WHAT?
Implementation: What do I do?

Why did God choose according to today's reading, to communicate the gospel through angels in the end times? The events that unfold in these last days get more amazing with each passing chapter of Revelation. In this chapter, we read about the unique way that God will communicate the gospel to people during the tribulation. According to this chapter, God will send three angels who will fly around, calling out with a loud voice to people on earth. One will be calling for people to glorify God; one will proclaim that Babylon is fallen; and one will warn people not to worship the beast or get its mark. In the midst of all the devastation that has gone on to this point, one would think that people would be ready to listen to an angel from Heaven. But, they won't and will continue in their sin, refusing to humble themselves before God. The resulting judgment of God climaxes in the battle of Armageddon where the blood will be 4½ feet deep for 180 miles (vs20). Do you find comfort knowing that you do not have to be a part of this horror? Tragically, there are those who will reject God no matter what the consequences.

★★★★

REV 14:7
..."Fear God and give him glory, because the hour of his judgment has come, and worship him who made heaven and earth, the sea and the springs of water."

WHO HAD BEEN VICTORIOUS

Chapter fifteen is an interlude before the most awesome of God's judgments against the world, which has yet to begin. In chapter sixteen we will begin reading about the seven bowl judgments, which are even worse than what you have read so far. In the midst of learning about what will be taking place in Heaven during this time, there is something important to keep in mind. Did you see it? It is found in verse two. As John looked across the sea, he saw a group of people. Note how he described them. They were a group of people who were victorious over the beast. It could easily feel as if Satan will be victorious over everyone during the tribulation. There still will be those, however, who will stand for God and be victorious over Satan. In fact, there will even be some who will still trust Christ as we read earlier. As we journey ahead in this book and as the bowl judgements unfold, keep in mind that there will always be a group of people resisting Satan and standing for God. If that is true in the future, how much more ought we in today's world stand firm for Christ and live victorious in spite of the influence and attacks of Satan.

★★★★

REV 15:2

And I saw what appeared to be a sea of glass mingled with fire—and also those who had conquered the beast and its image and the number of its name...

SAY WHAT?
Observation: What do I see?

SO WHAT?
Interpretation: What does it mean?

NOW WHAT?
Application: How does it apply to me?

THEN WHAT?
Implementation: What do I do?

BUT THEY REFUSED

SAY WHAT?
How does God reveal to you areas in which you need to repent?

SO WHAT?
In what areas do you see Him prompting you even now?

NOW WHAT?
How can you avoid developing a hard heart that refuses to repent?

THEN WHAT?
In light of this passage, what personal commitment can you make?

Why does God bring about these horrible judgments on the earth? We get part of the answer in today's reading. As we read through this chapter, we can't help but shudder at what it is going to be like to live on the earth during the bowl judgements. Imagine everyone having painful sores cover their bodies. People will not be pleasant. Imagine the smell when every living thing in the sea dies, and the rivers and springs become blood. Imagine the agony and outcry when people are not just sunburned, but are scorched and seared. Why do all of these things happen? According to verse six, they have shed the blood of saints and prophets. They, even in the midst of all these judgments, have refused to humble themselves before God or even behave civilly to those who serve Him. Even verse nine says that, in spite of their own physical pain from the sores and the sun, they refuse to repent or glorify God. How could someone be so foolish? These events end with an earthquake unlike any before it. Their response? - Still no repentance. Sin left undealt with can lead to unbelievable hardness. Make sure it doesn't happen to you.

★★★★

REV 16:11
...and cursed the God of heaven for their pain and sores. They did not repent of their deeds.

FALSE RELIGION

This is one of the chapters in Revelation that can be confusing to read. It helps to understand some of the symbols given here. The beast, of course, as we have learned earlier, is the Antichrist. The harlot is a symbol of the false religion that has been the world religion during the Tribulation. John explains that, during the beginning of the Tribulation, this false religion will flourish in the system of the world referred to as Babylon. It will center in Rome and will include other religious groups besides the Roman Catholic church. For the first half of the Tribulation, this religion will reign unchallenged; but in the middle of the Tribulation, the Antichrist will destroy this religion and will set himself up as the one to be worshiped. John describes for us what the religion of the tribulation will look like and how the world will follow it until it's destroyed by the Antichrist. In spite of all that has gone on to this point, people will still refuse the true God and worship the beast. They will simply adopt the new religion. It may look bleak, but God's victory is just around the corner. In fact, those of us in Heaven are ready to go to war.

SAY WHAT?
Observation: What do I see?

SO WHAT?
Interpretation: What does it mean?

NOW WHAT?
Application: How does it apply to me?

THEN WHAT?
Implementation: What do I do?

REV 17:15

And the angel said to me, "The waters that you saw, where the prostitute is seated, are peoples and multitudes and nations and languages.

SAY WHAT?

What circumstances do people face in this life that sap them of hope?

SO WHAT?

Why is it so hard to trust God in circumstances like those listed above?

NOW WHAT?

How can you use this passage to encourage others and yourself in difficult times?

THEN WHAT?

In light of this passage, what personal commitment can you make?

Today you have read the final aspect of the judgment of God on the world. In it we find some important and interesting truths. During the tribulation, Babylon will not only become the center of religion in the world, but it will also become the commercial center of the world. Chapter seventeen has revealed how the religion of Babylon will end. Chapter eighteen reveals how the economic and commercial aspects of Babylon will end. In spite of all the death and devastation on the earth so far, those remaining will continue to have hope because of the wealth and power of Babylon. Read verses eleven through thirteen to see the kind of luxury items that will still be available in this city. God will destroy it however, and they will finally realize that it is all about to end. As they see the city burning, they will know that Babylon and its power and wealth has fallen under the mighty hand of God's judgment. Fear will grip the hearts of people when they realize the end is near. As believers, we are reminded again that, although it may appear hopeless, appearances viewed through our eyes can be deceiving. God will always win, He's always victorious.

REV 18:20

"Rejoice over her, O heaven, and you saints and apostles and prophets, for God has given judgment for you against her!"

KING OF KINGS

What a difference between this chapter and the other chapters we have been reading this month. Did you notice as you read? Instead of gloom and doom, today we see the beginning of God's reign on the earth. As you read these events, remember that if you know Christ as your Savior, you will be participating in them. After the destruction of Babylon, Christ will come back to earth to set up His kingdom. Heaven will begin its rejoicing, knowing that the time is almost here. Christ will mount His white horse and come to earth to destroy Satan and his armies. The beast and false prophet will be captured and cast into the lake of fire. Imagine the armies of the earth gathering for one final battle and the excitement they feel as they all unite against God and His army. With this much might, they surely must believe God will be defeated. How that will all change when the beast and the false prophet are captured! All this was designed to prepare for God's rule. God's kingdom will be ready to begin its rule. Are you excited to live in a world that God is ruling, one in which all laws will honor Him? Will you be one who enters it?

REV 19:16

On his robe and on his thigh he has a name written, King of kings and Lord of lords.

SAY WHAT?
Observation: What do I see?

SO WHAT?
Interpretation: What does it mean?

NOW WHAT?
Application: How does it apply to me?

THEN WHAT?
Implementation: What do I do?

IF ANY WAS NOT FOUND WRITTEN

SAY WHAT?
When did you by faith trust Christ as your Savior?

SO WHAT?
What evidence do you see in your life that you have been truly saved?

NOW WHAT?
How can you tell that your actions are the result of your salvation and not just outward conformity to Christianity?

THEN WHAT?
In light of this passage, what personal commitment can you make?

Who are the rest of the dead referred to in verse five? Where do the people who side with Satan at the end of the 1,000 years come from? To answer these questions we must keep in mind some important facts. There are two resurrections mentioned in Scripture. The first is of those who were saved when they died. That will take place at the rapture. Those who have died without Christ will not be resurrected at this time. John was referring to these unsaved people in verse five. Only those who are saved will enter into the 1,000 year reign of Christ. However, Christians who are alive on the earth at the end of the tribulation will enter into the 1,000 year reign with their human bodies. These people will continue to have children throughout the 1,000 years. Although everyone will have to be obedient to Christ and His rule during this time, there will be some who will not turn to Christ for salvation. This proves that living in a perfect world and doing all the right things outwardly, are not enough to make you a child of God. Man's heart changes only when he turns to Christ for salvation. No amount of outward effort or conformity will do. Have you allowed God to change your heart?

★★★★

REV 20:15
And if anyone's name was not found written in the book of life, he was thrown into the lake of fire.

EVERYTHING NEW

These last two chapters of Revelation address what it will be like in eternity for those of us who have accepted Christ as our Savior. Chapter 21 deals with the city of Jerusalem, and chapter 22 shows the blessing for us who will be living on the earth forever. It is amazing as you read through it to discover all the wonderful things God has prepared for us. What makes this city even greater is not the material that is used, not the construction, not even its size. What makes it great is who will be there. It is a city where God will dwell. There will be no need for light because His glory will shine. There will be no need for a temple, for He will be present to worship. Think about what it will be like to live there with your saved loved ones and friends, all the saints of the Bible and especially Jesus Christ. It is going to be awesome! It is sobering however, to realize there are those who will not be going to live in glory. If this is you, allow both the horrors of God's judgment and the glory of our eternal home, to motivate you to trust Christ. If it is someone you know and care for, be motivated to share Christ with them. Either way, act today.

SAY WHAT?
Observation: What do I see?

SO WHAT?
Interpretation: What does it mean?

NOW WHAT?
Application: How does it apply to me?

THEN WHAT?
Implementation: What do I do?

REV 21:5

And he who was seated on the throne said, "Behold, I am making all things new." Also he said, "Write this down, for these words are trustworthy and true."

SAY WHAT?
Observation: What do I see?

SO WHAT?
Interpretation: What does it mean?

NOW WHAT?
Application: How does it apply to me?

THEN WHAT?
Implementation: What do I do?

Well, your journey through the book of Revelation is over. You have just completed reading this amazing book. Hopefully you leave it with a greater understanding of not only the end times, but of God as well. In the very first chapter, we read that blessings await those who read, hear and take to heart the words of this book. As we have read of both the horrible things that are ahead for the unsaved, and the wonderful things that are ahead for God's people, we have rejoiced knowing that we will not experience the horrible things that will take place. Hopefully, you have a greater motivation to serve God more faithfully. Hopefully you have gained a greater burden to reach the lost in your world with the message of salvation so that they may avoid the tribulation and an eternity without Christ. Our time is slipping away, and Jesus Christ will return soon. Make sure that you and the people in your life are ready for that day. Take some time today and reflect on what God has confronted you with as you have been reading Revelation this month. Don't walk away from it unchanged! Jot down some ways that you are committed to changing.

REV 22:1
Then the angel showed me the river of the water of life, bright as crystal, flowing from the throne of God and of the Lamb.

» MILITARYDEVOTIONAL.COM

 @MILITARYDEVOS

 FACEBOOK.COM/MILITARYDEVOS

MILITARY OTD

THE BOOKS OF
1 THESSALONIANS
2 THESSALONIANS
1 TIMOTHY
2 TIMOTHY
TITUS &
PHILEMON

JULY
★★★★

MONTHLY
PRAYER SHEET

"... THE PRAYER OF A RIGHTEOUS PERSON HAS GREAT POWER AS IT IS WORKING."

JAMES 5:16

I NEED TO REACH OUT TO...	HOW I WILL DO IT...	HOW IT WENT...

OTHER REQUEST	HOW ANSWERED	DATE

MONTHLY MISSION SHEET

>> Share your personal commitments with those who will help keep you accountable to them.

>> NAME: ....

This sheet is designed to help you make personal commitments each month that will help you grow in your walk with God. Fill it out by determining:

★ What will push you.
★ What you think you can achieve.

>> PERSONAL DEVOTIONS:
I will commit to read the OnTrack Bible passage and devotional thought .... day(s) each week this month.

>> CHURCH/CHAPEL ATTENDANCE:
I will attend Church/Chapel .... time(s) this month.
I will attend .... time(s) this month.

>> SCRIPTURE MEMORY:
I will memorize .... key verse(s) from the daily OnTrack Devotions this month.

>> OUTREACH:
I will share Christ with .... person/people this month.
I will serve my local church/chapel this month by ....
....
....

>> OTHER ACTIVITIES:
List any other opportunities such as events, prayer group, etc..., you will participate in this month. ....
....
....
....
....
....

Determine to begin today a journey that will last a lifetime,and will change your life forever.

TRUE CONVERSATIONS

How do you know if true conversion has taken place in the life of someone who has made a profession of faith? How can you tell if it is really a work of God or if he is simply responding to the way you have presented the gospel? Paul helps us in today's reading to answer these questions. He begins this book with the realization that this church responded to the power of the Holy Spirit, not to his words. He knows they are truly saved because he saw four characteristics in their lives. First, he saw that they were becoming imitators of Christ and were a people who walked with God. Second, they received the Word of God with joy and excitement. They wanted to attend church to learn what Scripture teaches. Third, their faith had become obvious to others because of the change demonstrated in their lives. Fourth, they had given up their former way of life and began serving the One True God. Paul used their daily lives as a measuring stick to determine whether or not they had turned to the true God. What changes have taken place in your life which demonstrate to others that God has worked? Is there evidence of salvation?

SAY WHAT?
In what ways do you imitate Christ?

SO WHAT?
What attitude do you display when the Word of God is being taught in chapel or church?

NOW WHAT?
What comments would other people make regarding your character?

THEN WHAT?
How has your life changed since you trusted Christ?

★★★★

1 THESS 1:5
...because our gospel came to you not only in word, but also in power and in the Holy Spirit and with full conviction. You know what kind of men we proved to be among you for your sake.

MILITARYDEVOTIONAL.COM
@MILITARYDEVOS

SAY WHAT?
Observation: What do I see?

SO WHAT?
Interpretation: What does it mean?

NOW WHAT?
Application: How does it apply to me?

THEN WHAT?
Implementation: What do I do?

Why was Paul's ministry so successful? What can we learn from him in this passage that will insure success in our ministries? Paul did not fail for some important reasons in spite of experiencing incredible obstacles. First,he had the right motives (vs3-6). He was not performing to please people. He served God because he desired to please God,who had given him a message to proclaim. Second, he used the right method (vs7-9). He not only communicated the truth of God's Word,but he also opened his life up to those he taught. He didn't just preach to them,he was involved in their lives and they in his. Third,he had the right message (vs10-12). He taught them to live worthy of God. At times, his message was to encourage, comfort, or urge, but always with the goal of enabling them to walk worthy before God. Are you successfully influencing your world for Christ? Take some time today and examine yourself in these three areas. What are your motives? What method are you using to reach people? What is the central message you present? our lives. Can they see the demonstration of the Spirit's power in your life? How can you take advantage of those opportunities?

1 THESS 2:5
For we never came with words of flattery, as you know, nor with a pretext for greed— God is witness.

LOVE FOR PEOPLE

On a scale of 1-10, how would you rate your love for people? If 10 was perfect, a Christlike love for people, and 1 was no love for people at all, where would you place yourself? How does your rating compare to the love Paul demonstrated in today's passage? He told the Thessalonians that he longed to see them and be with them. When he was apart from them, he missed them. Do you love people in this way? He wanted to encourage them in their faith. His desire was to help them move forward in their walks with God. Do you love people this way? He continually thought about them and was concerned that they might be tempted and led astray. He was filled with a desire to keep them from falling. Do you have this kind of concern for the people in your world? When he heard about their growth and how faithful they were in their walks with God, he rejoiced. To know that they were growing gave him joy even in the midst of personal difficulty. We often live our day to day lives only concerned about ourselves and unwilling to care for the needs of others. Look at Paul's example and compare it to your life. What conclusions do you come to?

SAY WHAT?

In what ways do you demonstrate this kind of love for people?

SO WHAT?

In what ways can you improve in your love for people?

NOW WHAT?

What steps can you take to begin improving in this area?

THEN WHAT?

In light of this passage, what personal commitment can you make?

1 THESS 2:19

For what is our hope or joy or crown of boasting before our Lord Jesus at his coming? Is it not you?

NEVER SATISFIED

SAY WHAT?
Observation: What do I see?

SO WHAT?
Interpretation: What does it mean?

NOW WHAT?
Application: How does it apply to me?

THEN WHAT?
Implementation: What do I do?

How do you feel about where you are spiritually right now? What words would you use to describe your walk with God? Have you seen growth over the past few months? In what specific areas have you seen that growth? Today, Paul reminds us of the need to keep growing in our relationship with God and not be satisfied with where we presently are. In verse one, Paul wrote that he knew the Thessalonians were living a life that pleased God. Keep in mind that this wasn't their opinion of themselves, but was the Apostle Paul's opinion. We can assume from this that their lives did please God. Notice though, what he wrote next. He told them to continue, "more and more." Even though they were living godly lives, Paul encouraged them to work harder at it. Likewise you should not be satisfied with living the life you now live, even if it is pleasing to God. Make it even more pleasing to God. We must never become satisfied with our spiritual lives. In order to please God, it is necessary that we continually examine our lives and improve in areas that are lacking. You may be doing well now, but there is always room to improve.

★★★★

1 THESS 4:1

...we ask and urge you in the Lord Jesus, that as you received from us how you ought to walk and to please God, just as you are doing, that you do so more and more.

BE READY

What facts about the second coming of Jesus does this section of Scripture teach us? If we look closely, we are given several. Number them in your Bible. First, we are assured that since Jesus has risen from the dead, those who trusted have died in Him will also rise (vs 14-15). That is, people who have trusted Christ before death will be raised again when Christ returns at the rapture. Second, we learn the sequence of the events (vs 16-17). Christ will come down from heaven with a shout and with a trumpet call of God. Then, those who were saved before they died will rise from their graves. Those who are alive on earth at this time will meet them and together go up to meet the Lord in the air. Third, we learn that after the second coming we will never again be separated from Christ (vs17). Fourth, we learn that the dates and times of His coming are not known by any man. And lastly, we learn that, since we do not know when the rapture will take place, we need to be ready for it to come at any time. Are you? If Jesus comes today, will you be ready to meet Him? Would the people you influence be ready? What would it take to be able to answer yes?

1 THESS 5:11

Therefore encourage one another and build one another up, just as you are doing.

SAY WHAT?
Observation: What do I see?

SO WHAT?
Interpretation: What does it mean?

NOW WHAT?
Application: How does it apply to me?

THEN WHAT?
Implementation: What do I do?

The book of Proverbs was designed to help us in "attaining wisdom and discipline; in understanding words of insight; in acquiring a disciplined and prudent life, doing what is right and just and fair; in giving prudence to the simple, knowledge and discretion to the young." As you read through this chapter, write down the verses that are most significant to you in your present circumstances.

VERSE | WHAT TRUTH IT COMMUNICATES | HOW IT IMPACTS MY LIFE

ALWAYS IN ALL?

Of all the final instructions in today's reading, which one affects you the most? Which one is the most difficult for you to obey? How about being joyful ALWAYS and giving thanks in ALL circumstances? Paul gave the Thessalonians (and us) a command that is extremely difficult to obey. It would have been easier had he used the words, "most of the time." One of the most common reasons for not obeying this command is that we do not often see our circumstances the way God sees them. We often forget that God is in control and He has an important purpose for our circumstances. He may be preparing us for something in our future. He may be giving us an opportunity to grow in an area of blindness. He may be providing us an opportunity to demonstrate to a lost world the difference He has made in our lives. When we rejoice and are joyful, we show that we believe what God has said and He will keep His Word. Are you facing a difficult circumstance that is robbing you of joy? What circumstances do you find yourself facing that make it hard to give thanks? What might God be trying to accomplish in your life through them?

1 THESS 5:18

...give thanks in all circumstances; for this is the will of God in Christ Jesus for you.

SAY WHAT?

Is there a situation you're facing that is robbing you of joy and thanksgiving?

SO WHAT?

List a few reasons for which you can give thanks.

NOW WHAT?

What can be done to help you follow God's expectations in this area?

THEN WHAT?

In light of this passage, what personal commitment can you make?

REASON FOR PRAISE

SAY WHAT?
What part of your life demonstrates that your faith is growing?

SO WHAT?
What qualities demonstrate that your love for others is growing?

NOW WHAT?
What shows that you persevere in faith in persecution and trials?

THEN WHAT?
In light of this passage, what personal commitment can you make?

If your friends were to talk about your life, what would they say? Would hearing what they say encourage or discourage you? Could your parents or friends say what Paul said about the Thessalonians in this first chapter? Paul first mentioned that he had noticed that their faith was growing more and more. Is your faith stronger today than it was at the beginning of this school year? Paul could see that their love for each other was also growing. Can you point to signs during this past year that show your love for others has also grown? Finally, Paul said that they were demonstrating perseverance and faith in the midst of persecution and trials. They hung in there and did not give up even when the going got tough. As you look back over the year so far, do you think this could be said about you? Have you demonstrated perseverance and faith in the midst of persecution and trials? As you look back over this year, can you see that your faith and your love for others is the same as it was when the year started? In what ways do you see it growing? Are you strong enough to persevere in hard times? What would it take to improve?

2 THESS 1:4

Therefore we ourselves boast about you in the churches of God for your steadfastness and faith in all your persecutions and in the afflictions that you are enduring.

SECOND CHANCE?

If you heard the gospel,rejected it, and therefore missed the rapture, is it possible to be saved during the Tribulation? Today's reading gives us helpful information to answer this frequently asked question. First,Paul tells us that the Holy Spirit will be taken away during the Tribulation. His influence and ability to hold back sin will no longer be a part of this world (vs7). Second, we learn that,during the Tribulation, Satan will perform counterfeit miracles,signs and wonders in an effort to deceive vulnerable people (vs9). These efforts will cause people to believe that he,not Jesus Christ,is the Messiah. Third, we learn that God allows a powerful delusion to deceive people so that they believe the lie. Whatever Satan will tell them about the events going on at this time they will believe. God will allow people who have rejected Christ to believe the lie of Satan. They will be condemned and will not become believers. This passage would seem to say that those who have rejected Christ before the rapture, will not accept Him during the Tribulation. To reject Christ is a very serious decision. One can't assume he will have an opportunity later.

2 THESS 2:11

Therefore God sends them a strong delusion, so that they may believe what is false,

SAY WHAT?
Observation: What do I see?

SO WHAT?
Interpretation: What does it mean?

NOW WHAT?
Application: How does it apply to me?

THEN WHAT?
Implementation: What do I do?

MILITARYDEVOTIONAL.COM
🐦 @MILITARYDEVOS

SAY WHAT?
Observation: What do I see?

SO WHAT?
Interpretation: What does it mean?

NOW WHAT?
Application: How does it apply to me?

THEN WHAT?
Implementation: What do I do?

Why could Paul speak so strongly about idleness in today's reading? One reason he was able to speak against idleness so strongly was because he wasn't an idle man. What does the word idle mean in this passage? How are we to respond to idle people? The word translated here is a military term which means "out of rank." It is a Christian who is acting "out of rank." In the context of this passage Paul was writing of the specific behavior of not working for a living. It refers to being lazy or unwilling to work. No one could ever say that about Paul. He knew that as a believer he should be the hardest of workers. He knew that being lazy and unwilling to work hard indicated a serious spiritual problem. We often see people today who are unwilling to work hard for anything. They can be lazy and seem to work harder getting out of work than they would by just getting the job done. Idleness characterizes every area PT and money to job proficiency and church attendance. God expects Christian teens to be hard workers. To be idle is to sin against God. How do you measure up to God's standard? Make an honest evaluation.

★★★★

2 THESS 3:6
Now we command you, brothers in the name of our Lord Jesus Christ that you keep away from any brother who is walking in idleness and not in accord with the tradition that you received from us.

KEY TO LOVE

Where does a heart of love come from? If you want to have a heart of love, what should you do? You could turn to today's reading and find out. This passage gives us a way to examine ourselves and determine if our love is what it ought to be. Mark these qualities in your Bible. In verse five, Paul says that love comes from having a pure heart, a good conscience and a sincere faith. First, a pure heart is one that is without sin and is wholly devoted to Christ. Is your heart pure? If you have sin in your life, or if other things are more important than God, we can't love as we should. Second, Paul's says that love comes from a good conscience. It is a conscience that does not bother you because of a relationship that is not right or sin that has not been confessed and forgiven. If your conscience is not good, you can not have love. Third, Paul says that love comes from a sincere faith. It is a faith that has no hypocrisy. If you live a hypocritical life, you can not love. How are you doing in these three areas? You can't have a heart of love without being successful in these areas. Use the questions below to examine your life and determine if you have real love.

SAY WHAT?

Is your heart pure? What changes are necessary for you to have greater love?

SO WHAT?

Is your conscience good? What changes are necessary for you to have greater love?

NOW WHAT?

Is your faith sincere? What changes are necessary for you to have greater love?

THEN WHAT?

In light of this passage, what personal commitment can you make?

★★★★

1 TIM 1:5

The aim of our charge is love that issues from a pure heart and a good conscience and a sincere faith.

MILITARYDEVOTIONAL.COM
🐦 **@MILITARYDEVOS**

STAYING TRUE

SAY WHAT?
Observation: What do I see?

SO WHAT?
Interpretation: What does it mean?

NOW WHAT?
Application: How does it apply to me?

THEN WHAT?
Implementation: What do I do?

Can you and I be guaranteed to fulfill the purpose God has for our lives? Is there a way to know for sure that we will not ruin our lives or fail to accomplish what God has for us? The answer is yes according to today's reading. In verse eighteen, Paul gave Timothy two instructions that would enable him to fulfill God's purpose for his life. First, Timothy had to hold on to faith. That is, he needed to remain loyal and committed to the revealed truth of God found in the Scriptures. Unlike those who had fallen away, Timothy was instructed to remain devoted to the Scriptures. He had to study the Scriptures, guard them, defend them and know them well. Second, if Timothy was going to stay the course, he had to hold on to a good conscience. That was only possible if he lived a pure life. If he allowed sin to enter his heart, he would fall away and fail to fulfill God's call on his life. Though it is by no means easy, staying true in our walks with God is simple. We too must stay true to the Scriptures. We must know them, obey them and share them. We must maintain a good conscience. We can not tolerate any sin in our lives. Are you committed to these?

★★★★

1 TIM 1:18
This charge I entrust to you, Timothy, my child, in accordance with the prophecies previously made about you, that by them you may wage the good warfare,

The book of Proverbs was designed to help us in "attaining wisdom and discipline; in understanding words of insight; in acquiring a disciplined and prudent life, doing what is right and just and fair; in giving prudence to the simple, knowledge and discretion to the young." As you read through this chapter, write down the verses that are most significant to you in your present circumstances.

VERSE | WHAT TRUTH IT COMMUNICATES | HOW IT IMPACTS MY LIFE

SAY WHAT?
Observation: What do I see?

SO WHAT?
Interpretation: What does it mean?

NOW WHAT?
Application: How does it apply to me?

THEN WHAT?
Implementation: What do I do?

How often do you pray for the unsaved? How often does your church pray for specific unsaved people? When we understand this chapter, we will understand the expectations for our prayer lives, individually and corporately. In today's reading Paul makes it clear that we as Christians, ought to make prayer for the unsaved a very high priority. Paul used the words first of all in verse one to indicate this. He gave several reasons in this section to pray for the unsaved. First praying for the unsaved is the right thing to do. Second, God desires for all to come to the knowledge of the truth and be saved. Third, we should pray for the unsaved because it is consistent with what God has called us to do. The reason we are still here on the earth is to be able to reach the world with the message of Christ. There is only one way to receive salvation and it is our responsibility to share this message. It is clear from this passage that we, as individuals and as specific groups of believers, ought to be praying for specific unsaved people. If you are not praying like this now, why not begin today? Ask God to give you a burden for the lost and a desire to share.

★★★★

1 TIM 2:1
First of all, then, I urge that supplications, prayers, intercessions, and thanksgivings be made for all people,

QUALIFICATIONS OF A PASTOR

What do we learn about pastors in today's reading? There is much beyond the specific list of qualifications. First, we learn that it is a very important calling. It is not something to be entered into lightly. Second, we learn that it is a limited calling. Becoming a pastor is not for everyone. It is limited in that it is not for women or for all men. Only a select few are qualified. Third, we learn it is a compelling calling. It is a calling that comes from God and results in an inner passion of the one called. Fourth, it is a responsible calling. It comes with great responsibility and a very high standard. Fifth, it is an honorable calling. It is the highest office to which one can be called and most important work one could do. Finally, it is a demanding calling. It takes a lot of effort and some simple, hard work. It is not something you can do halfheartedly. It is no wonder Paul lists the character qualities required for a man called to be a pastor. The position of a pastor is to be taken very seriously. The pastorate is not for everyone. It is for those whom God has chosen. Could you be one of those God is calling into vocational ministry as a pastor? Is God calling you to be a Chaplain? How will you know? Talk to your chaplain today. ★★★★★

1 TIM 3:2

Therefore an overseer must be above reproach, the husband of one wife, sober-minded, self-controlled, respectable, hospitable, able to teach...

SAY WHAT?
Observation: What do I see?

SO WHAT?
Interpretation: What does it mean?

NOW WHAT?
Application: How does it apply to me?

THEN WHAT?
Implementation: What do I do?

MILITARYDEVOTIONAL.COM
🐦 @MILITARYDEVOS

NEGLECTING SPIRITUAL GIFTS

SAY WHAT?
What spiritual gifts do you think God has given to you?

SO WHAT?
In what ways do people say you influence their lives?

NOW WHAT?
How can you make sure you do not neglect your spiritual gift(s)?

THEN WHAT?
In light of this passage, what personal commitment can you make?

How could someone neglect his spiritual gift? What would one have to do in order for this to be true of him? It must have been an important issue because Paul included this admonition in his charge to Timothy in this chapter. Timothy was told many things that are obviously important. But why did Paul mention neglecting his gift? Paul knew that even someone like Timothy could fall into the trap of neglecting the gifts God had given. How? He could neglect them by not using them. He could try to do things in his human strength. He could even overlook his gifts by being distracted into doing something other than what God wanted. Timothy could neglect them by falling into sin, and not be able to use them as God had intended. He could neglect his gift by desiring a different kind of gift. He could neglect his gift by determining to use it to minister in his own way, not the way God had intended. Neglecting his gifts would hinder or even cause the failure of his ministry. Could you be neglecting the gifts God has given to you in any of these ways? Do you even know what they are? How are you using them? Is it the way God intends for you to use them?

★★★★

1 TIM 4:10
For to this end we toil and strive, because we have our hope set on the living God, who is the Savior of all people, especially of those who believe.

CARING FOR FAMILY

As your parents get older, whose responsibility will it be to care for them? The answer is found in today's reading, and it might surprise you. Paul, in today's reading, gives Timothy some very clear instruction regarding specific groups of people. He explains to Timothy that he, as a pastor, is to instruct family members to take care of their mother if she becomes widowed. Her children and grandchildren have the responsibility to care for their mother/grandmother if she has lost her husband. The reason for this responsibility is found in verse four. It is a way of repaying her for the care she gave to her children while they were growing up. Paul makes it clear that when we leave home we do not leave the responsibilities for our parents behind. As our parents grow older, it becomes our responsibility to care for them as it was theirs to care for us when we were unable to care for ourselves. To neglect this responsibility is to disobey God's clearly stated command. As you grow older, do not forget God's expectations when the time comes to care for your parents. Acknowledge the sacrifices they made and the times they were inconvenienced for you while under their care.

1 TIM 5:8

But if anyone does not provide for his relatives, and especially for members of his household, he has denied the faith and is worse than an unbeliever.

SAY WHAT?

Observation: What do I see?

SO WHAT?

Interpretation: What does it mean?

NOW WHAT?

Application: How does it apply to me?

THEN WHAT?

Implementation: What do I do?

MILITARYDEVOTIONAL.COM
@MILITARYDEVOS

SAY WHAT?
Observation: What do I see?

SO WHAT?
Interpretation: What does it mean?

NOW WHAT?
Application: How does it apply to me?

THEN WHAT?
Implementation: What do I do?

How do you respond to those in authority over you? What if that person is harsh or cruel? What if he makes a decision which is unfair? What if he is a Christian? Paul tells us how we ought to answer those questions at the end of this passage. He instructed Timothy to teach his flock that they should treat their masters as people who are worthy of full respect. The reason? - So that God's name and the message of the gospel would not be slandered. Those watching their lives would notice the difference and would form opinions about Christ based on believer's actions. He also explained that those who have fellow believers as masters are not to treat them with less respect. It appeared that the Ephesians felt that if their masters were believers, they did not have to give them the same respect as they would if they were unbelievers. Paul corrected that thinking here. He wanted the believing masters to be treated better than unsaved masters. How do you respond to those who have authority over you who are saved? Does your behavior and testimony encourage them, or do you take advantage of them because they are saved? Look at your life and evaluate it.

★★★★

1 TIM 6:2
Those who have believing masters must not be disrespectful on the ground that they are brothers; rather they must serve all the better...

DANGER OF WEALTH

What is the most important priority in your life? If you could be anything, what would you choose to be? Would you chose to be wealthy and famous, or humble and godly? While most of us might say we would choose to be godly, the reality is that godliness is not the priority of most believers' lives. In this passage, Paul gave Timothy contrasting characteristics between those who choose the making of money a priority and those who choose godliness as their priority. Those who pursue money may acquire it, but they will also be filled with grief. They will find themselves in ruin and destruction (9-10). They may be very successful, but it will be success in that which does not matter. Those who pursue godliness will find righteousness, contentment, love, faith, endurance, and gentleness. They may not appear to be successful in the world's eyes, but they are in the things that really matter. What are you pursuing? What is your goal in life? Is your goal to be successful in what really matters or what doesn't (money)? We know by examining which fruits listed today are a part of your life. What does God's Word say are your priorities?

★★★★

1 TIM 6:10

For the love of money is a root of all kinds of evils. It is through this craving that some have wandered away from the faith and pierced themselves with many pangs.

SAY WHAT?

What is your goal in life? How does it demonstrate itself?

SO WHAT?

How can you tell if materialism is part of your goal?

NOW WHAT?

How can you keep yourself from pursuing what does not matter?

THEN WHAT?

In light of this passage, what personal commitment can you make?

MILITARYDEVOTIONAL.COM
@MILITARYDEVOS

The book of Proverbs was designed to help us in "attaining wisdom and discipline; in understanding words of insight; in acquiring a disciplined and prudent life, doing what is right and just and fair; in giving prudence to the simple, knowledge and discretion to the young." As you read through this chapter, write down the verses that are most significant to you in your present circumstances.

VERSE | WHAT TRUTH IT COMMUNICATES | HOW IT IMPACTS MY LIFE

BRINGING JOY

In what way does your life affect others? When a person remembers you or thinks of you,what comes to their mind? It surely must have encouraged Timothy's heart to know that he had positively influenced the life of the Apostle Paul. When Paul wrote this letter to Timothy,his life was difficult, and he already had endured much. He was in chains for his faith and according to verse 15, had seen everyone desert him. He must have been extremely discouraged at times. I am sure that some of the people who had deserted Paul were people in whom he had invested much time. Their rejection must have broken his heart. Timothy was different. Whenever Paul stopped to think of Timothy,he was filled with joy because of Timothy's faith. In the midst of great discouragement, Timothy brought Paul joy. Is your life such that those who think about you are filled with joy because of your walk with God? Or do you bring them sorrow and cause for concern due to the choices you are making? We need to strive to live the kind of life that encourages those who are close to us and love us. What traits in your life bring joy to those who love you? What traits do not? What needs to change?

★★★★

2 TIM 1:6-7

For this reason I remind you to fan into flame the gift of God, which is in you through the laying on of my hands, for God gave us a spirit not of fear but of power and love and self-control.

SAY WHAT?

List the people who have contributed to your life.

SO WHAT?

In what ways does your life encourage or discourage them?

NOW WHAT?

What can you do to continue to encourage them?

THEN WHAT?

What personal commitment can you make in light of this passage?

MILITARYDEVOTIONAL.COM
@MILITARYDEVOS

CIVILIAN PURSUITS

SAY WHAT?

What kind of "civilian pursuits" do you struggle with?

SO WHAT?

Why is it difficult to not become entangled in them?

NOW WHAT?

What steps can you take to avoid apathy in spiritual warfare?

THEN WHAT?

In light of this passage,what personal commitment can you make?

What was Paul intending to communicate by writing that soldiers do not get involved in civilian pursuits? The answer will help us stay the course and prevent us from becoming sidetracked in the ministry God has given us. The first notable phrase in this section is found in verse four, "no soldier." The implication is that we are serving as soldiers and not home on leave, resting. Paul wants us to remember that we are in battle and we can't take time off. In light of that,we must not get caught up in "civilian pursuits." We are at war and we can't be preoccupied by something else. We are serving as soldiers. We can't strive for good marks in order to pursue a career which may blind us to the ministry opportunities God gives to us. We are at war,and we must make sure that we do not get involved in things that divert our time, energy, and money from our tasks as soldiers. We must be able to give full attention to our service to God. What "civilian" things have you gotten caught up with? How can you become a good soldier again? Remember, we are at war with a fierce enemy! Do not allow yourself to become distracted.

2 TIM 2:4

No soldier gets entangled in civilian pursuits, since his aim is to please the one who enlisted him.

CHARACTERISTICS OF A WORKER

What two things did Paul want to be said of Timothy as a worker? Circle them in your Bible. How can we be sure these two things will be said of us? The first characteristic Paul wanted Timothy to be known for was a worker who did not need to be ashamed. Paul wanted Timothy to live a pure life so that he could hold his head high wherever he went. In order for Timothy to not be ashamed, he would need to make purity a priority. Are you a worker who is not ashamed? Is your life so clean that you are not ashamed in any place or with anyone? The second characteristic Paul wanted Timothy to be known for was as a worker who correctly handled the Word of truth. In order for this to be true, he had to read the Word, study it to discover what it is teaching, and memorize it to be able to use it at any time. Knowing God's Word has to be his priority. Are you a worker who can correctly handle the Word of truth? Do you spend time learning how to use God's Word? In order for you to be known for these characteristics, what changes do you have to make? Are these a priority in your life, or are you satisfied with the way things are?

SAY WHAT?
Observation: What do I see?

SO WHAT?
Interpretation: What does it mean?

NOW WHAT?
Application: How does it apply to me?

THEN WHAT?
Implementation: What do I do?

2 TIM 2:15

Do your best to present yourself to God as one approved, a worker who has no need to be ashamed, rightly handling the word of truth.

MILITARYDEVOTIONAL.COM
🐦 @MILITARYDEVOS

SAY WHAT?

What kind of persecution could one face if he were living a godly life?

SO WHAT?

Why do you think those who want to live godly lives face persecution?

NOW WHAT?

What needs to change in your life for you to become more godly?

THEN WHAT?

In light of this passage, what personal commitment can you make?

So often when we read our Bibles, we read over phrases that are packed with great meaning and contain important truth. We can miss the significance of those small phrases. Today, there is a small phrase tucked in the midst of this chapter which could change the way you view the Christian life. Did you notice it? Go back and read verse twelve again. Paul wanted Timothy to understand that he had been asked to endure suffering because of his faith. Paul reminded Timothy of the kinds of persecution he had experienced by the hands of the world. God's deliverance of Paul was to be an encouragement to Timothy to faithfully continue his ministry. Right in the middle of his charge he said, "everyone who wants to live a godly life... will be persecuted." This means that we too will suffer. Be prepared for it. It is a natural part of walking with God. It also means that, if we aren't facing persecution, we may not be living the life God wants us to live. How about you? Do you want to live a godly life even if it means you will face persecution from the world? Although it will come, God will always rescue us. What does your level of persecution reveal?

★★★★

2 TIM 3:12

Indeed, all who desire to live a godly life in Christ Jesus will be persecuted,

A SECOND CHANCE

Is it hard for you to forgive the mistakes of other people? Do you hold grudges towards people who have hurt you? If you answer yes to either of those questions, you will find encouragement from today's reading. To fully understand this, we must take time to review. In the book of Acts, Paul and Barnabas had taken with them on their missionary journey, a young man named Mark (Acts 12:25). During the trip,Mark became discouraged and left the group to return home. A few years later,Paul and Barnabas were about to embark on another journey. Barnabas wanted to take Mark,but Paul refused. He felt that since Mark had previously failed,they shouldn't give him a second chance. So, Paul took Silas, and Barnabas left with Mark (Acts 15:36-41). We don't hear any more about it until Paul's final comments in today's reading. In verse eleven, Paul asked Timothy to bring Mark because he had been helpful to Paul in ministry. Over time,Paul had forgiven him and once again valued his service. He didn't hold a grudge or stubbornly refuse to give him another chance. Do you need to forgive and restore the way Paul did?

2 TIM 4:11

Luke alone is with me. Get Mark and bring him with you, for he is very useful to me for ministry.

SAY WHAT?
Observation: What do I see?

SO WHAT?
Interpretation: What does it mean?

NOW WHAT?
Application: How does it apply to me?

THEN WHAT?
Implementation: What do I do?

WHY QUALIFICATIONS?

SAY WHAT?
Observation: What do I see?

SO WHAT?
Interpretation: What does it mean?

NOW WHAT?
Application: How does it apply to me?

THEN WHAT?
Implementation: What do I do?

In today's reading, Paul gave Titus a list of requirements for anyone who is being considered for the position of a pastor. Why are these requirements important? According to this passage, there are three reasons for this standard. The first reason Paul lists is found in verse seven. These men have been entrusted with God's work. What a pastor does is different than any other job a man can have. They are giving God's Word to people. They are responsible to study it, teach it, use it to correct and rebuke, and they have to be credible. Second, we are told in verse nine that these standards are important because they enable him to encourage others with the truth and refute those who are teaching or living in error. If his life is not what it ought to be, he loses his ability to do this. Third, these standards are vital because there are many rebellious people who teach error and are ruining households. A pastor must be the kind of man who can protect his people from the evil intent of these kinds of men. The job of a pastor demands a standard that is higher than any standard of any other job one might have. Could God be calling you to such a position?

★★★★

TITUS 1:7
For an overseer, as God's steward, must be above reproach. He must not be arrogant or quick-tempered or a drunkard or violent or greedy for gain,

The book of Proverbs was designed to help us in "attaining wisdom and discipline; in understanding words of insight; in acquiring a disciplined and prudent life, doing what is right and just and fair; in giving prudence to the simple, knowledge and discretion to the young." As you read through this chapter, write down the verses that are most significant to you in your present circumstances.

VERSE | WHAT TRUTH IT COMMUNICATES | HOW IT IMPACTS MY LIFE

SAY WHAT?

How is your spiritual condition impacting evangelism in your life?

SO WHAT?

What needs to change so you will be more effective in evangelism?

NOW WHAT?

What can you do to see your life help others come to know Christ?

THEN WHAT?

In light of this passage, what personal commitment can you make?

If you want to reach those around you for Christ, how would you do it? What strategy would be best to see them trust Christ as their Savior? The most effective evangelism strategy is found in today's reading, and it has been working for over 2,000 years. Did you notice it? Paul told Titus that the most effective way to influence the lost is to have the saved growing and walking with God. If you examine each of the "so thats" in today's reading, you see that at the heart of Paul's instruction is evangelism. Paul wanted Titus to teach women the right things so that their lives would not malign the Word of God. Paul wanted Titus to teach young men the right things so that those who opposed them would have nothing to say. Slaves are given instructions on how to live so that their lives would make the teachings about Christ attractive. You see, effective evangelism begins with godly people. If you have a youth group in which kids are walking wholeheartedly with God, then you have a youth group that can be effective in evangelism. Is your church ready to reach out with the message of Christ?

★★★★

TITUS 2:10

...not pilfering, but showing all good faith, so that in everything they may adorn the doctrine of God our Savior.

GOOD REMINDERS

We find in this chapter a wonderful description of salvation. You need to be familiar with this section so that when you have an opportunity to share your faith, you can use it. Or you might need a simple reminder today of what Jesus Christ has done in your life. Paul, in verse three, describes what we were like before we trusted Christ. It is not very flattering, is it? In verses four through six, he reminds Titus how we have been saved. Our salvation is the work of God in our lives and not something we can do for ourselves. This happened so that we might have the hope of eternal life. And what should our response be to all of this? - To devote ourselves to doing what is good (vs8). Titus needed to stress these truths to people so that they would not forget what had happened to them. When you stop to think of what Christ has done for you, how can you do anything but devote yourself to doing what is good? Reread this section and ask yourself what good you are doing in response to what God has done for you and what affect is your life having on the unsaved people you know. To understand the immensity of these truths will change your life and your view of the unsaved souls in your world. ★★★★

TITUS 3:8

...so that those who have believed in God may be careful to devote themselves to good works. These things are excellent and profitable for people.

SAY WHAT?
Observation: What do I see?

SO WHAT?
Interpretation: What does it mean?

NOW WHAT?
Application: How does it apply to me?

THEN WHAT?
Implementation: What do I do?

MILITARYDEVOTIONAL.COM
@MILITARYDEVOS

WHAT WE OUGHT TO DO

SAY WHAT?
Observation: What do I see?

SO WHAT?
Interpretation: What does it mean?

NOW WHAT?
Application: How does it apply to me?

THEN WHAT?
Implementation: What do I do?

Philemon is an excellent book on the issue of forgiveness. Paul gave us so much in this short book that will help us learn to forgive others. One of the areas he covers is our responsibility in forgiveness. First, we must be receptive (10-14). We must be willing to open ourselves up to the one who has offended us. If God has done a work in his heart and he seeks forgiveness, we must be open to it. Second, we must be willing to restore him (15-16). If he is truly repentant, we must be willing to not just forgive him, but bring him back to effective ministry and relationship with us. Third, we must be willing to see that restitution takes place. It may involve being willing to cancel a debt or allow the offender to work off what he owes. We must be willing to allow the wrong to be made right. All of these steps were part of our salvation the moment we trusted Christ. God was open to and desired our restoration to Him. He allowed us to become His children. He sent Jesus to this earth to pay the price for the debt we owed so that we could have all He offered. Are you willing to do the same? This book makes it clear that we need to show the same forgiveness that God showed us.

★★★★

PHILEMON 1:8

Accordingly, though I am bold enough in Christ to command you to do what is required,

The book of Proverbs was designed to help us in "attaining wisdom and discipline; in understanding words of insight; in acquiring a disciplined and prudent life, doing what is right and just and fair; in giving prudence to the simple, knowledge and discretion to the young." As you read through this chapter, write down the verses that are most significant to you in your present circumstances.

VERSE | WHAT TRUTH IT COMMUNICATES | HOW IT IMPACTS MY LIFE

"One of the most effective tools for changing lives I have ever seen... the perfect environment for God to work resulting in permanent life change."

WILDERNESS INSTITUTE FOR LEADERSHIP DEVELOPMENT

W.I.L.D.

SIMPLYPILGRIM.COM

» MILITARYDEVOTIONAL.COM

 @MILITARYDEVOS

 FACEBOOK.COM/MILITARYDEVOS

MILITARY
OTD

AUGUST
★★★★

MONTHLY
PRAYER SHEET

I NEED TO REACH OUT TO...	HOW I WILL DO IT...	HOW IT WENT...

OTHER REQUEST	HOW ANSWERED	DATE

★ MONTHLY
★ MISSION SHEET ★

≫≫ Share your personal commitments with those who will help keep you accountable to them.

≫ NAME: ....

This sheet is designed to help you make personal commitments each month that will help you grow in your walk with God. Fill it out by determining:

★ What will push you.
★ What you think you can achieve.

≫ PERSONAL DEVOTIONS:
I will commit to read the OnTrack Bible passage and devotional thought .... day(s) each week this month.

≫ CHURCH/CHAPEL ATTENDANCE:
I will attend Church/Chapel .... time(s) this month.
I will attend .... time(s) this month.

≫ SCRIPTURE MEMORY:
I will memorize .... key verse(s) from the daily OnTrack Devotions this month.

≫ OUTREACH:
I will share Christ with .... person/people this month.
I will serve my local church/chapel this month by ....
....
....

≫ OTHER ACTIVITIES:
List any other opportunities such as events, prayer group, etc..., you will participate in this month. ....
....
....
....
....
....

Determine to begin today a journey that will last a lifetime,and will change your life forever.

PURPOSE FOR TRIALS

Why do trials come into the life of a believer? At times it almost seems as if the closer we move toward God, the more difficult the circumstances become in our lives. In today's reading, Peter reveals one purpose God has for allowing trials to come into our lives. We should be encouraged and rejoice at the trials we face. In verse seven, we learn that sometimes trials come so that we can see that our faith is genuine. Trials help us know for certain that we are saved and give us greater confidence that we have a relationship with God. It takes our faith from theory to reality. It makes our faith something alive in us that affects the way we live. And what happens when our faith becomes real? According to verse seven, it results in praise and honor when Jesus Christ is revealed. God uses trials to show us the reality of our faith. Is your faith real to you? Do you know for certain that you are on your way to heaven? It may be that the trials you are facing have been placed there by God to give you the opportunity to make your faith real. Trials are the means to a deeper, more personal relationship with Christ. Do you view trials this way?

★★★★

1 PETER 1:7

...so that the tested genuineness of your faith—more precious than gold that perishes though it is tested by fire—may be found to result in praise and glory and honor at the revelation of Jesus Christ.

SAY WHAT?

What trials are you facing right now?

SO WHAT?

How can you use today's verses to help you face those trials and gain more authenticity in your walk with God?

NOW WHAT?

How can you use this passage to help someone you know who is going through trials?

THEN WHAT?

In light of this passage, what personal commtiment can you make?

MILITARYDEVOTIONAL.COM
@MILITARYDEVOS

EMPTY WAY OF LIFE

SAY WHAT?
Observation: What do I see?

SO WHAT?
Interpretation: What does it mean?

NOW WHAT?
Application: How does it apply to me?

THEN WHAT?
Implementation: What do I do?

Have you ever read a passage of Scripture in which the Holy Spirit showed you something that stuck with you for a while? We find one of those phrases in today's reading. Did you notice it in verse 18? Peter described life before trusting Christ as being empty. How true that is! Life without Jesus Christ is empty, even though it may be filled with lots of people and tons of activities. We may achieve fame; we may gain wealth, but it will all be empty. We may even gain power and freedom, but it will still be empty. Life with Christ however, is fulfilling even though we may not have much of what the world deems valuable. We may not have material wealth and may not be well known, but we will still have a very full life. We may not have power, but we are content. When we trust Christ and He becomes real to us, our lives are full and exciting. With a lack of real commitment to Christ, any life we choose will be empty. Christ came to give us life and give it to the full. If you know Christ as your personal Savior and He is real to you, you know what Peter meant. If your life is empty, something is wrong! Take a hard look at your life.

★★★★

1 PETER 1:18
...knowing that you were ransomed from the futile ways inherited from your forefathers, not with perishable things such as silver or gold,

BUT NOW...

Did anything you read today in this passage make you think of yesterday's reading? Look at the words,"but now." In today's reading, Peter talks more about our lives before we came to faith in Christ. Whom does he say we were before we trusted Christ? We were insignificant. We had nothing and were nothing. But now,we are the people of God. We have gone from being insignificant to being children of the King. He also tells us that before Christ we were objects of God's wrath. We were sinners in need of forgiveness. But now, we have received mercy and our sins have been forgiven since we, by faith, trusted Christ. Therefore,according to verse eleven,we should live as aliens in this world. In light of what God has done, we need to abstain from sinful desires. We should live such good lives that, even though the world accuses us of wrong doing, they still see our good deeds and glorify God. Our lives were empty because we were not the people of God and had not received mercy. But now our lives are full because we are the people of God and have found mercy through Jesus Christ. Circle the words "but now" in these verses.

1 PETER 2:10

Once you were not a people, but now you are God's people; once you had not received mercy, but now you have received mercy.

SAY WHAT?

Observation: What do I see?

SO WHAT?

Interpretation: What does it mean?

NOW WHAT?

Application: How does it apply to me?

THEN WHAT?

Implementation: What do I do?

SAY WHAT?

Write out the proverb that was most meaningful to you.

SO WHAT?

Why is this proverb so meaningful to you?

NOW WHAT?

How can you apply it this week?

THEN WHAT?

What personal commitment will you make?

The book of Proverbs was designed to help us in "attaining wisdom and discipline; in understanding words of insight; in acquiring a disciplined and prudent life, doing what is right and just and fair; in giving prudence to the simple, knowledge and discretion to the young." As you read through this chapter, write down the verses that are most significant to you in your present circumstances.

★★★★

PROV 26:1-2

Like snow in summer or rain in harvest, so honor is not fitting for a fool. Like a sparrow in its flitting, like a swallow in its flying, a curse that is causeless does not alight.

CHRIST'S EXAMPLE

How do you feel when you suffer for having done the right thing? You not only did nothing wrong,you actually did the right thing,but got punished anyway. Today's reading gives us some practical principles regarding this kind of situation as it comes into our lives. First of all,Peter explains that it really is no big deal for someone to endure punishment or suffering for doing something that is wrong. But, it is commendable to be someone who suffers for doing good. It should sober us to know that we should expect to suffer for doing good. It is something that we are called to do. Jesus Himself went through the same thing. He did so because He wanted to give us an example to follow. How close are you to that example? There was no deceit found in His mouth when he suffered. Is there any in yours? He hurled no insults to those who were mistreating Him. Do you? He did not retaliate when he was abused, but instead entrusted Himself to God the Father. What a powerful testimony this kind of life would be in our world today. What have you encountered that demands you follow the example of Christ?

SAY WHAT?

In what situations are you finding it difficult to respond as Christ did?

SO WHAT?

In what ways have you responded in an ungodly manner?

NOW WHAT?

How can you use today's reading to help you respond like Christ when faced with unjust opposition?

THEN WHAT?

In light of this passage,what personal commitment can you make?

1 PETER 2:21

For to this you have been called, because Christ also suffered for you, leaving you an example, so that you might follow in his steps.

SAY WHAT?
Observation: What do I see?

SO WHAT?
Interpretation: What does it mean?

NOW WHAT?
Application: How does it apply to me?

THEN WHAT?
Implementation: What do I do?

What is Peter referring to in his admonition to wives and husbands when he says, "in the same way?" When we stop to think about it, we realize that this passage teaches that husbands and wives are to respond to their spouses in the same way that Christ responded in yesterday's reading. When circumstances are difficult and unfair in marriage, husbands and wives are not to react with insults, deception or retaliation. When one spouse is not being godly, the other party should not make any threats. Instead, he is to entrust himself to God. He alone is in control, and He alone has the solution. God tells us that He judges justly, and He will respond. There is not a need to threaten, insult, or to retaliate EVER! Jesus Christ is the example, and we are to respond, "in the same way" in our marriages. When and if God allows you to enter into a marriage relationship, you must be prepared to respond as Christ did, no matter what. His example does not allow us the option of acting on our feelings. One way to prepare yourself, is to act "in the same way" in relationships now. How are you doing in this area?

1 PETER 3:4
...but let your adorning be the hidden person of the heart with the imperishable beauty of a gentle and quiet spirit, which in God's sight is very precious.

BLESSED BY SUFFERING

Today, Peter continues the topic of how to respond to suffering which is undeserved. That is, being punished for something we did not do. In this passage, we are challenged in our responses to those who are evil toward us or insult us. Peter instructs us to continue to respond with kindness and goodness toward those who are in opposition to us. We must understand that we have been called to face this kind of suffering. In fact, in verse fourteen, Peter tells us that if we face this kind of opposition, we are blessed. It is helpful to realize that our godly responses to this kind of suffering will often result in opportunities to share Christ with those who observe us. Peter tells us that we need to be prepared to share with people the reason we can respond with kindness. He tells us to not only be ready with the right message, but also be ready with the right attitude, with gentleness and respect. We need to be able to respond to unjust suffering in the way Peter has described. And then, we should be able to provide an answer for our hope. Finally, we must be prepared to share the message with the right attitude. Do you know what to say?

★★★★

1 PETER 3:14

But even if you should suffer for righteousness' sake, you will be blessed. Have no fear of them, nor be troubled,

SAY WHAT?
What can you do to prepare yourself for unjust suffering?

SO WHAT?
What can you do to prepare yourself to give an answer?

NOW WHAT?
What can you do to prepare yourself to respond with the right attitude?

THEN WHAT?
In light of this passage, what personal commitment can you make?

MILITARYDEVOTIONAL.COM
🐦 @MILITARYDEVOS

SAY WHAT?

Observation: What do I see?

SO WHAT?

Interpretation: What does it mean?

NOW WHAT?

Application: How does it apply to me?

THEN WHAT?

Implementation: What do I do?

In what way has God gifted you to serve and encourage the body of Christ? If you do not know the answer to that question, you can not fulfill what today's passage teaches us. In verse ten, we are told to use whatever gift we have received to serve others. We are to take the gifts God has given to us and use them to encourage and help the body of Christ. We are to allow them to be energized by the Holy Spirit. As Christians, we have already learned that we are called to face all kinds of unjust suffering. While we know our suffering produces positive results in our lives, it is nonetheless difficult. It is important, then, to be a part of the lives of our brothers and sisters by using our gifts to serve and encourage them. Verse ten lets us know it will come in various ways, but it must come from each of us. You can't just sit back and not take your place. God has a purpose for you. What role does God want you to be playing in your church? How can you use your gifts to serve the body of Christ? If you don't know what your gifts are, who can help you discover what they are and how you might serve the body? Your are needed!

1 PETER 4:10

As each has received a gift, use it to serve one another, as good stewards of God's varied grace:

NEVER GIVE IN

Before Peter closes this great book on suffering, he gives us a few final reminders. Did one of them stand out to you? Peter reminds us again that there are positive results from suffering. He reminds us that we are able to participate in what Christ faced and that suffering allows us to bear His Name. Insults, resulting from our witness, demonstrates that God's glory is upon us. We have an opportunity to not only impact this world and grow in our walks with God through suffering, but we also have the opportunity to impact our first meeting with Christ. Suffering allows us to prepare ourselves to be able to have that first meeting with Christ be one of great joy. The bottom line on suffering? It is found in verse 19. Underline it in your Bible. First, we are to commit our lives to Christ and trust Him. Do not fret and worry, but give everything to Him. Second, continue to do good. Don't give in, don't stop doing what is right even in the midst of suffering. Allow God to use it in your life and use it in the lives of those who are watching. Why not take some time today to memorize this verse to help you handle any suffering you experience.

SAY WHAT?

Name one principle on suffering that you will take from reading this book.

SO WHAT?

How can you apply it to your life right now?

NOW WHAT?

How can you better prepare yourself to respond correctly when suffering comes?

THEN WHAT?

In light of this passage, what personal commitment can you make?

★★★★

1 PETER 4:19

Therefore let those who suffer according to God's will entrust their souls to a faithful Creator while doing good.

INSIGNIFICANT & SMALL

SAY WHAT?

How does someone who is humble demonstrate it?

SO WHAT?

In what ways can you become more humble?

NOW WHAT?

How can you "clothe" yourself with humility each day?

THEN WHAT?

In light of this passage, what personal commitment can you make?

What does it mean to be humble? How do we clothe ourselves with it in our relationships with each other? The word translated here humble or humility means lowliness of mind. It literally means the esteeming of ourselves as small. It means seeing ourselves as someone who is small and insignificant. It is the opposite of seeing ourselves as the big shot or the best. Being humble is not bragging or trying to put ourselves forward. The word translated clothe in today's reading means what you might imagine. To cling to something in the same way we put clothes on in the morning. Peter admonishes us in this passage to be a humble people. We must view ourselves as small and not be prideful. We are then to get up each morning and cling to this kind of an attitude throughout the day. We need to consciously remember what Christ has done for us and seek to not exalt ourselves but others. Clothing ourselves with humility means to intentionally think of ourselves as small and not the most important or the best person. Are you living successfully in this area? How can you improve?

★ ★ ★ ★

1 PETER 5:6

Humble yourselves, therefore, under the mighty hand of God so that at the proper time he may exalt you,

The book of Proverbs was designed to help us in "attaining wisdom and discipline; in understanding words of insight; in acquiring a disciplined and prudent life, doing what is right and just and fair; in giving prudence to the simple, knowledge and discretion to the young." As you read through this chapter, write down the verses that are most significant to you in your present circumstances.

VERSE | WHAT TRUTH IT COMMUNICATES | HOW IT IMPACTS MY LIFE

SAY WHAT?
Observation: What do I see?

SO WHAT?
Interpretation: What does it mean?

NOW WHAT?
Application: How does it apply to me?

THEN WHAT?
Implementation: What do I do?

What is the difference between life and godliness in verse three? Why does Peter distinguish between the two? The word translated life in this verse means life in the physical sense. It refers to our conduct or manner of living. It includes everything we do in the course of a regular day. The word for godliness is the spiritual aspect of our life. It is a life that is acceptable to God. It is not inward holiness but the outward manifestation of a walk with God. Peter is saying that we have been given everything we need for the physical areas of life as well as the spiritual areas. When one becomes a Christian, he receives everything he needs to be effective in every area of his life, in both the spiritual and physical aspects. Some might think that the Bible and our walk with God have to do only with spiritual things. That is not true!! In salvation and in God's Word we have been given what we need both in the physical, day to day areas and the spiritual areas of our lives. We possess every thing we need to be a good husband or wife, a good student or employee and a good child and sibling. Are you accessing what you have in those areas?

★★★★

2 PETER 1:3

His divine power has granted to us all things that pertain to life and godliness, through the knowledge of him who called us to his own glory and excellence,

PAY ATTENTION

How reliable is an eyewitness account? While it is most likely reliable, it is not one hundred percent accurate. Why? Because even though we see something clearly, how we evaluate it or describe it can be impacted by many other factors. We may have been tired or upset. We each have our own opinions or biases which impact how we see something or interpret it. Knowing this makes the verses found in today's reading so important. Although Peter was an eyewitness to much of what is in Scripture, as were many of the authors, that is not why we can be sure that our Bibles are accurate. Peter tells us that the reason we can be sure that our Bibles are even more accurate than an eyewitness account is they were not written according to their own interpretation. God wrote the Scriptures, and it is He who makes them accurate. Men recorded what they had witnessed, but what they wrote was not their own opinions or interpretations of the events, but God's. You can have confidence that your Bible can be trusted and what you read is accurate. Therefore, according to verse nineteen, you will do well to pay attention to it. Do you give consideration to what you read?

SAY WHAT?

How might Peter's description of what he saw been impacted by other factors?

SO WHAT?

Why is this truth important to our understanding of Biblical inspiration?

NOW WHAT?

How can you use this to defend your view of Scripture with skeptics?

THEN WHAT?

In light of this passage, what personal commitment can you make?

2 PETER 1:19

And we have something more sure, the prophetic word, to which you will do well to pay attention as to a lamp shining in a dark place, until the day dawns and the morning star rises in your hearts,

GOD WILL DELIVER

SAY WHAT?
Observation: What do I see?

SO WHAT?
Interpretation: What does it mean?

NOW WHAT?
Application: How does it apply to me?

THEN WHAT?
Implementation: What do I do?

Have you ever been in the midst of a trial you thought would never end? Or, have you ever gotten to the point while enduring difficult circumstances that you felt like giving up? Have you ever wondered if God was even aware of the circumstances that were going on in your life? If so, then you will find encouragement in these verses. Peter reminds us that God knows how to rescue godly men from trials. Peter also lists for us a number of examples of how God has responded to sin in the past. He used the example of Lot. He lived in the midst of a horrible circumstance and had felt tormented for years. God delivered him from it. Peter makes the point that God is able to deliver you as well. He stands to defend us against the sin of our world that seeks to inflict trials upon our lives. Even in the midst of incredible sin and hardship, God will deliver the godly while holding the unrighteous accountable. Are there circumstances in your life that require the hope this passage provides to keep you pressing forward? Think of someone who needs this hope. Will you share it with him? Never forget that God knows where you are, and He cares.

2 PETER 2:9
then the Lord knows how to rescue the godly from trials, and to keep the unrighteous under punishment until the day of judgment,

FALSE TEACHERS

What can you learn about false teachers from this passage in 2 Peter? Certainly one thing we can learn is that God has a very grim view of them. Another thing we see in these verses is the list of the characteristics of false teachers. Did you notice them? The first is that they take real Christian fellowship and distort it in order to practice their ungodliness. Opportunities that are meant to be good times of fellowship become times for these false teachers to indulge their flesh. A second characteristic is that they use their positions and abilities to do spiritual work for personal gain. Their true motivation is to make money, not helping people. Although they had, at one time, displayed an appearance of godliness, the pattern of their lives illustrates that their true nature is far from God. We need to be careful in whom we place our trust and whose example we follow. In fact, we need to examine our teachers to make sure they are truly living according to God's standard. It is a blessing to have a teacher who is not like the men in this chapter. If your teacher is a godly man, write and thank him. It will encourage him!

2 PETER 2:22

What the true proverb says has happened to them: "The dog returns to its own vomit, and the sow, after washing herself, returns to wallow in the mire."

SAY WHAT?

Observation: What do I see?

SO WHAT?

Interpretation: What does it mean?

NOW WHAT?

Application: How does it apply to me?

THEN WHAT?

Implementation: What do I do?

MILITARYDEVOTIONAL.COM
@MILITARYDEVOS

SAY WHAT?
How can we be prepared for Christ's return?

SO WHAT?
How can we tell if we really believe He will come back soon?

NOW WHAT?
How are you working to help others be prepared for Christ's return?

THEN WHAT?
In light of this passage, what personal commitment can you make?

Why hasn't Christ returned yet? When will He come again? To some, His delay indicates that He is not coming back at all. Peter closes this book by addressing the scoffers who claim that Christ is not coming back and lets us know why His return has been delayed. He first addresses the scoffers and speaks to some of their points. Some scoffers say that proof that Christ will not return is that things have gone on the same since the beginning of time. But Peter reminds us that they have not taken into account how God has judged the world such as the flood, which illustrates the absurdity of their point. Things have not continued the same since the beginning of time. Then, Peter explains that to God a day is like a thousand years. So to Him, it has only been two days since He left the earth. Peter further explains that the return of Christ has been delayed to provide more people with the opportunity to be saved. His delay is not the neglect of His promise, but the fulfillment of it. When His patience has ended, He will come. The return of Christ has been delayed for people you know who will trust?

2 PETER 3:8
But do not overlook this one fact, beloved, that with the Lord one day is as a thousand years, and a thousand years as one day.

MILITARY OTD

IGNORANT PEOPLE

Why do people have different interpretations of the Bible? One answer, though not a very comfortable one for us, is found in today's reading. Peter concludes this book with an admonition to live a godly life and then encourages us in reading what Paul has written. Peter knows that some of what Paul wrote is not easy to understand. As a result, some people, who are ignorant and unstable, have distorted Paul's teachings and have led people astray with their wrong interpretations. We need to realize that sometimes people will share interpretations that are wrong, intentionally or unintentionally. They are wrong because those who make them are ignorant. They do not have the knowledge or skills they need to correctly handle the passage. It might also be wrong because they are unstable. They go back and forth between positions and beliefs. They are not firmly grounded in the Word. We need to be on our guard, lest we get carried away by false teaching. We need to make sure that our positions are based on solid interpretation principles and not just our ideas or opinions. It is very important.

★★★★

2 PETER 3:16

...There are some things in them that are hard to understand, which the ignorant and unstable twist to their own destruction, as they do the other Scriptures.

SAY WHAT?

Observation: What do I see?

SO WHAT?

Interpretation: What does it mean?

NOW WHAT?

Application: How does it apply to me?

THEN WHAT?

Implementation: What do I do?

MILITARYDEVOTIONAL.COM
@MILITARYDEVOS

The book of Proverbs was designed to help us in "attaining wisdom and discipline; in understanding words of insight; in acquiring a disciplined and prudent life, doing what is right and just and fair; in giving prudence to the simple, knowledge and discretion to the young." As you read through this chapter, write down the verses that are most significant to you in your present circumstances.

VERSE | WHAT TRUTH IT COMMUNICATES | HOW IT IMPACTS MY LIFE

SIGN OF OUR WALK

Today you begin a journey through the book of 1 John. This book contains important information about our salvation. It provides the characteristics of one who is truly saved and the characteristics of one who is not saved. It is a book that will confirm to your heart that you know Christ, or reveal that you are not really saved. With this in mind, why not read through 1 John with that central theme in mind, and record your discoveries. Each day, read the passage given and write down your observations on the chart below. Then, at the end of this book, examine your life to see if the fruits of true salvation are present. One important thing to keep in mind is the Christian life is a process. While you may still struggle in areas that reflect the life of an unbeliever, they should be diminishing with time. Are you seeing growth in those areas? You may not be happy with how much you have grown, but what is important, is that you have grown. Begin with prayer, asking God to reveal to your heart how you really stand before Him.

SAY WHAT?
What characteristics of a believer does John reveal?

SO WHAT?
What characteristics of an unbeliever does John reveal?

NOW WHAT?
What do those characteristics reveal about your salvation?

THEN WHAT?
In light of this passage, what personal commitment will you make?

1 JOHN 1:7
But if we walk in the light, as he is in the light, we have fellowship with one another, and the blood of Jesus his Son cleanses us from all sin.

MILITARYDEVOTIONAL.COM
🐦 @MILITARYDEVOS

SAY WHAT?
What characteristics of a believer does John reveal?

Continue the project we began yesterday. Read through today's passage and write down the characteristics John lists for believers and unbelievers. Ask God daily to reveal the true condition of your heart through your discoveries. Are you gaining assurance, or becoming concerned with your findings?

SO WHAT?
What characteristics of an unbeliever does John reveal?

NOW WHAT?
What do those characteristics reveal about your salvation?

THEN WHAT?
In light of this passage, what personal commitment will you make?

★★★★

1 JOHN 2:3
And by this we know that we have come to know him, if we keep his commandments.

SIGN OF LOVING THE WORLD

Continue today the project we began in 1 John. Read through this passage carefully and write down the characteristics John gives for believers and unbelievers. Ask God today to reveal to you what your discoveries tell you about your own condition. What have you been learning so far? Are you gaining assurance or becoming more concerned? Who can you share this with?

SAY WHAT?
What characteristics of a believer does John reveal?

SO WHAT?
What characteristics of an unbeliever does John reveal?

NOW WHAT?
What do those characteristics reveal about your salvation?

THEN WHAT?
In light of this passage, what personal commitment will you make?

1 JOHN 2:15

Do not love the world or the things in the world. If anyone loves the world, the love of the Father is not in him.

SAY WHAT?

What characteristics of a believer does John reveal?

SO WHAT?

What characteristics of an unbeliever does John reveal?

NOW WHAT?

What do those characteristics reveal about your salvation?

THEN WHAT?

In light of this passage, what personal commitment will you make?

Continue today the project we began in 1 John. Read through this passage carefully and write down the characteristics John gives for believers and unbelievers. Ask God today to reveal to you what your discoveries tell you about your own condition. What have you been learning so far? Are you gaining assurance or becoming more concerned? Who can you share this with?

1 JOHN 3:7

Little children, let no one deceive you. Whoever practices righteousness is righteous, as he is righteous.

SIGN OF OBEDIENCE

Continue today the project we began in 1 John. Read through this passage carefully and write down the characteristics John gives for believers and unbelievers. Ask God today to reveal to you what your discoveries tell you about your own condition. What have you been learning so far? Are you gaining assurance or becoming more concerned? Who can you share this with?

SAY WHAT?
What characteristics of a believer does John reveal?

SO WHAT?
What characteristics of an unbeliever does John reveal?

NOW WHAT?
What do those characteristics reveal about your salvation?

THEN WHAT?
In light of this passage, what personal commitment will you make?

1 JOHN 3:11

For this is the message that you have heard from the beginning, that we should love one another.

MILITARYDEVOTIONAL.COM
@MILITARYDEVOS

SIGN OF LOVE

SAY WHAT?
What characteristics of a believer does John reveal?

Continue today the project we began in 1 John. Read through this passage carefully and write down the characteristics John gives for believers and unbelievers. Ask God today to reveal to you what your discoveries tell you about your own condition. What have you been learning so far? Are you gaining assurance or becoming more concerned? Who can you share this with?

SO WHAT?
What characteristics of an unbeliever does John reveal?

NOW WHAT?
What do those characteristics reveal about your salvation?

THEN WHAT?
In light of this passage, what personal commitment will you make?

1 JOHN 4:7
Beloved let us love one another, for love is from God, and whoever loves has been born of God and knows God.

The book of Proverbs was designed to help us in "attaining wisdom and discipline; in understanding words of insight; in acquiring a disciplined and prudent life, doing what is right and just and fair; in giving prudence to the simple, knowledge and discretion to the young." As you read through this chapter, write down the verses that are most significant to you in your present circumstances.

VERSE | WHAT TRUTH IT COMMUNICATES | HOW IT IMPACTS MY LIFE

THE SIGN OF OVERCOMING

SAY WHAT?

What characteristics of a believer does John reveal?

Continue today the project we began in 1 John. Read through this passage carefully and write down the characteristics John gives for believers and unbelievers. Ask God today to reveal to you what your discoveries tell you about your own condition. What have you been learning so far? Are you gaining assurance or becoming more concerned? Who can you share this with?

SO WHAT?

What characteristics of an unbeliever does John reveal?

NOW WHAT?

What do those characteristics reveal about your salvation?

THEN WHAT?

In light of this passage, what personal commitment will you make?

1 JOHN 5:4

For everyone who has been born of God overcomes the world. And this is the victory that has overcome the world—our faith.

SIGN OF FORSAKING SIN

Continue today the project we began in 1 John. Read through this passage carefully and write down the characteristics John gives for believers and unbelievers. Ask God today to reveal to you what your discoveries tell you about your own condition. What have you been learning so far? Are you gaining assurance or becoming more concerned? Who can you share this with?

SAY WHAT?

What characteristics of a believer does John reveal?

SO WHAT?

What characteristics of an unbeliever does John reveal?

NOW WHAT?

What do those characteristics reveal about your salvation?

THEN WHAT?

In light of this passage, what personal commitment will you make?

★★★★

1 JOHN 5:18

We know that everyone who has been born of God does not keep on sinning, but he who was born of God protects him, and the evil one does not touch him.

MILITARYDEVOTIONAL.COM
 @MILITARYDEVOS

SAY WHAT?

What in your life shows that you are truly saved?

SO WHAT?

Are any characteristics of the unsaved also true of you?
Have you observed growth in these areas?

NOW WHAT?

Where do you stand in relationship to God based on your answers?

THEN WHAT?

What do you need to do now? How will you do it?

We have just completed reading through this great book, jotting down our observations of believers and unbelievers. John closed this book with the statement "I write these things to you...that you may know that you have eternal life." As you read through it, did you see evidence of your salvation? Use this sheet to help summarize what you have learned. Be honest about what you have found, and then talk to someone who can help you understand what it means as well as how to respond in a right way. Be a doer of the Word.

1 JOHN 5:13

I write these things to you who believe in the name of the Son of God that you may know that you have eternal life.

WALKING IN TRUTH

What does it mean to walk in the truth? When the Apostle John knew people were walking in the truth, it brought him great joy. How do we know if we are? Walking in the truth simply means that you have ordered your life according to the Word of God. You know what it says, and you are obeying it in every area of your life. In fact, according to verse six, our love for Christ is demonstrated by our obedience to His commands. To disobey what the Word says is to show that we do not truly love Christ. Walking in the truth means that people who observe us see an individual who is honest. Walking in the truth means we do not gossip or make fun of others. Walking in the truth means that we are obedient to our authorities and show them respect even when they are not around to hear what we are saying. Walking in the truth means that our speech always reflects Christ. Walking in the truth means that our lives and conduct are consistent with what the Scriptures teach. Could it be said of you that you walk in the truth? Are there areas of your life in which you do not? Does your walk bring joy to those who teach you?

2 JOHN 1:4

I rejoiced greatly to find some of your children walking in the truth, just as we were commanded by the Father.

SAY WHAT?
Observation: What do I see?

SO WHAT?
Interpretation: What does it mean?

NOW WHAT?
Application: How does it apply to me?

THEN WHAT?
Implementation: What do I do?

MILITARYDEVOTIONAL.COM
@MILITARYDEVOS

SAY WHAT?

In what ways are you like Diotrephes?

SO WHAT?

In what ways are you unlike Diotrephes?

NOW WHAT?

What can you do to make your life less like this man's life?

THEN WHAT?

In light of this passage,what personal commitment can you make?

Who do people say you remind them of? The answer to that question could reveal a lot to you about yourself. John shares in this short book that we are to imitate what is good. That is, we ought to remind people of good things and good people. We should not be imitating people or things which are wrong. John uses Diotrephes as an example. He was someone who obviously imitated evil. John tells us that he was a man who loved to be first. He must have been a very selfish man if others observed this in him. Would people in your world describe you this way? John also wrote that he was someone who gossiped maliciously about others. What conclusions would we come to if we listened to what you talked about today? To make matters even worse,Diotrephes refused to welcome other brothers. Do you? When someone new comes to your unit,do you reach out to him and make him feel more comfortable? Diotrephes wouldn't have. Does this sound at all like you? It is shameful to be known as this man was. What kind of reputation do you have? Do your friends think of you as selfish or unkind?

★★★★

3 JOHN 1:9

I have written something to the church, but Diotrephes, who likes to put himself first,does not acknowledge our authority.

PRAYING IN THE SPIRIT

What does it mean to pray in the Spirit? How does one do that? There is often confusion about what Jude is asking us to do in this passage, but the answer is really quite simple. To pray in the Spirit means to be guided and led by Him. It means that we are not led by our own selfishness when we pray. That would not be praying in the Spirit but praying in the flesh. We also pray in the flesh when we pray using our own intellect. We request what seems to make sense to us and do not pray according to God's wisdom. Praying in the flesh also includes asking God to energize what we want instead of seeking His will. Praying in the Spirit is not some mystical thing that only very spiritual people can do. It is something we all can and should do. How do we accomplish this? By letting God control our wants and seeking His will rather than our fleshly desires. Examine your prayer life. Are you praying in the flesh or in the Spirit? Is it God's will you are seeking or your own? Are you selfishly asking God to conform to you or asking Him to conform you to what He desires? What needs to change in order for you to pray in the Spirit?

JUDE 1:20

But you, beloved, building yourselves up in your most holy faith and praying in the Holy Spirit,

SAY WHAT?

How can you determine if you pray in the flesh?

SO WHAT?

In what ways can you determine that you are praying in the Spirit?

NOW WHAT?

What can you do to begin to eliminate your flesh from dominating your prayer life?

THEN WHAT?

In light of this passage, what personal commitment can you make?

YOU ARE ALREADY **A LEADER...**
EARN THE DEGREE TO MATCH.

Pilgrimage offers a unique opportunity to earn a master's degree in **ORGANIZATIONAL LEADERSHIP from an accredited Christian college or university,** while working in your professional field of choice... even while you continue to serve in the military.

Our **experience-based distance learning model** uses your current leadership context as the classroom for learning... and applies essential organizational leadership skills that convert to any role or environment.

Put your GI Bill benefits to work for your future!

Need an undergraduate degree? Ask about our undergrad programs or the accelerated graduate degree program.

Get started today on your next steps at **ORG-LEADERSHIP.COM.**

LEARN MORE OR APPLY ONLINE AT:

ORG-LEADERSHIP.COM

 **PILGRIMAGE**

PILGRIMAGE EDUCATIONAL RESOURCES / CLARKS SUMMIT, PA
P: 570.504.1463 / E: INFO@SIMPLYAPILGRIM.COM / SIMPLYAPILGRIM.COM

» MILITARYDEVOTIONAL.COM

 @MILITARYDEVOS

 FACEBOOK.COM/MILITARYDEVOS

MILITARY OTD

SEPTEMBER
★★★★

MONTHLY PRAYER SHEET

I NEED TO REACH OUT TO...	HOW I WILL DO IT...	HOW IT WENT...

OTHER REQUEST	HOW ANSWERED	DATE

MONTHLY MISSION SHEET

>>> Share your personal commitments with those who will help keep you accountable to them.

>>> NAME: ....

This sheet is designed to help you make personal commitments each month that will help you grow in your walk with God. Fill it out by determining:

★ What will push you.
★ What you think you can achieve.

>>> PERSONAL DEVOTIONS:

I will commit to read the OnTrack Bible passage and devotional thought .... day(s) each week this month.

>>> CHURCH/CHAPEL ATTENDANCE:

I will attend Church/Chapel .... time(s) this month.
I will attend .... time(s) this month.

>>> SCRIPTURE MEMORY:

I will memorize .... key verse(s) from the daily OnTrack Devotions this month.

>>> OUTREACH:

I will share Christ with .... person/people this month.
I will serve my local church/chapel this month by ....
....
....

>>> OTHER ACTIVITIES:

List any other opportunities such as events, prayer group, etc..., you will participate in this month. ....
....
....
....
....
....

Determine to begin today a journey that will last a lifetime,and will change your life forever.

HE MUST INCREASE

What characteristics do you observe in John the Baptist in this chapter? What characteristics does he specifically demonstrate in verses 15 and 26-27? It becomes clear as you read this section of Scripture that John was not the kind of person who tried to make himself look better than he really was. He was not jealous of anyone who received more attention than he did. He seemed to have no trouble allowing Christ and His ministry to exceed his own. He even encouraged people to follow Christ instead of him. When asked about himself, he told people the truth. He would not allow people to think something about him that was not true. Do you try to draw attention to yourself or to others? When people ask questions, do you make what you have done seem better than it really is? Would you allow someone in your youth group to get more attention than you get for similar accomplishments? Do you direct the attention and glory to God or to yourself? In what areas of your life do you need to be more like John? Use the opportunities God brings to point others to Christ.

SAY WHAT?
Observation: What do I see?

SO WHAT?
Interpretation: What does it mean?

NOW WHAT?
Application: How does it apply to me?

THEN WHAT?
Implementation: What do I do?

★★★★

JOHN 1:15

John bore witness about him, and cried out, "This was he of whom I said, 'He who comes after me ranks before me, because he was before me.'")

SAY WHAT?

What kinds of prejudice do you see in your unit?

SO WHAT?

In what way do you see that prejudice demonstrated?

NOW WHAT?

What kinds of prejudice has God spoken to you about?

THEN WHAT?

What should you do about what you have written on this page?

Circle the names of the disciples who were called in this section? What were they like? As you read through the Gospels, you find they were ordinary people with the same strengths and weaknesses we have. In this passage we see Nathanael demonstrate a glaring and obvious sin. Did you notice it? It was prejudice. He didn't want to come with Philip to meet Christ because Jesus Christ was from Nazareth (vs46). Even during the time of Christ, people judged others based on origin, color of skin and manner of dress. It would have been a tragedy to have missed an opportunity to be impacted by the message of Christ because the person who could share or the one who needed to hear was hindered by prejudice. Prejudice destroys what Christ came to do. In what ways do you or your youth group demonstrate prejudice? Ask God to enable you, and help your group, view people as God does. Thank God for teaching us through the example of Nathanael that He does break down the walls of prejudice and uses us to impact others. How do you need to change?

★★★★

JOHN 1:46

Nathanael said to him, "Can anything good come out of Nazareth?" Philip said to him, "Come and see."

EXCITING OR BORING?

How many days have passed since these disciples began following Christ? Circle the days in your Bible. What has happened in these few, short days? What an incredible journey it must have been for these disciples who were with Christ. They saw other disciples called. They saw Jesus give specific details about someone He had never seen before. They saw Him turn water into wine. They ended their first week with Christ by clearing out the temple. They were probably overwhelmed. They must have been filled with anticipation and excitement about following Christ. Could it be as exciting for us walking with God? What a thrill to watch God do great things every day -- answering prayer, giving you comfort, or providing opportunities to be a witness. If your walk with God is not exciting, it indicates something about you, not God. He wants to fill each day of our lives with excitement. Make a list of those things you have noticed He has done in your life this past week. If that list is small, talk to someone about how you can become a person who enjoys all the Christian life has to offer. You will not regret it!

JOHN 2:11

This, the first of his signs, Jesus did at Cana in Galilee, and manifested his glory. And his disciples believed in him.

SAY WHAT?

Observation: What do I see?

SO WHAT?

Interpretation: What does it mean?

NOW WHAT?

Application: How does it apply to me?

THEN WHAT?

Implementation: What do I do?

HOW TO GET TO HEAVEN

SAY WHAT?

Name religious people you know that may not go to heaven.

SO WHAT?

How can you let them know what the Bible says?

NOW WHAT?

How can you be more aware of opportunities to share with them?

THEN WHAT?

In light of this passage, what personal commitment can you make?

Who was Nicodemus? Why do you think he came to Jesus by night? Though he was not brave enough to seek Jesus publicly during the day, he was determined to know the truth. Though he wanted to know the truth, and was a member of the Jewish ruling council, he did not know how to get to heaven. Jesus demonstrated His surprise at this by His response in verses ten through twelve. He felt Nicodemus should have known. We, too, think that because people go to church, even your church, that they know all about salvation and how to get to heaven. The problem is that they do not. People who appear to be very religious on the outside may have no clue whatsoever as to what the Bible really says about heaven and how to receive eternal life. We often think that everyone living in America knows how to get to heaven. All around us are people, both religious and nonreligious, who do not know how to have a relationship with God. They need someone who will care enough to tell them. With whom can you share what Christ shared with Nicodemus? Don't miss an opportunity because you think he/she already knows. They may not.

JOHN 3:10

Jesus answered him, "Are you the teacher of Israel and yet you do not understand these things?

WHY SAMARIA?

Why do you think the disciples "had to" go through Samaria? Could it be that Christ knew the woman in today's reading would be at the well just when He would arrive, and He wanted to share the gospel with her? What makes this account even more amazing was that she was a Samaritan, and He was a Jew. You see, Jews hated Samaritans and would not even talk to them. Jews would walk miles out of their way to avoid Samaria. But here we find Christ, traveling through Samaria in order to share salvation with this woman. As a result of Christ's love and compassion, this women trusted Christ as her Savior and ran to tell the whole town, where "many" believed. An entire town came to salvation because Jesus was willing to love a person whom others refused to reach out to in love. What kinds of people in your world do you feel uncomfortable around or avoid altogether, who have never heard the message of Christ? Drug addicts? Homosexuals? Others in your unit? Everyone needs to hear the gospel, and we should be willing to share it with them.

SAY WHAT?
Observation: What do I see?

SO WHAT?
Interpretation: What does it mean?

NOW WHAT?
Application: How does it apply to me?

THEN WHAT?
Implementation: What do I do?

JOHN 4:9
The Samaritan woman said to him, "How is it that you, a Jew, ask for a drink from me, a woman of Samaria?" (For Jews have no dealings with Samaritans.)

The book of Proverbs was designed to help us in "attaining wisdom and discipline; in understanding words of insight; in acquiring a disciplined and prudent life, doing what is right and just and fair; in giving prudence to the simple, knowledge and discretion to the young." As you read through this chapter, write down the verses that are most significant to you in your present circumstances.

VERSE | WHAT TRUTH IT COMMUNICATES | HOW IT IMPACTS MY LIFE

POWER OF YOUR STORY

How is the gospel presentation this woman gave when she went back into town different from the one Christ gave in this chapter and in chapter three? How would you describe her method of sharing? One of the great lessons we can learn from what this women said is how to communicate the gospel to those around us. She simply ran home and told people what Christ had done in her life. She gave to them her testimony of how she had met a Man who told her everything she had ever done. This Man changed her life, and she wanted them to know about it. We often make sharing the gospel complicated when all it needs to be is one person sharing what has happened in their life with someone else. The need to be able to share a full Gospel presentation is important to learn, but anyone can share his personal story of the difference Christ has made. Take some time today to write out the difference Jesus Christ has made in your life. Then pray and ask God to give you an opportunity today to share your "story" with someone. People need to hear what God has done and is doing in our lives. This is the hope the world needs to know about.

JOHN 4:39

Many Samaritans from that town believed in him because of the woman's testimony, "He told me all that I ever did."

SAY WHAT?

What was your life like before you were saved? Or, how is your life different than an unsaved person's because you were saved as a child?

SO WHAT?

How did you come to trust Christ as your Savior?

NOW WHAT?

How is your life different since you trusted Christ?

THEN WHAT?

How can you share this with someone this week?

SAY WHAT?
Observation: What do I see?

SO WHAT?
Interpretation: What does it mean?

NOW WHAT?
Application: How does it apply to me?

THEN WHAT?
Implementation: What do I do?

Circle all the different people or items which Jesus said testify about who He was in verses 31-40. Since there were many powerful testimonies about who He was, why didn't the people believe? The answer is found in verses 41-44. In these few verses, Christ told them their unbelief was because they were more interested in what people thought about them than what God thought. In fact, Jesus said that He knew that they weren't saved because they made no effort to obtain praise from God, but only the praise that comes from men. This incident may tell you something about your personal walk with God. A common problem among Christians is that we have the ability to see the reality of who God is, but miss it because we care more about what people think than we do about what God thinks. Do you consider your friend's opinion more important than God's? Can you think of a time when you did something only to please God? If not, it is time to act on what God wants for you, not what others want. If you do not consider what pleases Him, you may not be saved. Seek only the praise that comes from God, not the praise of men.

★★★★

JOHN 5:44
How can you believe, when you receive glory from one another and do not seek the glory that comes from the only God?

ANDREW'S MINISTRY

Which specific disciples are mentioned by name in this passage? It is fascinating to look closely at how Jesus talks to the different disciples in this chapter and what that may tell us about their personalities. Christ asked Philip where they could buy bread for the people; He did not ask James or Matthew. Think about Andrew. He was the disciple who brought people to Christ. In today's reading, we see that he was the one who brought the little boy with the five loaves and two fish to Jesus. Although that was not a lot of food, he must have thought Jesus could do something with it. He was not one of the obvious leaders in the group. He did not write a book of the Bible. He did not deliver any powerful messages in Scripture. He just quietly brought people to Christ - from his brother Peter - to a little boy with a small lunch. What an example to us! How often do you bring people to Christ? Maybe you are not one of the "up front" leaders in your youth group or church, but you can bring people to meet Christ. Train your mind to think like Andrew, and see what God will do with your life if you allow Him to use you.

SAY WHAT?
Observation: What do I see?

SO WHAT?
Interpretation: What does it mean?

NOW WHAT?
Application: How does it apply to me?

THEN WHAT?
Implementation: What do I do?

JOHN 6:8-9

One of his disciples, Andrew, Simon Peter's brother, said to him, "There is a boy here who has five barley loaves and two fish, but what are they for so many?"

SAY WHAT?

What would your reaction have been to what Christ said?

SO WHAT?

Why is it so hard for people to be 100% sold out for Christ?

NOW WHAT?

What part of your life is the most difficult for you to give to Christ?

THEN WHAT?

What would you need to change to be totally dependent on Christ?

What was the response to Jesus' statements in verses 53-59? Why? At first glance, it almost seems as if Jesus were asking them to be involved in cannibalism. But a closer examination reveals exactly what He was saying and why the disciples had such a hard time accepting it. Jesus was clearly stating that in order to follow Christ one would need to be totally committed. Jesus was not looking for half-hearted commitment or people who just wanted a part of Him. He wanted only those who would take all of Him. Jesus' point was that we should be so committed that just as food nourishes, sustains, and energizes our physical bodies, so must Christ nourish, sustain and energize our spiritual lives. As dependent as we are on food, we are to be that dependent on Jesus Christ. In other words, we must realize that Jesus Christ demands control of every area in our lives. When some of the disciples understood the level of commitment He was asking for, they checked out. Christ does not want a part of our lives, or even most of it. He demands all of it. Does He have all of you? What needs to change for you to be 100% committed?

JOHN 6:60

When many of his disciples heard it, they said, "This is a hard saying; who can listen to it?"

RESPONDING TO MOCKERY

When was the last time someone said something to you in a mocking tone? What was your response? In today's reading we see that Jesus faced this very situation, and from it we can learn how we ought to respond to mockery. This particular circumstance was even more painful because it was His family that was mocking Him. Their comments about showing Himself to the world at the feast must have been humiliating. It must have caused Him pain to hear and feel their sarcasm and unbelief. Notice His response. He did not become angry or defensive. He did not give a sarcastic comment in return, but patiently and lovingly responded to their attack. He simply told them that He was not going and why. What an example! Is this how you have recently responded to your family? We are prone to defend ourselves and our actions. We need to follow this example of Christ and always respond with love and patience. Circumstances like these give us great opportunities to demonstrate the difference that Christ has made in our lives. Both positive and negative responses will be noticed. Why don't you do the right thing?

SAY WHAT?

Name someone who responds to you like Jesus' family did in today's reading?

SO WHAT?

Why is it so difficult to respond in a positive way to people who mock you?

NOW WHAT?

How can you use today's reading to help you respond correctly to them in the future?

THEN WHAT?

Make a personal commitment of how you will respond in the future.

JOHN 7:6

Jesus said to them, "My time has not yet come, but your time is always here.

SAY WHAT?

Observation: What do I see?

SO WHAT?

Interpretation: What does it mean?

NOW WHAT?

Application: How does it apply to me?

THEN WHAT?

Implementation: What do I do?

How many times did Jesus refer to Himself using the phrase, "I am?" Circle them in your Bible. Sometimes Christians have the mistaken belief that Jesus never claimed to be God. We find however, that He said it over and over in this section of Scripture. Every time He used the phrase,"I am," He was calling Himself by a name that the Jews knew was reserved only for God. He was not trying to trick or confuse them. He came right out and let people know exactly who He was,and why He had come to this earth. What He said in verses 27-28 must have haunted them after His death. Jesus claimed to be God, sent to pay the penalty for their sins. He said that He would die, and then He would rise from the dead,which would prove His claims. How could those people miss a message so clearly given and proven? How have you responded to His message? Have you trusted Christ as your Savior, or have you rejected Him as these did? Today, you can be like those mentioned in verse three and put your faith in Him. If you have already trusted Christ,how can you share what the Bible says about Jesus Christ with a world that needs to know?

JOHN 8:28

So Jesus said to them, "When you have lifted up the Son of Man, then you will know that I am he, and that I do nothing on my own authority, but speak just as the Father taught me.

The book of Proverbs was designed to help us in "attaining wisdom and discipline; in understanding words of insight; in acquiring a disciplined and prudent life, doing what is right and just and fair; in giving prudence to the simple, knowledge and discretion to the young." As you read through this chapter, write down the verses that are most significant to you in your present circumstances.

VERSE	WHAT TRUTH IT COMMUNICATES	HOW IT IMPACTS MY LIFE

SAY WHAT?

Observation: What do I see?

SO WHAT?

Interpretation: What does it mean?

NOW WHAT?

Application: How does it apply to me?

THEN WHAT?

Implementation: What do I do?

Have you ever wondered if you are really saved? Have you ever believed you were saved but then wondered if you have done or could do something to lose your salvation? If you answered yes to either of these two questions, you will find a small but powerful phrase that should reassure you of the certainty of God's promise. Did you see it when you read verse 35? The Bible teaches in many places that our relationship to God is one of a Father and His "sons." If you have been saved, you are a son of God. According to verse 35, a slave has no permanent place in a family. A son, however, belongs to the family forever! Nothing can ever change the fact that a son is a son and a member of the family. When I became a child of God, I became a son and a member of God's family forever. Why? According to verse 36, when we are set free by the Son, we are free indeed. So if I have been truly saved, nothing can cause me to lose my salvation or remove my name from the family. If you have truly been saved, you are a child of God, you are a son, and sons are forever! Memorize verses 34 & 35 to recall in times of doubt. Share it with a friend.

★★★★

JOHN 8:35

The slave does not remain in the house forever; the son remains forever.

REASON FOR DIFFICULTY

Have you ever wondered why difficult things happen? Why do some people have illness and disease? While there can be a variety of specific reasons, all have one basic purpose - to provide an opportunity to have the works of God demonstrated. In today's reading, Jesus illustrated this concept. The disciples, like many people today, thought that when tragedy occurred,it was because the "victim" had done something wrong. They believed difficult things were God's way of punishing people for having committed a sin. When the disciples saw the blind man,they wanted to know whose sin was responsible for it. Surely it was a result of some sin. Jesus told them that sin had nothing to do with this man's blindness. He was blind so that God could demonstrate the difference that Jesus Christ makes in a life. Problems provide opportunities to demonstrate God's power. Often, difficult circumstances are allowed for positive reasons. What does God want to show the people in your world through your present circumstances? Underline verse three to remind you of the potential your problems bring.

SAY WHAT?
What difficult circumstances are part of your life?

SO WHAT?
What positive reasons could God have for allowing them?

NOW WHAT?
How should you respond to what He is doing in your life?

THEN WHAT?
Based on this passage,what commitment will you make?

★★★★

JOHN 9:3
Jesus answered, "It was not that this man sinned, or his parents, but that the works of God might be displayed in him.

MILITARYDEVOTIONAL.COM
@MILITARYDEVOS

TELL YOUR STORY

SAY WHAT?
Observation: What do I see?

SO WHAT?
Interpretation: What does it mean?

NOW WHAT?
Application: How does it apply to me?

THEN WHAT?
Implementation: What do I do?

What words would you use to describe the three main characters in today's reading; the Pharisees, the blind man and his parents? It is great to read how excited the blind man was about what Jesus Christ had done for him. He wanted everyone to know that Jesus Christ was responsible. He did not back down at all when the Pharisees doubted and criticized him or when his parents did not support him. He knew,like his parents,that to acknowledge that Jesus was the Christ would mean he would be put out of the synagogue. Still,he would not deny the fact that Jesus Christ had done a work in his life,and he wanted to share it,even if that meant he would face punishment. No matter what the question or the response was,he basically said the same thing - that he was blind,but now he could see. He is a great example to us - share our faith without fear or shame. We seem to think that we have to always give a thorough gospel presentation when in a spiritual conversation. When at times, all we really need to do at first is simply tell people what Jesus Christ has done in our lives. Why not look for an opportunity to do just that today?

★★★★

JOHN 9:25
He answered, "Whether he is a sinner I do not know. One thing I do know, that though I was blind, now I see."

GOOD SHEPHERD

In today's reading, Jesus used a metaphor of a shepherd and his sheep to demonstrate how much He loved them. How many different illustrations does He use? Put a star next to the different ways Jesus shows He loves you. Of all the different examples in this chapter, which ones mean the most to you. Maybe it is knowing that, just like a shepherd calls his own sheep by name, Jesus Christ knows your name. You are not just a number, but "somebody." He even knows how many hairs you have on your head. It may be that He always walks ahead so that the path you travel is one that He knows is just right for where you are in life. Your favorite example may be that Jesus offers life - life to the fullest rather than the death and destruction offered by the thief. Maybe it is knowing that, unlike some in your life, Jesus is not a hired hand and will never leave you, regardless of the cost to Him. It has already cost Him His life, and our shepherd is ready and willing to give us anything we need. Regardless of the example you've chosen, clearly you are deeply loved by God. Underline the verses that mean the most to you, and think about them today.

JOHN 10:11

I am the good shepherd. The good shepherd lays down his life for the sheep.

SAY WHAT?

Observation: What do I see?

SO WHAT?

Interpretation: What does it mean?

NOW WHAT?

Application: How does it apply to me?

THEN WHAT?

Implementation: What do I do?

SAY WHAT?

Write out who you believe Jesus Christ to be.

SO WHAT?

Why do you believe that what you wrote above is true?

NOW WHAT?

How should someone respond to who Jesus Christ is?

THEN WHAT?

With whom will you share this information?

Imagine you are having a conversation with some friends, and it suddenly turns to religion. During the discussion, one of your friends asks you who you believe Jesus Christ is. How would you answer him? That is the most important question which could be asked - one all of us must be able to answer. Who you believe Jesus Christ to be and how you respond to Him determines where you will spend eternity. This chapter contains verses which clearly state that Jesus Christ declares Himself to be God. In fact, Jesus Himself, said in verse 4 that Lazarus' death was permitted by God to reveal this very fact. In order to receive eternal life, we must come to realize that Jesus Christ is God, and His death made eternal life possible for those who believe. As you read through the rest of this book, write in the margin of your Bible the word "Deity" every time you read something that illustrates that Jesus Christ is God. It will help prepare you to tell others who He is. As you discover more about the life of Jesus Christ and what He has done for us, look around at the people in your world. They need you to share what you are learning, with them.

JOHN 11:14-15

Then Jesus told them plainly, "Lazarus has died, and for your sake I am glad that I was not there, so that you may believe. But let us go to him."

GREATEST HYPOCRITE

What words would you use to describe Judas Iscariot? One of the great advantages of having the Scriptures is that we have the inside scoop not available to those who were there at the time. This passage is even more incredible when you realize that no one in the story knew the events taking place, except Jesus Christ. Judas chose his words very carefully when he objected to Mary's actions in order to prevent anyone from knowing the true motivation of his heart. He was so successful that no one ever suspected he was not what he claimed to be. The disciples trusted him explicitly. He even controlled their money. When Jesus said that one of them would deny Him, they suspected themselves, not Judas. He is one of the greatest examples of a hypocrite. He led people to believe something about him that was not true. Are you in any way like Judas? Are there areas of your life in which you carefully choose words so as not to reveal the true condition of your heart? Is what people believe about you really true? If not, take the first step today to end hypocrisy in your life. Ignore it and there will be serious consequences someday.

SAY WHAT?
Observation: What do I see?

SO WHAT?
Interpretation: What does it mean?

NOW WHAT?
Application: How does it apply to me?

THEN WHAT?
Implementation: What do I do?

JOHN 12:6

He said this, not because he cared about the poor, but because he was a thief, and having charge of the moneybag he used to help himself to what was put into it.

GREATEST HYPOCRITE

SAY WHAT?
Observation: What do I see?

SO WHAT?
Interpretation: What does it mean?

NOW WHAT?
Application: How does it apply to me?

THEN WHAT?
Implementation: What do I do?

What request did the Greeks make of Philip in verse 21 of today's reading? Why didn't he grant their request? Instead of taking them to Jesus, Philip took them to Andrew. Although he did not take the Greeks to Jesus himself, he did take them to see someone who could. In doing so, he illustrates a lesson helpful to many people. There are some who, for whatever reason, do not feel that they can lead a person to Christ, or tell them the way of salvation. In light of that, they often do not even share how Jesus Christ has changed their lives for fear they will be unable to completely communicate the plan of salvation. What they fail to see is that while they may not be able to personally share the message of Christ, they can always take people to someone who can. Like Philip, they can take him to an Andrew. One could just simply say, "I can't explain everything myself, but, if you want, I can call someone at my church, or one of my friends who can explain it clearly." If you find yourself in this position, don't hesitate to take a friend to someone who can share Christ with them. In the meantime, work to develop the ability to share the gospel.

★★★★

JOHN 12:21
So these came to Philip, who was from Bethsaida in Galilee, and asked him, "Sir, we wish to see Jesus."

The book of Proverbs was designed to help us in "attaining wisdom and discipline; in understanding words of insight; in acquiring a disciplined and prudent life, doing what is right and just and fair; in giving prudence to the simple, knowledge and discretion to the young." As you read through this chapter, write down the verses that are most significant to you in your present circumstances.

VERSE	WHAT TRUTH IT COMMUNICATES	HOW IT IMPACTS MY LIFE

JUST A FOOT WASHING

SAY WHAT?

When did you have your "whole body washed" (experience salvation)?

SO WHAT?

What "part of your body" has become dirty in recent days? How?

NOW WHAT?

How can it become clean again?

THEN WHAT?

How can you prevent it from becoming dirty in the future?

What lessons can one take from the account in this chapter of the washing of the disciples feet by Jesus? An important lesson, but one often overlooked, is taken from Christ's conversation with Peter in verses six through eleven. Christ went to Peter and began to wash his feet. Peter objected. In the conversation, Christ told Peter that a person who has taken a bath need have only his feet washed when they become dirty, not his whole body. Christ is illustrating an important spiritual principle that we all must understand. At the moment of salvation, our "whole body" was cleaned - a bath, if you will. When we get dirty on "parts" of our bodies, by sinning, we do not need a whole bath, salvation, again. We simply need to clean the part that has become dirty by seeking forgiveness for the sin we committed. We may feel like we need a bath and may even feel that we have lost or deserve to lose our salvation. But all we need is to confess our sin and allow God to clean the part that has been dirtied. Is there some part of your life that needs to be cleaned? Why not wash your "feet" today!

★★★★

JOHN 13:10

Jesus said to him, "The one who has bathed does not need to wash, except for his feet, but is completely clean. And you are clean, but not every one of you."

OBEY COMMANDS

What is the difference between a command and a teaching? In today's reading, we see how our obedience to both, demonstrates how much we truly love God. Commands are the direct admonitions. Examples would be do not lie, do not commit adultery, etc. How well do you obey Jesus' commands? Do you even know what they are? To know His commands you must take the time to read His Words. It means making personal devotions the primary goal of one's life. How well do you obey Jesus' teachings? His teachings go another step. They are not direct commands but those things He taught out of the Scriptures - to love your neighbor, to give to the Lord's work, to forgive those who have sinned against you, to serve others, you are the light of the world, etc. Does your life reflect the obedience to His teachings as well as His commands? Does it demonstrate that you truly love Jesus? Are you being obedient in those areas that you know Christ has commanded you? How are you doing in those areas in which He has been teaching you? In what areas do you need to improve?

SAY WHAT?
Observation: What do I see?

SO WHAT?
Interpretation: What does it mean?

NOW WHAT?
Application: How does it apply to me?

THEN WHAT?
Implementation: What do I do?

★★★★

JOHN 14:23

Jesus answered him, "If anyone loves me, he will keep my word, and my Father will love him, and we will come to him and make our home with him.

SAY WHAT?

Identify one area in which you are having a difficult time remaining?

SO WHAT?

Why do you struggle in this area?

NOW WHAT?

What can you do to help yourself remain in this area?

THEN WHAT?

How will you be able to tell if you are remaining?

How many times does Jesus use the word "remain" in today's reading? Circle them in your Bible. What does it mean to remain? If you were to look up the definition for the word remain, you would find that it means to stay in place, to continue to exist, or to hold fast. In other words, it means that we continue to walk and grow with God. To remain with God is to have a consistent walk with Him. It is not walking close for a month and then going a month without having devotions. To remain means having steady constant growth. The Christian walk is not to be an up/down or hot/cold sort of relationship but one of staying with it, being persistent over time. As a branch stays on the vine and gains all its sustenance from the vine, so are we to remain with Christ in our walk, gaining daily from Him. For too long, we have accepted the fact that the Christian life is up/down and hot/cold. Consequently we tolerate it in our lives. That is not at all how God intended for us to live. Would God define your personal walk as a one that is remaining? How can you become more consistent in remaining in your relationship? How can others help you?

★★★★

JOHN 15:5

I am the vine; you are the branches. Whoever abides in me and I in him, he it is that bears much fruit, for apart from me you can do nothing.

HELP TO UNDERSTAND

How would you feel, if every time you sat down to take a test, the teacher sat down next to you and gave you all the answers for the test? Sounds pretty crazy doesn't it? But amazingly, that is very similar to what this passage of Scripture tells us the Holy Spirit does for us. The disciples were promised that, when the Holy Spirit came, He would guide them into ALL truth. That is, He would be there to teach them and guide them to understand what Scripture says. Since the Holy Spirit lives inside of us, and since He was the author of Scripture, He gives us an awesome opportunity. He takes the responsibility of guiding us into understanding what a passage of Scripture means and how it applies to our lives. We must begin by praying for God's help and guidance every time we read Scripture. We need also to be very careful to keep our lives pure so we do not miss this privilege by stifling His ministry in our lives. We must remember that every time we read the Bible, the Author is with us, wanting to help us understand what the passage says. He desires to have an intimate relationship with you. Ask Him to help you today.

SAY WHAT?
Observation: What do I see?

SO WHAT?
Interpretation: What does it mean?

NOW WHAT?
Application: How does it apply to me?

THEN WHAT?
Implementation: What do I do?

★★★★

JOHN 16:7

Nevertheless, I tell you the truth: it is to your advantage that I go away, for if I do not go away, the Helper will not come to you. But if I go, I will send him to you.

SAY WHAT?

Observation: What do I see?

SO WHAT?

Interpretation: What does it mean?

NOW WHAT?

Application: How does it apply to me?

THEN WHAT?

Implementation: What do I do?

If someone came up to you today and asked you what eternal life was, how would you answer him? Suppose he asked you if you had eternal life and how you knew you did? What would you say? Being able to answer these two questions is very important for the believer. Being able to answer them properly might determine his destiny as well as yours. In today's reading, Christ gives us a very simple and important definition for what eternal life is. It is found in verse three. According to this verse, eternal life is knowing God and Jesus Christ whom He sent. In other words, it is having a personal relationship with God. The question you need to ask yourself is "do you know God?" not "have I prayed a prayer at one point in my life?" Is God real to you? Many kids may think they are on their way to heaven when, in fact, all they really have is a type of religion. If I have eternal life, God is real to me, and, instead of a religion, I have a relationship. He will not just be a God I know a lot about; He will be a God who is real to me personally. Ask God to make Himself real to you in a way He never has before. He will amaze you.

★★★★

JOHN 17:3

And this is eternal life, that they know you the only true God, and Jesus Christ whom you have sent.

IT'S A SMALL WORLD

Have you ever read a passage of Scripture, and, while it may not have contained some incredible truth, it did contain something that seemed interesting to you. We find one of those nuggets in today's passage. It is a little piece of information John gave to us in verse 26. This incredible night began in the upper room where Peter told Christ he would die for Him. It continued with the events in the garden when Peter cut off the ear of the servant of the High Priest. Then, we find in verse 26, that the girl who came to him and accused him of being a follower of Christ was a relative of the man who had his ear cut off. Why would John give us this interesting little fact? I am sure Peter had no idea how his behavior in the garden would affect so many people. Or, that he would have another opportunity to impact this man and his family. What a small world it is! What things have you done without stopping to consider the impact they might have on those who may be watching you? Or what opportunities has God sent your way in order that you might influence lives for Him?

SAY WHAT?

Have your actions ever had a greater effect on someone than you thought that they might?

SO WHAT?

What effect did they have?

NOW WHAT?

How can you become more aware of the potential impact your actions can have?

THEN WHAT?

Write out a prayer asking God to help you in this area.

JOHN 18:26

One of the servants of the high priest, a relative of the man whose ear Peter had cut off, asked, "Did I not see you in the garden with him?"

MILITARYDEVOTIONAL.COM
@MILITARYDEVOS

FOR ME!

SAY WHAT?
--

SO WHAT?
--

NOW WHAT?
--

THEN WHAT?
--

Today you have read the account of what Jesus went through for you. What amazing love Jesus Christ demonstrated! Today, instead of taking time to read a devotional thought or answer questions on the left side of this page, go back through the passage and at the end of each verse say, "for me." Example: Then Pilate took Jesus and had him flogged "for me". It could change your life. How should you respond to such love? In what way can you show Him how thankful you are?

★★★★

JOHN 19:30

When Jesus had received the sour wine, he said, "It is finished," and he bowed his head and gave up his spirit.

UNLOCK THE DOORS

What specific things do you observe the disciples doing in this chapter that demonstrate that they had very little faith? Put an * in your Bible next to those examples. One unbelievable example is found in verse 26. Keep in mind as you read this verse that the disciples had already seen Jesus Christ alive by the time they were gathered again. He had already talked to them and shown them the scars on His body. They gathered again, and verse 26 tells us that the doors were locked just as they had been in verse 19. Why? Could it be that they were still afraid of the Jews? Wouldn't you assume after experiencing all they had up to that point, they would have had no fear and would have left the doors wide open? How similar we act today. We have had God do the miraculous in our lives, and yet we later find ourselves overcome with fear wondering what will happen next. Could you have an area of your life where you have the doors locked in fear? How can you allow what you know to be true of God begin to open the doors in your life?

SAY WHAT?
Observation: What do I see?

SO WHAT?
Interpretation: What does it mean?

NOW WHAT?
Application: How does it apply to me?

THEN WHAT?
Implementation: What do I do?

JOHN 20:26

Eight days later, his disciples were inside again, and Thomas was with them. Although the doors were locked, Jesus came and stood among them and said, "Peace be with you."

A SECOND CHANCE

SAY WHAT?
Observation: What do I see?

SO WHAT?
Interpretation: What does it mean?

NOW WHAT?
Application: How does it apply to me?

THEN WHAT?
Implementation: What do I do?

Describe the different emotions Peter must have experienced in this chapter. From overwhelming guilt over his denial to overwhelming hope that he could be forgiven and still used by God. Peter denied Christ in public, in a dreadful way. He had denied Christ by telling people he did not even know Him. As a result, he had given up and gone back to fishing, even taking some of the disciples with him. He had been given a position of leadership. He had every opportunity to become someone who accomplished great things for God. But, he blew it. Jesus took Peter aside and let him know that he was forgiven and could be given another chance. In a word, he got a "do over." Christ told him He still expected him to take care of His sheep. Everyone of us can have the same opportunity. Like in Peter's life, God's forgiveness provides for us a "do over" - an opportunity to confess our sin and have God put our lives back together. As you look forward to next month, spend time today reviewing this past month. Confess your sin and begin tomorrow with a clean slate.

JOHN 21:19
(This he said to show by what kind of death he was to glorify God.) And after saying this he said to him, "Follow me."

>> MILITARYDEVOTIONAL.COM

 @MILITARYDEVOS

 FACEBOOK.COM/MILITARYDEVOS

MILITARY
OTD

OCTOBER

★★★★

MONTHLY
PRAYER SHEET

"... THE PRAYER OF A RIGHTEOUS PERSON HAS GREAT POWER AS IT IS WORKING."

JAMES 5:16

I NEED TO REACH OUT TO...	HOW I WILL DO IT...	HOW IT WENT...

OTHER REQUEST	HOW ANSWERED	DATE

MONTHLY
★ MISSION SHEET ★

≫ NAME: ....

This sheet is designed to help you make personal commitments each month that will help you grow in your walk with God. Fill it out by determining:

★ What will push you.
★ What you think you can achieve.

≫ PERSONAL DEVOTIONS:

I will commit to read the OnTrack Bible passage and devotional thought .... day(s) each week this month.

≫ CHURCH/CHAPEL ATTENDANCE:

I will attend Church/Chapel .... time(s) this month.
I will attend .... time(s) this month.

≫ SCRIPTURE MEMORY:

I will memorize .... key verse(s) from the daily OnTrack Devotions this month.

≫ OUTREACH:

I will share Christ with .... person/people this month.
I will serve my local church/chapel this month by ....
....
....

≫ OTHER ACTIVITIES:

List any other opportunities such as events, prayer group, etc..., you will participate in this month. ....
....
....
....
....
....

Determine to begin today a journey that will last a lifetime, and will change your life forever.

YOUR REPUTATION

If you were not around and people were talking about you, what would they say? What words would they use to describe you? Would they talk about how committed to Christ you are? Would they say they respect you? In today's reading, we learn something about the Christians in Rome that hopefully can be said about each of us. Paul wrote to the Romans to explain the gospel, the message of Christ. He told them he had been faithfully praying for them and that he thanked God for them because their "faith is being reported all over the world." What an incredible statement! When conversation turned to the Christians in Rome, it was about their great faith. In fact, their commitment to Christ was known by people all over the world. It must grieve the heart of God when we claim to be believers in Jesus Christ yet are not known as people of faith. It ought to be said of each of us as individuals and corporately as a church, that we are people of faith. The world ought to be able to know just by observing a believer that he loves and serves God. It is a poor testimony if the world can't see our faith lived out in every circumstance in our lives.

★★★★

ROMANS 1:8

First, I thank my God through Jesus Christ for all of you, because your faith is proclaimed in all the world.

SAY WHAT?
Observation: What do I see?

SO WHAT?
Interpretation: What does it mean?

NOW WHAT?
Application: How does it apply to me?

THEN WHAT?
Implementation: What do I do?

NO EXCUSE

SAY WHAT?
How do we see God's eternal power in the world?

SO WHAT?
How is God's divine nature seen in the world?

NOW WHAT?
How can you help an unbeliever see God in this world?

THEN WHAT?
In light of the passage, what personal commitment can you make?

According to this passage, what can people conclude about God just by general things they observe in the world? This section of Scripture teaches us an important truth and reveals two things that can be discovered about God just by observing our world. God has created a world that reveals to everyone, no matter where he lives, that there is a God. In fact, the created world reveals to all of us God's otherwise invisible qualities. The first invisible quality seen in the world is God's eternal power. Mankind can look all around him and see that God is omnipotent. His power is unlimited. Second, the created world reveals God's divine nature to mankind. It demonstrates that God is a God of love and mercy. He cares about us as individuals. And who is able to see these things about God? Everyone! God has not hidden them but has made it plain to all men. If they miss it, they do so because they have suppressed the truth in their own minds. All of mankind will stand before God without excuse because God has made known to man that He does exist. How we respond to this knowledge determines where we will be spending eternity.

★★★★

ROMANS 1:20

For his invisible attributes, namely, his eternal power and divine nature, have been clearly perceived, ever since the creation of the world, in the things that have been made...

The book of Proverbs was designed to help us in "attaining wisdom and discipline; in understanding words of insight; in acquiring a disciplined and prudent life, doing what is right and just and fair; in giving prudence to the simple, knowledge and discretion to the young." As you read through this chapter, write down the verses that are most significant to you in your present circumstances.

VERSE | WHAT TRUTH IT COMMUNICATES | HOW IT IMPACTS MY LIFE

SAY WHAT?
Observation: What do I see?

SO WHAT?
Interpretation: What does it mean?

NOW WHAT?
Application: How does it apply to me?

THEN WHAT?
Implementation: What do I do?

What attribute of God's character often leads people to repentance? We might think that it would be His justice or His wrath. We might think what God needs to do is hammer people into repentance. In today's reading however, we realize it is something different. According to verse four, it is God's kindness that leads people to repentance. It is incredible to grasp the contrast shown here between God's kindness and man's stubbornness. Paul wrote in the previous chapter that all men stand before God condemned. Man cannot save himself and is guilty before God. Although every man deserves hell, God's kindness has provided a way of escape. God sent His Son to the earth that we might find forgiveness of sin. According to Paul, God's riches, tolerance, and patience ought to bring us to the point of repentance. Instead, man responds to such kindness with stubbornness and with an unrepentant heart. Instead of seeking after God, man is self seeking and rejects the truth. Man, by nature, would rather follow after evil than live by the plan of God. How have you responded to God's kindness and grace? Does it lead you to greater service?

ROMANS 2:4
Or do you presume on the riches of his kindness and forbearance and patience, not knowing that God's kindness is meant to lead you to repentance?

PRACTICE WHAT YOU PREACH

How is Paul's message in today's reading true of Christians today? Do you notice any similarities between your church and these Jews? Paul criticized the Jews for an attitude that is not only wrong, but one which could cost them eternity. They thought that because they were Jews by birth, it gave them certain privileges. They were Jews who were familiar with the law; therefore they believed that their knowledge gave them a relationship with God which made them superior to others. They felt that they had the right to instruct others and even guide people in issues of life. But Paul revealed the error of their attitude. Just because the knowledge they claimed was God's truth, it had not changed them. They taught that it was wrong to steal, but they stole. They bragged about their relationship with God, yet dishonored Him with their actions. Christians often have this same attitude. They feel superior to others because they "know" the truth. They talk as if they have a relationship with God, yet live lives no differently than the unbelievers who surround them. Would this described you?

SAY WHAT?

In what ways are Christians like the Jews in today's reading?

SO WHAT?

Why is it so easy for Christians to fall into this trap?

NOW WHAT?

What can you do to prevent this kind of attitude from developing in your own heart or in the hearts of others?

THEN WHAT?

In light of this passage, what personal commitment can you make?

ROMANS 2:24

For as it is written, "The name of God is blasphemed among the Gentiles because of you."

SAY WHAT?
Observation: What do I see?

SO WHAT?
Interpretation: What does it mean?

NOW WHAT?
Application: How does it apply to me?

THEN WHAT?
Implementation: What do I do?

If you were to condense the point of today's reading into one sentence, what would it be? Paul is trying to illustrate to us that all men stand before God condemned and can be forgiven only by faith in Jesus Christ alone. The Jews believed that in order to be right with God, one had to observe the Old Testament law. Paul is showing them that they could not earn their way into heaven, even by observing the law. Paul demonstrated that the law showed people only that they stood before God condemned. It was designed to reveal how much they needed a Savior, not to provide them with a means to "earn" salvation. In verse 28, he said again that one is declared righteous by faith alone and not works. He has shown that this salvation is available to everyone. Everyone is a sinner, condemned before God and everyone can find forgiveness through faith in Jesus Christ. You can't attain heaven or a relationship with God by your effort or your merit, even if your effort includes very good things. Who, in your world, needs to know that he stands before God condemned, and that Christ has provided a way for him to be forgiven? Will you tell them?

★★★★

ROMANS 3:28
For we hold that one is justified by faith apart from works of the law.

NOT BY WORKS

Up to this point in his letter, Paul has been working to convince the Romans that salvation was by grace and not by works. How does today's passage support this position? Paul illustrates it by using Abraham, the father of the Jews, and someone about whom they would have knowledge. In Abraham's life, salvation came through grace and not as a result of his works. If salvation came to Abraham by grace, then certainly our salvation would come by grace as well. Paul quoted from the Old Testament in verse three to prove this point. He used the Old Testament account to show the readers that Abraham was not even circumcised when God declared him righteous. That alone would demonstrate to the Jews that his works could not have made him righteous, because he was declared righteous before he obeyed the law. Paul also uses another significant man in Jewish history, David. He illustrates from David's own words that righteousness comes by grace through faith. Realizing that standing righteous before God is nothing we can earn, our hearts ought to be filled with humble gratitude to God for providing salvation through Jesus Christ.

★★★★

ROMANS 4:3

For what does the Scripture say? "Abraham believed God, and it was counted to him as righteousness."

SAY WHAT?

Observation: What do I see?

SO WHAT?

Interpretation: What does it mean?

NOW WHAT?

Application: How does it apply to me?

THEN WHAT?

Implementation: What do I do?

MILITARYDEVOTIONAL.COM
🐦 @MILITARYDEVOS

GREAT FAITH

SAY WHAT?

In what areas of your life is your faith weak?

SO WHAT?

How does it show up?

NOW WHAT?

What can you do to begin growing in your level of faith?

THEN WHAT?

In light of this passage, what personal commitment can you make?

How would you describe your faith? On a scale of 1--10, 1 being no faith and 10 being never any doubt, how would you rate it? Today, we read an impressive statement about Abraham's faith. Verse 21 tells us that Abraham was, "fully persuaded that God had the power to do what He had promised." God said it, and Abraham simply believed God would do what He had said. Abraham was a 10. He did not doubt or wonder if what God said was true. He did not build into his life something to fall back on in case God's plan didn't work out. He just believed God. We can't help but be impressed with a faith that demanded he leave home and go to a land that God would show him, believe God would give him a child in his old age and then be willing to sacrifice that only child. How does your faith compare to Abraham's? How does your level of faith show up in your daily living? It is sobering to realize that without faith, it is impossible to please God. What would it take for you to become a person of great faith? What can you do today to begin the process of seeing your faith grow? Why not find someone who can help you take those first steps of growth.

ROMANS 4:21

...fully convinced that God was able to do what he had promised.

PERSEVERENCE

Why would perseverance be worth suffering for? Paul tells the Romans in today's reading that they should rejoice in their suffering because it produces perseverance. The definition of perseverance is steadfast endurance, standing our ground, never giving up. James 1:2-4 tells us that, in order for us to be mature and complete, not lacking in anything, perseverance must finish its work. Perseverance is a quality then, which is necessary to be spiritually mature. In this passage, Paul tells us that perseverance produces character, and character produces hope. We can conclude then, that without suffering we have no perseverance, and without perseverance we have no maturity, no character, and no hope. Without perseverance we are lacking in many areas of our spiritual lives. In light of how important perseverance is to our spiritual lives, Paul encourages us to rejoice when suffering comes our way. It is the only way to acquire perseverance and it is a part of life. How are you responding to the suffering that God has allowed you to experience in your life? Rejoice, your suffering is producing character that will change you!

★★★★

ROMANS 5:3

More than that, we rejoice in our sufferings, knowing that suffering produces endurance,

SAY WHAT?

Observation: What do I see?

SO WHAT?

Interpretation: What does it mean?

NOW WHAT?

Application: How does it apply to me?

THEN WHAT?

Implementation: What do I do?

MILITARYDEVOTIONAL.COM
🐦 @MILITARYDEVOS

The book of Proverbs was designed to help us in "attaining wisdom and discipline; in understanding words of insight; in acquiring a disciplined and prudent life, doing what is right and just and fair; in giving prudence to the simple, knowledge and discretion to the young." As you read through this chapter, write down the verses that are most significant to you in your present circumstances.

VERSE | WHAT TRUTH IT COMMUNICATES | HOW IT IMPACTS MY LIFE

RESISTING SIN

One of the greatest struggles we have as Christians is gaining victory over sin. In today's and tomorrow's reading, we will learn five keys to being able to gain victory over sin. Mark them in your Bible. First, Paul says that we must know the right things. We must understand and believe what Scripture teaches. It tells us that we were baptized into Christ; therefore, we have new life. We also know that our old self was crucified with Christ. It is dead and has no control over us. Second, we must count ourselves dead to sin. The word "count" here means letting what you know to be true in your head make its way down to your heart. Third, offer yourselves to God. The progression Paul has in mind is to know the truth, feel it in your gut, and then give yourself to God and do not let sin have any control in your life. Yield to God, not to sin. You can say no to sin and live a victorious Christian life. We must know the truth, believe the truth, and then live out the truth. Of these three, which one do you need to begin working on today? What can you do to start the process? Who can you ask to help you? Living victoriously is not only possible, it is worth it.

ROMANS 6:2

By no means! How can we who died to sin still live in it?

SAY WHAT?
Observation: What do I see?

SO WHAT?
Interpretation: What does it mean?

NOW WHAT?
Application: How does it apply to me?

THEN WHAT?
Implementation: What do I do?

OVERCOMING SIN

SAY WHAT?

What precepts from this chapter do you need to grasp as truth?

SO WHAT?

What can you do to help this truth to make its way to your heart?

NOW WHAT?

In what ways can you be more obedient rather than sin?

THEN WHAT?

How can you serve righteousness as a slave in your day to day living?

In today's reading Paul gives to us the final ingredients for being able to gain victory over sin. If you have not read the first part of the chapter or the devotional thought from yesterday go back and read it so that you can understand the entire flow of this chapter. The fourth thing we must do to gain victory over sin is to obey. Sin is not your master and you do not have to obey it. In fact since you are now a slave to righteousness, having been saved, you must now obey God and not give in to sin. The reality is that you have a choice. You have been set free. You can just say no to sin and yes to righteousness! Fifth, Paul says to serve righteousness as if you were a slave. Paul did not say that you will never sin, but that you do not have to sin. We are not helpless against sin's dominance after trusting Christ. Since you have become a slave to righteousness, serve it as a slave. As we have seen from this text, to gain victory one must know the truth believe it in his heart, offer himself to God, obey what He commands and serve righteousness as a slave. Use the sheet below to help you make the changes you should to live victoriously.

ROMANS 6:18

...and, having been set free from sin, have become slaves of righteousness.

THE LAW

Why did God give the Law to the nation of Israel? What did He want them to see from having it? If we follow what Paul wrote in this chapter without thinking through it, we may come to the conclusion that he thought the Law was a negative thing. Paul anticipated this conclusion and addressed it by giving to us four facts concerning the Law. First, he explains that the Law reveals what sin is. Without the Law, we would not know what God considers sin. Second, the Law stirs sin in people. When we know what God expects or what His Law states, our sinful nature desires to disobey it. Third, the Law left man ruined. Man realized that he had no power over sin and gave in to it. Fourth, the Law shows the sinfulness of man. It clearly demonstrates that, without a Savior, man is doomed. There is no way man can overcome sin and fulfill the righteous requirements of the Law without the Savior. Without the Law we don't see our need for help or turn to God as the only way of solving our sin problem. God desires that all of us come to the point where we acknowledge who we are and what He has done. You cannot live righteously without the Savior. The law proved it.

ROMANS 7:24

Wretched man that I am! Who will deliver me from this body of death?

SAY WHAT?

Observation: What do I see?

SO WHAT?

Interpretation: What does it mean?

NOW WHAT?

Application: How does it apply to me?

THEN WHAT?

Implementation: What do I do?

SAY WHAT?
List characteristics of those who live by the Spirit.

SO WHAT?
List characteristics of those who do not live by the Spirit.

NOW WHAT?
Which characteristics from each of the above lists describe you?

THEN WHAT?
What personal commitment will you make today?

What happens to those who trust Christ as Savior? Today's reading gives us the answer to that question. These verses give us a clear contrast of those who live by the Spirit and those who do not. Use the chart below to record the characteristics of those who live by the Spirit and those who do not. As you do, ask yourself which ones describe your life. What you discover will help you know the steps you need to take in order to progress in your walk with God. Be honest.

ROMANS 8:2
For the law of the Spirit of life has set you free in Christ Jesus from the law of sin and death.

BECOMING LIKE CHRIST

The substance of what we have learned to this point from reading Romans is incredible. These verses are no different. Paul's letter has demonstrated to us that we can have victory over sin and live a righteous life. Today we see that the process of becoming like Christ is guaranteed! Although it is a difficult process, and we may wonder at times if we will ever get there, God has guaranteed that it will happen. Paul tells us in verses 28-30 that God works out "everything" for good. You see, those God saved, He has predestined to be conformed to the likeness of His Son. You and I who know Jesus Christ as our Savior will become like Jesus Christ. The events of salvation are not only enough to save us and get us to heaven, but are also enough to make us like Christ. To drive the point home, Paul listed the kinds of things we fear might keep us from becoming like Christ. In verse 37 he states that we are more than conquerors. He re-emphasized that we will become like Christ. Not only is our salvation guaranteed but our sanctification is as well. Use these facts to encourage yourself and others to press on. All things work together for good.

★★★★

ROMANS 8:37

No, in all these things we are more than conquerors through him who loved us.

SAY WHAT?
Observation: What do I see?

SO WHAT?
Interpretation: What does it mean?

NOW WHAT?
Application: How does it apply to me?

THEN WHAT?
Implementation: What do I do?

SAY WHAT?

Why do people have such a hard time grasping the idea election?

SO WHAT?

What impact does this truth have on how we view our salvation?

NOW WHAT?

How should you respond in light of the fact that God chose

THEN WHAT?

What personal commitment will you make based on today's reading?

Does God choose some to be saved? According to today's reading the answer is yes. Does that mean that God chooses some people to go to hell? According to this passage the answer is no. While this might seem to be a contradiction, this passage helps us understand election more clearly. Paul tells us that men come to Christ according to God's purpose, not because of what they have done. He illustrates this truth with the life of Rebekah. Before the twins, Esau & Jacob, were even born and could do good or evil, God chose Jacob over Esau. Does that make God unjust? No. All men throughout all time deserve to go to hell. No one who goes to hell can say he deserved anything else. God has simply chosen to bestow mercy on some. We can accuse God of having selective mercy, but we can never accuse Him of being unfair because we all deserve hell. God wants those of us who have received Christ by faith to know we had nothing to do with our salvation. We should have hearts that are filled with humble gratitude for what God has given to us and serve Him with love and devotion every day of our lives. We have what we don't deserve!

★★★★

ROMANS 9:16

So then it depends not on human will or exertion, but on God, who has mercy.

The book of Proverbs was designed to help us in "attaining wisdom and discipline; in understanding words of insight; in acquiring a disciplined and prudent life, doing what is right and just and fair; in giving prudence to the simple, knowledge and discretion to the young." As you read through this chapter, write down the verses that are most significant to you in your present circumstances.

VERSE	WHAT TRUTH IT COMMUNICATES	HOW IT IMPACTS MY LIFE

BY FAITH ALONE

SAY WHAT?
Observation: What do I see?

SO WHAT?
Interpretation: What does it mean?

NOW WHAT?
Application: How does it apply to me?

THEN WHAT?
Implementation: What do I do?

When the portion of this letter from Saturday was read to the Jews it must have shocked them. In fact, Paul says as much in verses 30 and 31. How could the Jews, who pursue righteousness with a great deal of effort, miss salvation? Even more astonishing, how could the Gentiles, who did not pursue righteousness, obtain salvation? The key to understanding this truth is what the motives were for pursuing righteousness and how it was pursued. The Jews were trying to obtain righteousness through good works. In their pride, they refused to accept the fact that righteousness was out of their reach. Their pride was so great that instead of allowing the Law to demonstrate salvation could not be earned, they continued to try to earn it. The Gentiles came to God by faith knowing they could never earn salvation on their own. Pride did not get in the way of their salvation. The Gentiles in humility, received by faith what the Jews sought after with great effort, but failed to receive. Salvation is available to those who realize they could never earn their way into heaven. Are you one of those people? Pride will prevent many from accepting God's gift.

★★★★

ROMANS 9:30
What shall we say, then? That Gentiles who did not pursue righteousness have attained it, that is, a righteousness that is by faith.

HOW WILL THEY HEAR?

Since God chooses those who are going to be saved,does that mean we do not have to do our part to witness to people? You might conclude so if you failed to read this chapter. While it is true that those who are to be saved will become saved because of what God does,we still must do our part to share the message of Christ with them. We find in these verses two principles that confirm our responsibility. First,in verse eleven we see that everyone who calls on the name of the Lord will be saved. There is no difference between Jew or Gentile. Salvation is available to everyone and we must demonstrate that by sharing the message of the gospel with all people. Second,verses fourteen and fifteen clearly state that people will only respond to the message if they first hear it. The means by which God has chosen to make the message known is through His children. You and I have the awesome responsibility of taking the message to people so that God can enable them to respond. These verses should motivate us to spread the gospel to every corner of the world. People who are waiting to hear the message. Will you be the one to tell them?

SAY WHAT?

How can you better prepare yourself to share the message of the Gospel with anyone at any time?

SO WHAT?

How can you maximize your opportunities to share the Gospel with people?

NOW WHAT?

Name some friends and family members who need to hear the Gospel. How and when will you tell them?

THEN WHAT?

In light of this passage,what personal commitment can you make?

★★★★

ROMANS 10:14

How then will they call on him in whom they have not believed? And how are they to believe in him of whom they have never heard? And how are they to hear without someone preaching?

MILITARYDEVOTIONAL.COM
🐦 @MILITARYDEVOS

SAY WHAT?
Observation: What do I see?

SO WHAT?
Interpretation: What does it mean?

NOW WHAT?
Application: How does it apply to me?

THEN WHAT?
Implementation: What do I do?

Are God's promises to Israel changed in light of what we have been learning in Romans? Are those promises transferred to those of us who have accepted Christ? After hearing the letter, some of the Jews must have wondered if the church was going to replace Israel in light of God's promises. Paul clearly states that God has not rejected the Jews or shut them out from salvation. He will keep for Himself a remnant who have accepted Christ, and will fulfill the promises He made through these Jews. God is currently allowing Gentiles to be saved and enjoy what He first offered to the Jews. Since many Jews have rejected the Gospel, God has permitted Gentiles the opportunity to be "grafted in." We who are not Jews should be humbled to know that we have been given this opportunity to be saved along with the Jews. God is not finished with the Jews, nor has He rejected them. The promises He made to them through Abraham and David will one day be fulfilled. Likewise, we can be sure that the promises He made to us will also be fulfilled. We too will enjoy the blessings of His promises. Do His promises motivate you to share the good news?

ROMANS 11:1
I ask, then, has God rejected his people? By no means! For I myself am an Israelite, a descendant of Abraham, a member of the tribe of Benjamin.

OUR PERSONAL DOXOLOGY

What is a doxology? A doxology is an expression of praise to God. It is the response of a heart filled with the wonder of God. It is often found in Scripture after a description of truth such as we find in today's reading. Paul has written about the wonder of salvation for many chapters. He explained in his letter to the Romans how God made it possible for all to have eternal life and to have their sins forgiven. The more he wrote and described all God did for us, the more praise flowed from his heart. This doxology flows out under the inspiration of the Holy Spirit. As we read it, we can see how Paul viewed his God and the incredible things God had done for him. Have you ever written a doxology? Have you ever been so moved by what you heard or discovered that you wanted to tell God how wonderful He is or how good He has been? Why not take time today to do just that. Think back on what God has been teaching you and how much He has blessed your life with. Write your own doxology to Him. Why not also take some time to share it with a friend.

★★★★

ROMANS 11:33

Oh, the depth of the riches and wisdom and knowledge of God! How unsearchable are his judgments and how inscrutable his ways!

SAY WHAT?

God you are:

SO WHAT?

--

NOW WHAT?

I praise You because You have:

THEN WHAT?

--

BEING TRANSFORMED

SAY WHAT?
Observation: What do I see?

SO WHAT?
Interpretation: What does it mean?

NOW WHAT?
Application: How does it apply to me?

THEN WHAT?
Implementation: What do I do?

In today's reading, Paul makes a major shift in how he has been writing in this book. Did you notice it? He has been discussing doctrinal issues and how we ought to live in light of the truth he has described. He now begins with the practical ways these truths ought to impact our lives. One of the ways found in this section is to not allow ourselves to be conformed to the world. And how do we keep ourselves from being conformed to the world? The answer to that question is simple. It is just hard to accomplish. To keep ourselves from being conformed to the world, we must be transformed. How? According to verse two, we are transformed by renewing our minds. This is the key to not allowing ourselves to be conformed to the world. We renew our minds by saturating it daily with God's Word, the Scripture. We renew our minds by memorizing Scripture so that we can recall it when we need to. We renew our minds by refusing to allow the pollution of the world to enter it. Renewing our minds means controlling what we allow to enter into it. It is simple to do, but hard to carry out. We must all be aware of what we allow in our minds. Have you been?

★★★★

ROMANS 12:2
Do not be conformed to this world, but be transformed by the renewal of your mind, that by testing you may discern what is the will of God, what is good and acceptable and perfect.

OUR "ASSOCIATIONS"

If we looked at the people you spend your time with, what would we discover? What does their spiritual condition tell us about yours? What does their popularity tell us about you? What does how popular the people I hang around with have to do with who I am? According to today's reading, the answer to all those questions is: a lot! Paul gives us instructions about dealing with people. He talks about those who persecute you and those who are your enemies. Then, in verse sixteen he makes an important statement. He says, "be willing to associate with people of low position." Paul realized that pride will keep you from doing just that. If you only hang around with the popular or beautiful people, then you are proud. Paul tells us to stop being proud and be willing to spend time with people of low position. He wants you to invite them to a party you are planning to attend. Ask them to sit with you at church. Sit by them in the chow hall. The question still remains, what do the people you always spend your time with tell you about yourself? When is the last time you associated with or felt compassion for people of low position?

SAY WHAT?

How can you better "associate" with people of low position?

SO WHAT?

Why is it that you do not do this more often?

NOW WHAT?

What needs to change in your life for you to fulfill God's expectations in this area?

THEN WHAT?

In light of this passage, what personal commitment can you make?

★★★★

ROMANS 12:16

Live in harmony with one another. Do not be haughty, but associate with the lowly. Never be wise in your own sight.

The book of Proverbs was designed to help us in "attaining wisdom and discipline; in understanding words of insight; in acquiring a disciplined and prudent life, doing what is right and just and fair; in giving prudence to the simple, knowledge and discretion to the young." As you read through this chapter, write down the verses that are most significant to you in your present circumstances.

VERSE | WHAT TRUTH IT COMMUNICATES | HOW IT IMPACTS MY LIFE

THE 13/14 PRINCIPLE

What do you think about during the day? If we could play a video of your thoughts today, would you be comfortable if anyone saw it? In today's reading, we have one of the most important principles in the Bible in our battle against sin. It is found in verse fourteen. In fact, you could call it the 13/14 principle. In this verse, Paul tells us to clothe ourselves with the Lord Jesus Christ and to not even think about how to gratify the desires of our sinful nature. It goes beyond the act of sin, to actually keeping us from thinking of ways to entertain or contemplate sin. The implication here is that while channel surfing by stations we know something sinful is about to appear, we do not "accidentally" pass that channel again, but skip it all together. When we could mistakenly see something in a store or hear something if we linger, we move quickly away so that we do not see or hear. It is making our priority the prevention of any impure sight or sound from entering our minds. We do not put ourselves in a position which makes it easy to sin. We guard our minds and allow no thought to enter which dishonors God. How are you doing in your life with the 13/14 principle?

★★★★

ROMANS 13:14

But put on the Lord Jesus Christ, and make no provision for the flesh, to gratify its desires.

SAY WHAT?

Observation: What do I see?

SO WHAT?

Interpretation: What does it mean?

NOW WHAT?

Application: How does it apply to me?

THEN WHAT?

Implementation: What do I do?

MAKING GOOD CHOICES

SAY WHAT?
What are some choices you currently have to make?

SO WHAT?
How can you make sure you are motivated by pleasing God?

NOW WHAT?
How can you make sure to remember you will give an account for your decision?

THEN WHAT?
In light of this passage, what personal commitment can you make?

When you are faced with an important decision, how do you decide what to do? If you currently find yourself in a situation which requires a decision, you will find great encouragement from today's reading. Paul tells us that when we need to make choices in our lives, we need to keep two important thoughts in mind. First, our motives need to be pure and our lives, lived unto the Lord. Our desire ought to be to please Him and bring glory to His name, not what appears to be the most comfortable or easiest for us. Even in areas that are seemingly unimportant, like eating. Second, we must keep in mind that we will all appear before the judgment seat to give an account for the choices we have made. It is not others who evaluate the choices we make, it is God Himself who will evaluate each of our choices. With these two thoughts in mind, how do the choices you have made recently measure up? Have you thought about what other people are doing and what they might think of your decisions as opposed to what God thinks? Remember, do everything as unto the Lord, and never forget it is before Him you will stand to give an account. Pleasing Him is all that matters.

ROMANS 14:12
So then each of us will give an account of himself to God.

MAKING GOOD CHOICES

Today we find an important principle directing how we ought to respond to our brothers and sisters in Christ. It is one that is often misunderstood. Paul tells us that in light of what he previously wrote, we are to stop judging their choices and make up our minds to not put a stumbling block or obstacle in our brother's way by our own. What implications does that have? It means that we are not to engage in any activity that would result in a weaker brother being led into sin. We should carefully consider what we do in light of what a young Christian would think. We may tempt him to sin. How would we do this? It's often in areas like music or movies. Many times a weaker brother evaluates right or wrong based on the choices of those he looks up to. Some things, which may be fine for us, may not be for someone else. Soon he may be making unwise decisions. Some may also stumble when our actions violate their consciences. We may engage in an activity which makes them uncomfortable. If and when you do, do you justify your actions, belittle him, or stop what you are doing? Our choices should always be regulated by their impact on others. Are yours?

★ ★ ★ ★

ROMANS 14:13

Therefore let us not pass judgment on one another any longer; but rather decide never to put a stumbling block or hindrance in the way of a brother.

SAY WHAT?

Observation: What do I see?

SO WHAT?

Interpretation: What does it mean?

NOW WHAT?

Application: How does it apply to me?

THEN WHAT?

Implementation: What do I do?

MILITARYDEVOTIONAL.COM
🐦 @MILITARYDEVOS

THE KEY TO ENDURANCE

SAY WHAT?
In what ways has Scripture changed your life?

SO WHAT?
What passages have you read recently that have given you hope?

NOW WHAT?
What have you read recently that has helped you endure a difficult situation?

THEN WHAT?
What personal commitment can you make about your Bible reading?

What impact does Scripture have on you? Make a list of some of the ways it has changed you recently. An important way Scripture ought to influence you is found in verse four of today's reading. Did you notice it? One reason God deals with the many topics, issues, and expectations in Scripture is to encourage us and to increase our endurance. As we read and spend time in it, Scripture enables us to endure painful circumstances. It provides us the strength to keep pressing on. People who spend little or no time in the Scripture are people who are more prone to quit or give up under pressure. And the result in their life? They lose HOPE! God wants to give us hope, and He gives it through His Word. When we feel like giving up, we need to go to the Word. When we are discouraged, we need to go to the Word and in it find encouragement and endurance. As a result, God will flood our hearts with hope. Too often, when we are discouraged or feel like giving up, Scripture is the last place we go. Make the reading of God's Word THE priority of your life. Contained in the pages is everything you need. With every need, open the Word. Don't go a day without reading it.

★★★★

ROMANS 15:4
For whatever was written in former days was written for our instruction, that through endurance and through the encouragement of the Scriptures we might have hope.

WHAT ARE YOU KNOWN FOR?

If a friend of yours was asked to list three characteristics that you're known for, which ones would he choose? Hopefully, the traits would be the three that Paul used in today's reading to describe the Romans. First, he said that they were full of goodness. They were morally right and were known for their virtue. Would people describe you in this way? Second, they were complete in knowledge. That did not mean that they had arrived and knew everything about the Bible, but that they were doctrinally sound. They must have spent time in the Word and paid attention to solid Bible teaching. Would people say you are complete in knowledge? Third, they were competent to instruct. The word used here for instruct is most often translated admonish. It is not teaching or leading a Bible study, but giving counsel, encouragement, warning, or a rebuke to people as you have opportunity. Are you competent to instruct others? Is your lifestyle and level of Biblical knowledge such that you could encourage or counsel others? What would it take for you to become someone who is known by these characteristics? What will it take to become like the Romans?

SAY WHAT?

What would you need to change to become one konwn for being full of goodness?

SO WHAT?

What would it take for you to be known for being complete in knowledge?

NOW WHAT?

What would it take for you to be competent to instruct?

THEN WHAT?

In light of this passage, what personal commitment can you make?

ROMANS 15:14

I myself am satisfied about you, my brothers, that you yourselves are full of goodness, filled with all knowledge and able to instruct one another.

MILITARYDEVOTIONAL.COM
@MILITARYDEVOS

ENCOURAGING OTHERS

SAY WHAT?
Observation: What do I see?

SO WHAT?
Interpretation: What does it mean?

NOW WHAT?
Application: How does it apply to me?

THEN WHAT?
Implementation: What do I do?

Think through the past few years and name the people who have been an influence in your life. Have you taken the time to let them know how much you appreciated it? In this chapter Paul did just that. He closed his letter by naming individuals who had encouraged and influenced his life. How encouraging it must have been for Phoebe to know that she had touched the life of Paul and have her name written in this letter. When the letter was read publicly, those whose names were mentioned must have really been blessed and encouraged. Too often, we do not take the time to let people know the affect they have had on our lives. In fact, the people who have touched our lives the most probably do not even know they have done so. Why not take some time today to tell someone you know how much you appreciate them and the influence they have had on your life. It would encourage them so much. Why not also think of ways you can become a person who is touching the lives of others more often. It would go a long way to help keep the church encouraged.

ROMANS 16:2
that you may welcome her in the Lord in a way worthy of the saints, and help her in whatever she may need from you, for she has been a patron of many and of myself as well.

The book of Proverbs was designed to help us in "attaining wisdom and discipline; in understanding words of insight; in acquiring a disciplined and prudent life, doing what is right and just and fair; in giving prudence to the simple, knowledge and discretion to the young." As you read through this chapter, write down the verses that are most significant to you in your present circumstances.

VERSE | WHAT TRUTH IT COMMUNICATES | HOW IT IMPACTS MY LIFE

» MILITARYDEVOTIONAL.COM

 @MILITARYDEVOS

 FACEBOOK.COM/MILITARYDEVOS

MILITARY
OTD

NOVEMBER
★★★★

MONTHLY PRAYER SHEET

I NEED TO REACH OUT TO...	HOW I WILL DO IT...	HOW IT WENT...

OTHER REQUEST	HOW ANSWERED	DATE

MONTHLY
MISSION SHEET

>> Share your personal commitments with those who will help keep you accountable to them.

>> NAME: ....

This sheet is designed to help you make personal commitments each month that will help you grow in your walk with God. Fill it out by determining:

★ What will push you.
★ What you think you can achieve.

>> PERSONAL DEVOTIONS:
I will commit to read the OnTrack Bible passage and devotional thought .... day(s) each week this month.

>> CHURCH/CHAPEL ATTENDANCE:
I will attend Church/Chapel .... time(s) this month.
I will attend .... time(s) this month.

>> SCRIPTURE MEMORY:
I will memorize .... key verse(s) from the daily OnTrack Devotions this month.

>> OUTREACH:
I will share Christ with .... person/people this month.
I will serve my local church/chapel this month by ....
....
....

>> OTHER ACTIVITIES:
List any other opportunities such as events, prayer group, etc..., you will participate in this month. ....
....
....
....
....
....

Determine to begin today a journey that will last a lifetime, and will change your life forever.

THE COST OF FOLLOWING

Imagine while walking home from school, a stranger comes to you and asks you to leave everything to follow him. What would you do? What questions would you ask yourself before making such a decision? From today's reading, we see that this is almost what happened to some of the disciples when Jesus called them to follow Him. What questions do you think they might have asked before making such a commitment? From this passage, we learn that these men left everything to follow Christ. They left their homes, families, jobs, and friends to follow Him. In fact, Scripture says that they not only left, but they did it without delay. They had to be very committed in order to make such a decision. Make a list of three important things in your life. Look at them and ask yourself, "Am I willing to leave these to follow Christ?" Is there an area of your life that you are unwilling to leave behind in order to follow Christ - friends? job? car? Circle the words without delay in verse twenty to remind you of the Godly example of the disciples. God may never ask us to leave our lives behind, but we must be willing to do just that.

★★★★

ROMANS 1:18

And immediately they left their nets and followed him.

SAY WHAT?

What things are people unwilling to leave to follow Christ?

SO WHAT?

Why do you think it is difficult for some to leave those things?

NOW WHAT?

What areas do you need to evaluate in order to be more like the disciples in this passage?

THEN WHAT?

In light of this passage, what personal commitment can you make?

SAY WHAT?
Observation: What do I see?

SO WHAT?
Interpretation: What does it mean?

NOW WHAT?
Application: How does it apply to me?

THEN WHAT?
Implementation: What do I do?

Why did Jesus get up "very early in the morning, while it was still dark" to have His devotions (vs35)? Could it be that it was the only time that He could be alone, not fighting a lot of distractions? Or maybe because He knew they were important and didn't want to begin a day without His time with the Father? Jesus knew each day would be filled with opportunities, and He wanted to be ready to take advantage of them. He knew each day would be filled with temptations, and He wanted to be prepared to resist them. His personal time with God was so important that even though it meant getting up "very early in the morning, while it was still dark," He did so. If it were that important to Jesus, how important does that make it for you and me? Often, we wait until the last part of the day to spend time with God, after we have finished everything else. We never miss a favorite TV show, or time on the phone, or a good meal, but we miss our personal devotions. How important is your time with God each day? What changes do you need to make to be more effective - having them in the morning or more often each week?

★★★★

MARK 1:35

And rising very early in the morning, while it was still dark, he departed and went out to a desolate place, and there he prayed.

The book of Proverbs was designed to help us in "attaining wisdom and discipline; in understanding words of insight; in acquiring a disciplined and prudent life, doing what is right and just and fair; in giving prudence to the simple, knowledge and discretion to the young." As you read through this chapter, write down the verses that are most significant to you in your present circumstances.

VERSE | WHAT TRUTH IT COMMUNICATES | HOW IT IMPACTS MY LIFE

SAY WHAT?

Name someone whom you have a great burden for?

SO WHAT?

What specifically would you like to see God do in his/her life?

NOW WHAT?

What can you do to be used of God to see it happen?

THEN WHAT?

What commitment can you make about what you have written above?

What thoughts do you suppose went through the minds of the men who brought the paralytic to Christ and found when they arrived they could not get in? When they realized the situation, they did not give up, but found another way to get the man to Jesus. They were so convinced that Jesus could heal him and so committed to helping this man that they didn't give up even when it got tough. It is obvious that these men not only believed that Jesus could heal their friend, but were willing to go the extra mile to make it happen. Christ was so impressed with their actions that He healed the paralytic because of the faith of the men on the roof, not the man He healed (vs5). What a thrill to know that likewise, my faith can impact those around me. God does respond to others because of my faith. What a great opportunity this gives us. What actions, similar to what these men did, have you recently taken on behalf of someone else? For whom has God been burdening your heart, letting you know that you need to take steps to help him/her? Circle the words "their faith" in your Bible to remind you of the potential of reaching out.

★★★★

MARK 2:5

And when Jesus saw their faith, he said to the paralytic, "Son, your sins are forgiven."

STUBBORN HEARTS

Why did Jesus become angry with the Pharisees (vs5)? In what way did they demonstrate this attitude in the account that Mark records for us? Jesus performed a miracle right before their eyes, and instead of seeing it for what it was, they saw it as a violation of the law. Unbelievable! They were so stubborn, they were willing to join forces with the terrorists of their day, the Herodians, who were willing to murder people in order to overthrow Rome. These Pharisees missed an exciting miracle because their stubborn hearts would not allow them to see it. How blind they were to the needs of hurting people, and yet so focused on "getting" Jesus. Christ chose to meet the needs of people even if it violated other people's religious traditions and customs. In what way do you demonstrate a stubborn unbelieving heart? Is there someone in your world who has experienced a miracle, but your focus is only on what was wrong with it or why he didn't deserve it? Do you look beyond the circumstances to see hurting people? Could God be angry with you? If you see signs of a stubborn heart, begin to change it today.

SAY WHAT?
Observation: What do I see?

SO WHAT?
Interpretation: What does it mean?

NOW WHAT?
Application: How does it apply to me?

THEN WHAT?
Implementation: What do I do?

MARK 3:5

And he looked around at them with anger, grieved at their hardness of heart, and said to the man, "Stretch out your hand." He stretched it out, and his hand was restored.

MILITARYDEVOTIONAL.COM
@MILITARYDEVOS

THE WILL OF GOD

SAY WHAT?

What do you know to be God's will for your life this week.

SO WHAT?

How can you fulfill the will of God in those areas this week?

NOW WHAT?

What can you do to make sure you are fulfilling the will of God each week in those important areas?

THEN WHAT?

In light of this passage, what personal commitment can you make?

How do you think Jesus' mother and brothers felt when they heard Him say what He did in verses 33-35? What did Jesus mean when He spoke of doing God's will? Sometimes we make doing God's will so much more complicated than it should be. When someone mentions the will of God, some of us get nervous and think of something off in the future. We think it implies life changing decisions like whom to marry, where to go after the military, whether or not to re-enlist, right? NO!!! God's will is simply doing what He says each day of my life. It is living my life every day to please Him and obeying what He tells me in His Word. Whom to marry, what to do next, etc. are decisions based on God's will, but I can be sure I am choosing God's will in those future decisions by making sure I act upon God's will today. It means being faithful today by having my devotions, living consistently at work, resisting temptation, obeying authority, fulfilling commitments I have made, etc. What area of your life should you completely submit to God's control? Begin doing what we know His will is for today and let tomorrow take care of itself.

MARK 3:35

For whoever does the will of God, he is my brother and sister and mother.

LESSONS FROM THE SOIL

In the parable of the sower, identify what the different items represent. What does the seed illustrate? Who is the farmer? What do the soils illustrate? This parable demonstrates to us that people respond to the Gospel message in very different ways. Some reject it immediately after they hear it. Others may appear as if they have accepted it, but over time we see that they did not. The Scriptures teach that over time you will see the true response people have had to the gospel. Another group we see in this parable, are those who walk away from their commitment to Christ when trouble or persecution because of their faith comes. Others get caught up in the desire for money, fame, sports, music, etc. and soon those things take over God's place in their lives. What kind of response have you had to the message of Christ? Has time revealed that you really did accept Christ, or is time telling you that maybe you did not? Take a few minutes today to look at your life and examine the fruit to see what it tells you about your faith. What kind of soil are you? What conclusion have you come to and what are you going to do?

MARK 4:13

And he said to them, "Do you not understand this parable? How then will you understand all the parables?"

SAY WHAT?
Observation: What do I see?

SO WHAT?
Interpretation: What does it mean?

NOW WHAT?
Application: How does it apply to me?

THEN WHAT?
Implementation: What do I do?

ASLEEP AT THE WHEEL

SAY WHAT?
Are you facing a frightening circumstance?

SO WHAT?
What are you afraid will happen?

NOW WHAT?
What has God said in His Word about those things?

THEN WHAT?
What do you need to do to trust Him with this circumstance?

Do you remember the last time you were so frightened that you thought your heart would beat right through your chest or may even stop? What thoughts went through your mind? What do you think went through the minds of the disciples when the storm hit and they were out in the middle of the lake? From their response we see that they thought they were going to die, and they were terrified. Why were they so afraid knowing that Christ was in the boat? Is it possible that even after spending so much time with Him that they did not really understand His capabilities as the Son of God or remember what He had told them? He told them they were going to the other side (vs35). He didn't say "Let's go to the middle of the lake," or "Let's try to get to the other side of the lake." They had either forgotten what He said or they did not trust what He said. In the storm, they did not believe He would protect them. They saw Him sleeping and assumed He did not know or care what was going on in their lives. Are you facing a storm? If it appears that Christ is sleeping, He still has it under control. Don't ignore or forget what He has told you!

★★★★★

MARK 4:40
He said to them, "Why are you so afraid? Have you still no faith?"

TELLING YOUR STORY

Can you imagine the anguish this demon-possessed man must have experienced living in such torment? How horrible his cries in the night must have sounded! No wonder that when he saw Jesus at a distance, he came running. He knew that Jesus Christ could deliver him from his torment and restore him to a new life. Realizing what Christ had done for him by healing him, he came to Jesus later and begged Jesus to let him go with Him. Why do you think Jesus said "no?" Could it be that this man had a story to tell? The story about what Jesus Christ did in his life, the story he could tell better than anyone else? Going away with Jesus would take him from the very people God wanted him to reach out to. So Christ said "no" and sent him back to his world to tell there what God had done for him. He did, and Scripture tells us that all the people were amazed when they realized what God had done for him. Who needs to hear what Christ has done in your life? When was the last time you told anyone what God has done for you? People desperately need to hear our stories so they can know that God will change their lives, too.

★★★★

MARK 5:19

And he did not permit him but said to him, "Go home to your friends and tell them how much the Lord has done for you, and how he has had mercy on you."

SAY WHAT?

Write the name of someone you have a burden for.

SO WHAT?

In what way is your story similar to theirs?

NOW WHAT?

What has God done for you that you would like to see God do for them?

THEN WHAT?

When can you share with that person what God has done for you and the hope that He is offering to them?

MILITARYDEVOTIONAL.COM
@MILITARYDEVOS

The book of Proverbs was designed to help us in "attaining wisdom and discipline; in understanding words of insight; in acquiring a disciplined and prudent life, doing what is right and just and fair; in giving prudence to the simple, knowledge and discretion to the young." As you read through this chapter, write down the verses that are most significant to you in your present circumstances.

VERSE | WHAT TRUTH IT COMMUNICATES | HOW IT IMPACTS MY LIFE

TAKE IT TO GOD

Have you ever been faced with a problem that just never seems to go away? If so, you can find great encouragement from today's reading. In this section of Scripture, we read of a woman who had been struggling with a problem for a very long time. In fact, she had been struggling with it for twelve years and, although she had tried everything to correct it, she found no relief from her suffering. Why do you think she went to Christ? Do you think she had tried everything else, and nothing had worked? All too often we treat our problems this same way. We struggle and struggle trying to correct the problem and never seem to be able to fix it. As a last resort, we take it to God. Then we wonder why we waited so long to give it to Him. What problem are you now facing that you need to turn over to God - an illness? your friends? your future? your family? your career? It is awesome to finally find relief when we give it to Christ! Write down some problems you are facing which you need to give to Christ. Pray, asking God to take them from you. Then, take that sheet of paper and throw it away to remind yourself that they are God's problems now.

★★★★

MARK 5:33

But the woman, knowing what had happened to her, came in fear and trembling and fell down before him and told him the whole truth.

SAY WHAT?

Observation: What do I see?

SO WHAT?

Interpretation: What does it mean?

NOW WHAT?

Application: How does it apply to me?

THEN WHAT?

Implementation: What do I do?

MILITARYDEVOTIONAL.COM
@MILITARYDEVOS

FOLLOW INSTRUCTIONS

SAY WHAT?
Observation: What do I see?

SO WHAT?
Interpretation: What does it mean?

NOW WHAT?
Application: How does it apply to me?

THEN WHAT?
Implementation: What do I do?

What specific instructions did Jesus give to the twelve in today's reading? Why did He give those particular instructions to them? Jesus Christ had a goal in mind for the disciples. He knew what they would face and what they would need to do in order to be successful. According to the passage, it would seem that they went out and followed Christ's instruction, and as a result, many people were helped. How would the results have been different if they had not obeyed the instructions? What if the disciples thought Christ's instructions were stupid and didn't make sense? What if they thought the instructions were unnecessary? Had they not responded to Christ's instructions as they did, they would not have been successful. How well do you follow and obey instructions from your Chain of Command? Maybe the reason you are struggling in certain areas is that you are not following instructions. Today, follow the instructions that God allows to come into your life with an attitude that He would approve of. He has a purpose for everything He does. You will be amazed with the results!

★★★★

MARK 6:12-13
So they went out and proclaimed that people should repent. And they cast out many demons and anointed with oil many who were sick and healed them.

MISSION IMPOSSIBLE

When was the last time you were asked to do something that seemed impossible? In fact, you wondered what in the world was wrong with the person who asked you to do such a thing. For example, feeding 5,000 people when you had little money and almost no food? That is exactly what the disciples were asked to do in this passage. Jesus turned to them and said that He did not want to send the people home hungry and wanted the disciples to feed them all, over 5,000 of them. Although it seemed impossible, the impossible was exactly what Christ had in mind. They looked at the task and decided it could not be done. What they failed to see was the power of God in the midst of the impossible. What is impossible for man is possible with God. What request has God been making of you that, when you think about it, causes you to respond the way the disciples did? What miracle might you be missing because you are concentrating on the impossible and not on God's ability to respond? Ask God to enable you to trust Him and allow Him to do what to you might seem like the impossible. Then watch him work.

MARK 6:37
But he answered them, "You give them something to eat."

SAY WHAT?
In what areas do you find it difficult to trust God?

SO WHAT?
Why is it so hard for you to trust God in those areas?

NOW WHAT?
How can you use today's reading to help you in those areas?

THEN WHAT?
In light of this passage, what personal commitment can you make?

DEFINING A HYPOCRITE

SAY WHAT?
Observation: What do I see?

SO WHAT?
Interpretation: What does it mean?

NOW WHAT?
Application: How does it apply to me?

THEN WHAT?
Implementation: What do I do?

Write out a definition of what a hypocrite is. How close does your definition come to the one Isaiah gives in this passage (vs.7)? He says, basically, that a hypocrite is one who honors God with his lips, or by what he says, but his heart is far from God. A hypocrite is someone whose true walk does not match his talk. The way he acts on the outside is not really what is going on inside. At church he looks very spiritual, but at work no one knows he is a Christian. He sings the songs and talks the talk, but inside he knows that his heart is far from God. How close are you to the definition given here? If we could see the true condition of your heart, would we conclude that your walk matches your talk? Do you talk and act like a Christian, but inside your heart you are really far from God? Simply playing games with people and leading them to a wrong conclusion about you is pitiful. What would it take for you to change your hypocrisy? Make a list of the areas of your life in which you struggle the most with saying the right thing, but not doing the right thing. Make a plan today to begin to change all that and stop being a hypocrite.

★★★★

MARK 7:6
This people honors me with their lips, but their heart is far from me;

CONFUSING INSTRUCTIONS

Where did Jesus take the deaf man in order to heal him? Why did Christ give those instructions to him after He had healed him (vs36)? One would assume that Christ would want everyone to see Him heal the deaf man. One would think that after He healed the man,He would want him to tell everyone what had been done for him. In this case, however, Jesus did not react that way. It must have been hard for the man to follow the instructions and hard to understand why they had been given. What do you imagine, was on Christ's mind that led Him to make such a request. One thing we do know is that it was the best way to respond to what had happened. The hardest times to obey God's commands occur when they seem to make no sense to us. As in this case,He asks us to do something that is difficult. It is important to remember that God knows what is best, and, while it might not make sense to you, His ways are always best. In what areas are you struggling right now to do what God has asked of you? Rather than try to figure out why He is asking that or trying to logically make sense of the situation,just decide do it.

★★★★

MARK 7:36

And Jesus charged them to tell no one. But the more he charged them, the more zealously they proclaimed it.

SAY WHAT?

What is the hardest thing God ever asked you to do? What made it hard?

SO WHAT?

As you look back on it now,why do you think God asked you to do it?

NOW WHAT?

What is the hardest thing for you to trust God with right now? Why is it hard?

THEN WHAT?

Write out a prayer of commitment to begin to obey and submit to God in this area.

SAY WHAT?

Observation: What do I see?

SO WHAT?

Interpretation: What does it mean?

NOW WHAT?

Application: How does it apply to me?

THEN WHAT?

Implementation: What do I do?

Have you ever spoken to someone about a concern you had with what he was doing and he continues to repeat the behavior? Maybe you've asked others to stay out of your stuff? How does it make you feel to have explained something many times to someone who continues to repeat the behavior? How do you respond? In this passage, the disciples find themselves in the same position as they were earlier, with Jesus' wanting to feed a large group of people with little food. Obviously, they did not learn the lesson that Jesus tried to teach them when He fed 5,000 people in 6:30-44. It is interesting to observe Christ's response to them. He did not yell at them, get tense or have any of the reactions we so often use when people fail at something we have talked to them about. He is our example of how to respond to someone who does not learn the first time. Who in your world needs to see a more Christ-like response from you in this area? Your family, friends or comrades? Maybe you need to ask their forgiveness for responses you have already demonstrated. Start today being more like Christ when others fail.

★★★★

MARK 8:4

And his disciples answered him, "How can one feed these people with bread here in this desolate place?"

The book of Proverbs was designed to help us in "attaining wisdom and discipline; in understanding words of insight; in acquiring a disciplined and prudent life, doing what is right and just and fair; in giving prudence to the simple, knowledge and discretion to the young." As you read through this chapter, write down the verses that are most significant to you in your present circumstances.

VERSE	WHAT TRUTH IT COMMUNICATES	HOW IT IMPACTS MY LIFE

SAY WHAT?

What thoughts seem to occupy your mind the most lately?

SO WHAT?

What impact do they have on your response to God's Word when you read it or hear it?

NOW WHAT?

How can you avoid missing what God may be saying to you?

THEN WHAT?

In light of this passage, what personal commitment can you make?

How did Peter react to what Christ told the disciples about His coming suffering and death? Why do you think Peter responded the way he did? Regardless of what we might think his motives were, his response was wrong. In fact, Christ tells him that his response indicated that he did not have the things of God in mind. What things did Peter have in mind? Did he respond in that particular way because he did not want someone he loved to suffer? Was he considering the implications on his life were Christ to die? Was he afraid to be left without Him? Peter was so intent on what Christ said in the beginning that he missed what Christ said at the end: "...and after three days rise again." He heard the first part, but totally missed the most important part; he missed the point Jesus was making. Do you see yourself making the same mistakes that Peter made here? Are you missing the point that God is making because you're convinced that you've already gotten the whole message? It is frustrating to allow other ideas or attitudes to cause us to miss the point God is trying to make in our lives. Are you listening to the whole message?

★★★★★

MARK 8:33

But turning and seeing his disciples, he rebuked Peter and said, "Get behind me, Satan! For you are not setting your mind on the things of God, but on the things of man."

LISTEN!

What do you suppose went through the minds of Peter, James, and John at the transfiguration? Think of how you would have felt at that moment, and then on top of everything else going on,Moses and Elijah appear. The privilege of witnessing that moment may have made those men wonder what God had in mind for them. Not only did they witness an unbelievable event and see Jesus in the supernatural, but God the Father audibly spoke. Notice what God said in the midst of this awesome moment. He told the disciples to "listen to Him," not go and tell everyone what had happened on the mountain. They were not told, "Now you have arrived;" they were told to listen! Could it be that the whole point of this moment was to get Peter, James, and John to listen to Christ? How well do you listen to what God is saying to you through your devotions or a message from your pastor or Chaplain? We often have so much going on around us,that we fail to listen to what God is saying to us. The more we realize who God is,the more it should motivate us to listen. In what ways can you improve your listening skills in your walk with God? He has a lot to say.

SAY WHAT?
Observation: What do I see?

SO WHAT?
Interpretation: What does it mean?

NOW WHAT?
Application: How does it apply to me?

THEN WHAT?
Implementation: What do I do?

MARK 9:7
And a cloud overshadowed them, and a voice came out of the cloud, "This is my beloved Son; listen to him."

INFLUENCING PEOPLE

SAY WHAT?
Observation: What do I see?

SO WHAT?
Interpretation: What does it mean?

NOW WHAT?
Application: How does it apply to me?

THEN WHAT?
Implementation: What do I do?

Think of someone you really look up to. How has he/she impacted your life? What is it about him/her that has had an influence on you? Is he someone who has been with you through difficult times, someone who has given you some much-needed advice or led you to Christ? Who, when asked those same questions, would give your name as someone who has impacted him? If we could honestly look at the influence you have on the people in your world, would it be positive, negative or just neutral? In today's reading, we hear from Christ how He feels about those who use their influence on people to lead them into sin. How sobering to know that each of us have people watching us every day. Often we do not even realize the kind of influence we are having on the people around us. God clearly states in this passage that anything that influences people to sin, even if it is a part of our own body, should be removed. What would you need to change in your life if you want to influence people to do what is pleasing to God? Honestly examine your life; make the changes in order to be an influence for good.

★★★★

MARK 9:42
Whoever causes one of these little ones who believe in me to sin, it would be better for him if a great millstone were hung around his neck and he were thrown into the sea.

WHAT MUST I DO?

If someone came to you and asked the same question that Christ was asked in verse seventeen, what would you say? Would you give the answer that Christ gave? While the man said he came to find eternal life, he left discouraged with the answer Christ gave him. It would seem that although the man wanted to have eternal life, he did not want to give up what Christ indicated was necessary in order to get it. Christ clearly demands that we give up everything to follow Him. For some, becoming a Christian is not an easy thing to do. God does not want to just be part of our lives. Christ desires to be all of our lives. When we come to Christ, we are committing to allow Him to be the leader of our lives. What do you have right now that you have been unwilling to give up in order to follow Christ with your whole heart - friends? popularity? How comforting to then read verses 29-31 and realize that in reality we do not give anything up. In the margin of your Bible next to verses 29-31, write down what you find the most difficult to relinquish totally in order to follow Christ. Then pray that God will enable you to give it to Him.

SAY WHAT?

What do you think people feel they have to give up in order to follow Christ?

SO WHAT?

Why would someone be willing to give up those things?

NOW WHAT?

What is keeping you from following Christ with your whole heart?

THEN WHAT?

Write a prayer to God telling Him your fears and asking Him to enable you to give up whatever is necessary.

MARK 10:17

And as he was setting out on his journey, a man ran up and knelt before him and asked him, "Good Teacher, what must I do to inherit eternal life?"

WHAT ANGER REVEALS

SAY WHAT?
Observation: What do I see?

SO WHAT?
Interpretation: What does it mean?

NOW WHAT?
Application: How does it apply to me?

THEN WHAT?
Implementation: What do I do?

When was the last time you became really upset about something? What does your response in those circumstances tell you about yourself? You can learn a lot about someone by looking at the kinds of things that make him angry. Some people get mad every time they do not get what they want or get left out of something. Others get mad when someone does not do what they think he should do. What conclusions can we come to about Jesus by looking at the circumstances in this passage that made him angry. We see that He cared deeply about the Lord's house, and, when the actions of people demonstrated disrespect to God or His house, He became angry. His anger was never caused by something that someone did or did not do for Him. It wasn't about getting His own way. He cared about how people treated and responded to each other. He demonstrated that He cared more about how people responded to His Father and others than He cared about Himself. Make a list today of those things that have gotten you angry in the past two weeks. Ask yourself why and what your anger tells you about yourself.

★★★★

MARK 11:15
...And he entered the temple and began to drive out those who sold and those who bought in the temple, and he overturned the tables of the money-changers and the seats of those who sold pigeons.

SAYS WHO?

Why did the Pharisees ask the question they did in verse 27? Did they really want to know the answer Christ had for them? Although it is a very important question, they apparently did not want the answer. They did not like what Jesus was telling them, so by questioning His authority, they weren't obligated to listen to Him. People ask the same questions today. They usually ask the questions when they do not want to do what the Bible requires. They say, "Who gives you the right to tell me that?" Or, for example, a friend shares an area of concern from Scripture, and the attitude is: "Why should I listen to you?" or "Who do you think you are telling me that?" We must realize the answer to the question is often, "Almighty God!" He has given us the Bible as the absolute authority in our lives, and we must follow it. God has placed parents and others over us and He has given them their authority. All authorities in our lives have been placed there by God, and we should treat them with the respect that He demands. We may not like that answer, but it dictates our behavior. He expects our obedience. Respond as unto the Lord.

SAY WHAT?
Observation: What do I see?

SO WHAT?
Interpretation: What does it mean?

NOW WHAT?
Application: How does it apply to me?

THEN WHAT?
Implementation: What do I do?

MARK 11:28

...and they said to him, "By what authority are you doing these things, or who gave you this authority to do them?"

The book of Proverbs was designed to help us in "attaining wisdom and discipline; in understanding words of insight; in acquiring a disciplined and prudent life, doing what is right and just and fair; in giving prudence to the simple, knowledge and discretion to the young." As you read through this chapter, write down the verses that are most significant to you in your present circumstances.

VERSE | WHAT TRUTH IT COMMUNICATES | HOW IT IMPACTS MY LIFE

EVALUATION GIVING

Why was Jesus so impressed with what the widow gave in today's reading? In what way was her offering different from the offerings of the rich? This section of Scripture gives us an important and also encouraging principle. Jesus was not impressed with the amount that the widow gave, but with the heart in which it was given and with how much she gave in relationship to how much she had. She gave it because she wanted to, and it was all she had to give. Although the rich people gave much more than the poor widow, Christ knew how wealthy they were and how little she had. When Christ compared what they had against what she gave, He concluded that she gave much more. If that same standard were applied to your giving, how did God feel about what you gave in church this past Sunday? How does He feel about the amount you have given to your church this past year? Maybe today would be a good time for you to think about what you give and how to be sure that it is pleasing to God. Starting this Sunday, give God what He would be pleased with in light of what He has given you. He is watching you!

SAY WHAT?

List reasons why you feel God wants you to give to the church.

SO WHAT?

What words would you use to describe your attitude towards giving to the church?

NOW WHAT?

What words would you use to describe how much you give in relationship to how much you have?

THEN WHAT?

What do you need to do in order to improve in the area of giving?

MARK 12:44

For they all contributed out of their abundance, but she out of her poverty has put in everything she had, all she had to live on.

SAY WHAT?
Observation: What do I see?

SO WHAT?
Interpretation: What does it mean?

NOW WHAT?
Application: How does it apply to me?

THEN WHAT?
Implementation: What do I do?

What question did Peter, James, John, and Andrew ask Christ in verse four? How many different signs did Jesus give them? Put an * in your Bible next to each one of the different signs He gave. If we study those signs and compare them to the events of these days we live in, we should conclude that the end is closer than we realized. In fact, the reality is that there are no other signs yet to take place. Every sign Jesus mentioned has already taken place, so the next event on the Biblical calender is Christ's return. It was crucial for the disciples, knowing the end was at hand, to be ready. Jesus wanted them to live each day as though it were their last. Are you ready for Christ's return? Is your walk with God such that you are ready to meet Him and not be ashamed? Have you shared Christ with those in your world so that they are ready to meet Christ, or would you need more time? The return of Christ could come at any moment! What areas in your life do you need to work on before you are ready to meet the Savior? Do you have a plan to begin improving in those areas? Make a list of the steps you need to take to be ready for His return.

MARK 13:4
"Tell us, when will these things be, and what will be the sign when all these things are about to be accomplished?"

KEEP WATCH

What request did Jesus give to His disciples in verse 34? Why did He want them to keep watch for Him? While we always think about the physical suffering Christ endured at the crucifixion we often forget about the emotional pain of moments like the one in today's reading. That might be the key reason why Christ wanted them with Him. Think about it. He was betrayed by Judas, whom He had loved for three years. He was really hurting and told those close to Him that He was "overwhelmed with sorrow to the point of death." He asked those who were close to Him to pray for Him during this very emotional time. They not only failed to pray for Him, but fell asleep two times. When He needed their support and encouragement, they failed. Have you ever felt like Christ must have felt at that moment? You may have been really discouraged and needed prayer and support, but no one seemed to care. It is a great comfort that Christ knows exactly how you feel. When no one else cares, He always does. He is never too busy or too weary to help. He is always available. Are you? Who needs your encouragement?

MARK 14:38

Watch and pray that you may not enter into temptation. The spirit indeed is willing, but the flesh is weak.

SAY WHAT?
Observation: What do I see?

SO WHAT?
Interpretation: What does it mean?

NOW WHAT?
Application: How does it apply to me?

THEN WHAT?
Implementation: What do I do?

AN UNEXPECTED RESPONSE

SAY WHAT?

What are some responses that you have seen others give that have amazed you?

SO WHAT?

Why did they amaze you?

NOW WHAT?

What situations have you recently faced where your response could have impacted people this same way?

THEN WHAT?

What do you need to do to be better prepared to respond in a way that shows people what Jesus Christ can do?

What character in this passage was the most noticeable to you? While we often think about Christ when we read through this passage, today think about another person--the servant of the High Priest. He must have overheard many conversations about Christ while working, all of which had to be negative. We can only imagine how he must have felt about Him. With that in mind, put yourself in his shoes. You followed the High Priest to the garden and, just as you had anticipated, there was resistance. One of Jesus' men drew his sword and cut off your ear. The actions of the disciple would confirm who you thought Jesus was and that the punishment coming was well deserved. Then, to your amazement, (according to Luke 22:51), Jesus rebuked the one who cut off your ear and put it back on your head. That must have confused the servant at the very least and surely had to have an unbelievable impact on him. Do you impact people this way? When people seek to harm you, do you respond as Christ did? What opportunities do you have each day to demonstrate the difference Jesus has made?

★★★★

MARK 14:47

But one of those who stood by drew his sword and struck the servant of the high priest and cut off his ear.

RESPONSE TO LOVE

What did Jesus Christ go through in this chapter? How many different ways did they punish Him? Start with the first one, and then number in your Bible all the different things He had to endure. Of all the ones on your list, which one do you think was the most painful? It is amazing to realize that Jesus Christ went through all that for you. Everything found in this chapter was endured for you. His beard was ripped out for you. A crown of thorns was pressed into His head for you. That is amazing love! How do you respond to such love? With a life of apathy? Today, instead of having you do a lot of writing or studying, the sheet below has been designed to help you list the things from this chapter which Christ endured for our sake. Read over it a few times and simply meditate on how much Jesus Christ loves you. Then think about how you need to respond to such incredible love. Find a new way today to say thank you for all the suffering He endured for you.

SAY WHAT?

List the different things that happened to Christ in this chapter.

SO WHAT?

Write a note to God expressing how that list makes you feel.

NOW WHAT?

How can you demonstrate your thankfulness today?

THEN WHAT?

In light of this passage, what personal commitment can you make?

MARK 15:2

And Pilate asked him, "Are you the King of the Jews?" And he answered him, "You have said so."

OVERCOMING FAILIURE

SAY WHAT?
Observation: What do I see?

SO WHAT?
Interpretation: What does it mean?

NOW WHAT?
Application: How does it apply to me?

THEN WHAT?
Implementation: What do I do?

What instructions did the angel give to Mary in today's reading? Why do you think he added the phrase, "and Peter?" It would seem that when God sent the message, he especially wanted to comfort and encourage Peter after his specific failure to take a stand for Christ. How thrilling it must have been, after what Peter had done, how he had failed the Lord, to know that the angel wanted Mary to specifically tell Peter. Could it be that God wanted Peter to know that his failure had been forgiven and that He still loved him? Could God have added that small but significant phrase in this chapter to communicate to us as well that, no matter how badly we fail the Lord, He still loves us and wants us to know that He wants to use us? God had not given up on Peter. Christ knew that Peter was hurting because of his denial. He wanted him to know that he was not forgotten, but was still useful to God. What past failure have you allowed to hinder you from being used by God? Underline the phrase to remind you that no matter what you have done, God still loves you and still desires to use you when you seek His forgiveness.

★★★★★

MARK 16:7
But go, tell his disciples and Peter that he is going before you to Galilee. There you will see him, just as he told you.

MILITARY
OTD

» MILITARYDEVOTIONAL.COM

 @MILITARYDEVOS

 FACEBOOK.COM/MILITARYDEVOS

MILITARY
OTD

THE BOOKS OF
HEBREWS &
JAMES

DECEMBER
★★★★

MONTHLY
PRAYER SHEET

I NEED TO REACH OUT TO...	HOW I WILL DO IT...	HOW IT WENT...

OTHER REQUEST	HOW ANSWERED	DATE

MONTHLY
MISSION SHEET

>>> Share your personal commitments with those who will help keep you accountable to them.

>>> **NAME:** ....

This sheet is designed to help you make personal commitments each month that will help you grow in your walk with God. Fill it out by determining:

★ What will push you.
★ What you think you can achieve.

>>> **PERSONAL DEVOTIONS:**
I will commit to read the OnTrack Bible passage and devotional thought .... day(s) each week this month.

>>> **CHURCH/CHAPEL ATTENDANCE:**
I will attend Church/Chapel .... time(s) this month.
I will attend .... time(s) this month.

>>> **SCRIPTURE MEMORY:**
I will memorize .... key verse(s) from the daily OnTrack Devotions this month.

>>> **OUTREACH:**
I will share Christ with .... person/people this month.
I will serve my local church/chapel this month by ....
....
....

>>> **OTHER ACTIVITIES:**
List any other opportunities such as events, prayer group, etc..., you will participate in this month. ....
....
....
....
....
....

Determine to begin today a journey that will last a lifetime, and will change your life forever.

WHO IS JESUS CHRIST?

If someone at in your unit asked you who Jesus Christ is, what would you tell him? The book of Hebrews was written to clearly communicate who He is and what He has done. In today's reading, we see that Jesus Christ is superior to every living thing. Specifically, He is superior to angels. Verses one through three teach us that Jesus Christ is God. He is the exact representation of God. The word "representation" translated here means that He is equal to God in every way. He radiates the glory of God because He is totally God in every way. He is, therefore, not like the angels. He is not a higher form of an angel. He is superior to angels in every way because He is totally God. The book of Hebrews further demonstrates this truth by showing us that the Father talks to Jesus in ways He has never used to speak to angels. We see also that angels are not to be worshiped,but Jesus Christ is. Angels do not rule on thrones,but Jesus Christ does. Jesus Christ will never change or fail us. He alone,not angels, is to be worshiped and adored. Since angels are a common topic of conversation today, use the opportunity to share Christ?

HEBREWS 1:8

But of the Son he says, "Your throne, O God, is forever and ever; the scepter of uprightness is the scepter of your kingdom.

SAY WHAT?
Observation: What do I see?

SO WHAT?
Interpretation: What does it mean?

NOW WHAT?
Application: How does it apply to me?

THEN WHAT?
Implementation: What do I do?

MILITARYDEVOTIONAL.COM
@MILITARYDEVOS

WHY BECOME A MAN?

SAY WHAT?

What temptations are you now facing?

SO WHAT?

How is your temptation like one that Jesus faced?

NOW WHAT?

How did Jesus respond to His temptations?

THEN WHAT?

Write a prayer asking Jesus to give you victory over specific temptations.

Why did Jesus Christ have to become a man? In today's reading, we are given some very important reasons why Jesus had to come to earth as a man. One of those is found in verses nine and seventeen. Jesus Christ became a man so that He could die on behalf of all of us. He paid the price for our sin so that we do not have to pay it ourselves. A second reason is given in verse fourteen. Jesus Christ became a man so that He might destroy Satan and his power over death in order to free us from the fear of death. A third reason is given in verses seventeen and eighteen. This reason is so important for our daily living but few seem to realize it is true. We are told that Jesus Christ became a man so that He might become a merciful and faithful High Priest. Because He willingly became a man, He knows the daily experiences of a man and responds to us out of His personal knowledge of what we face. Verse eighteen tells us that He is able to help us when we are tempted because He has faced the same temptations. Jesus not only knows what we face today, but He is able to help each of us resist temptation. What temptation are you facing that you can take to Him for help?

★★★★

HEBREWS 2:17

Therefore he had to be made like his brothers in every respect, so that he might become a merciful and faithful high priest in the service of God, to make propitiation for the sins of the people.

A HARD HEART

So far in our reading of the book of Hebrews,we have come across two strong warnings to pay careful attention to the moving of God in our lives. We are further warned that when He does move in our lives,we need to respond. In the first four verses of chapter two, we are warned to not miss salvation. In today's reading we are given another warning: not to harden our hearts and miss salvation. God knows it is possible to grow up in a Christian environment and be able to recite the truth and yet not have trusted Christ. God also knows it is possible to grow up around godly people and influences and yet allow our hearts to become hardened toward God. How do we avoid a hardened heart? According to verse seven, we should respond to God's prompting. The author tells us that if we hear the voice of God today, we must respond immediately and not wait until another time. We must not excuse or justify a delay. When God convicts our hearts we must not wait until tomorrow to respond. If we don't act upon conviction, we are heading for hardened hearts. Has God convicted you of an area that you have not yet responded to?

HEBREWS 3:13

But exhort one another every day, as long as it is called "today," that none of you may be hardened by the deceitfulness of sin.

SAY WHAT?
Observation: What do I see?

SO WHAT?
Interpretation: What does it mean?

NOW WHAT?
Application: How does it apply to me?

THEN WHAT?
Implementation: What do I do?

SAY WHAT?

How would you describe the time you spend in God's Word?

SO WHAT?

In what way has God used His Word recently to move in your life?

NOW WHAT?

What is in the way of God's Word being more active in your life?

THEN WHAT?

In light of this passage, what personal commitment can you make?

What words would you use to describe the Bible? Write down what you came up with in the margin of your On Track. What words did you use? Did you choose the same words the Holy Spirit used in this passage of Scripture? - Living and active? Why did He choose these two specific words? He wanted us to understand that the Bible is unlike any other book. It is not stagnant, just words on a page. It is alive and can penetrate even to our souls. God's Word is what judges our hearts and reveals to us areas that need work. God's Word is what judges our thoughts and attitudes to make sure they are in line with what God desires. Everything is laid bare before God and His Word when we read it. We must be diligent to read and study this Book so it can do its work in our hearts. It will change our lives as we read it. How much time do you spend in God's Word each day? Do you make the effort every day? Are you spending the kind of time that allows it to do its work in your heart? If we neglect our time, we will lack the ability to examine our lives and guidance in our decision making. Neglecting Scripture is dangerous.

HEBREWS 4:12

For the word of God is living and active, sharper than any two-edged sword, piercing to the division of soul and of spirit, of joints and of marrow, and discerning the thoughts and intentions of the heart.

OUR HIGH PRIEST

In these next few chapters, the author writes about Jesus being our High Priest. Why is it important for us to understand this truth? The answer is important in order to properly understand Scripture. In the Old Testament, people needed a mediator between God and themselves, someone who would go to God on their behalf. Under the New Covenant, Jesus Christ became that person. We are under the New Covenant and therefore, do not need to go to a priest for forgiveness. We can go directly to Jesus Christ. We do not need to ask a priest to talk to God on our behalf. Jesus Christ is our High Priest and He does that for us. While there are other religions today who still believe one must go to God through a human priest, this section of Scripture makes it clear that this position is not Biblical. Jesus Christ was God who became a man. He was our High Priest and offered Himself as our sacrifice. His sacrifice was all that was needed to provide us access to God. He now sits at the right hand of God, interceding for us. When we want to confess sin or need help, we go to Him. He is our High Priest. Are you getting to know Him more?

HEBREWS 4:15

For we do not have a high priest who is unable to sympathize with our weaknesses, but one who in every respect has been tempted as we are, yet without sin.

SAY WHAT?

Observation: What do I see?

SO WHAT?

Interpretation: What does it mean?

NOW WHAT?

Application: How does it apply to me?

THEN WHAT?

Implementation: What do I do?

The book of Proverbs was designed to help us in "attaining wisdom and discipline; in understanding words of insight; in acquiring a disciplined and prudent life, doing what is right and just and fair; in giving prudence to the simple, knowledge and discretion to the young." As you read through this chapter, write down the verses that are most significant to you in your present circumstances.

VERSE | WHAT TRUTH IT COMMUNICATES | HOW IT IMPACTS MY LIFE

BEING A BABY

Have you ever tried to explain something to someone who should have been able to understand what you were saying, but he did not get it? He didn't get it even though the expectation was that he should have had information which would enable him to understand. In this passage, the author of Hebrews faces this same challenge. He expresses in verse eleven, a desire to share more fully, but slowness of learning prohibits him from doing so. Why? They had not been growing in their walks with God and were still babies. They just could not understand. It was not because it was difficult or complicated, as some might say, but because they had failed to grow in their knowledge of God's Word. By this point they should have been teachers, but were still spiritual babies. Where are you in your walk with God? Does your pastor have to talk simply to you because you have not grown in your faith and in knowledge? How much have you grown spiritually since you trusted Christ? If you are still a baby, and can't understand God's truths, what do you need to do to in order to grow as God desires? Who can help you?

SAY WHAT?

Why do so many Christians fail to grow in their walks with God?

SO WHAT?

How can we begin to consistently grow in our walks with God?

NOW WHAT?

How can you grow in your understanding of His Word?

THEN WHAT?

In light of this passage, what personal commitment can you make?

★★★★

HEBREWS 5:11

About this we have much to say, and it is hard to explain, since you have become dull of hearing.

RESULT OF CHANGE

SAY WHAT?
Observation: What do I see?

SO WHAT?
Interpretation: What does it mean?

NOW WHAT?
Application: How does it apply to me?

THEN WHAT?
Implementation: What do I do?

What does verse twleve of today's reading mean when it says that because of a new priesthood the law has changed? A closer look reveals the answer. The word translated "change" in this verse means to put one thing in the place of another. The point is that Christianity has been put in the place of Judaism. Jesus' Priesthood was not "added" to the Old Testament line of Aaron; He "replaced" it. The ceremonial system of the law was changed since Jesus Christ had become the High Priest. God's moral law, however, did not change. God's standard of righteousness remained the same. While we no longer need to go to the Temple to offer our sacrifices under the ceremonial law, the definition of sin, the moral law, remains the same. In fact, under the new system of Christ, the moral law of God has been strengthened. It is now a higher standard of righteousness. Now we are accountable for our attitudes and motivations, not just our actions. We now have direct access to God. We now can have full and complete forgiveness of sins. Jesus Christ has done what the law could not. Jesus has taken the place of the old system.

★★★★

HEBREWS 7:12
For when there is a change in the priesthood, there is necessarily a change in the law as well.

NEW IS BETTER

What makes the New Covenant,(the New Testament system) superior to the Old Covenant, (the Old Testament system)? In this chapter, the author lists many reasons. Three examples are found in verse ten. The Old Covenant was basically established on external behavior. Obedience was usually a result of the fear of punishment. God's law was given on tablets of stone. The Holy Spirit, however, was not yet given to believers in the way the New Covenant allowed. After the Holy Spirit was given to the believers, the law of God was written on their hearts. True religion was no longer an external ritual but an internal relationship. We see in verse eleven that the New is better because it is personal. God lives within the hearts of all who by faith, have trusted Christ. We can have a personal relationship with Christ. In verse twelve, the New Covenant is superior because it brings total forgiveness. The promise of the Old Testament was fulfilled. The Old Covenant only covered sin. Jesus Christ washed away our sin. How thankful are you for what Christ has done? Who needs to know what the New Covenant provides?

★★★★

HEBREWS 8:13

In speaking of a new covenant, he makes the first one obsolete. And what is becoming obsolete and growing old is ready to vanish away.

SAY WHAT?

What is the difference between external religion and internal religion?

SO WHAT?

How can you tell if one's foundation of life is based on an external or an internal faith?

NOW WHAT?

How can you prevent your true religion from becoming external,like the old covenant?

THEN WHAT?

In light of this passage,what personal commitment can you make?

SAY WHAT?
Observation: What do I see?

SO WHAT?
Interpretation: What does it mean?

NOW WHAT?
Application: How does it apply to me?

THEN WHAT?
Implementation: What do I do?

Is it possible to have a clear conscience even if you have committed horrible sin? We can have one if we understand what the new system has done for us! This section of Scripture is one of the greatest we can use to give hope to our world. The author explains that the gifts and sacrifices under the Old Testament law were not able to "clear the conscience." Can you imagine that? One committed a sin and even though it was covered by the blood of an animal, his conscience was not clean. Because we have a new system, our consciences can be clean. Verse fourteen tells us that, because Jesus Christ shed His blood on the cross for us, and offered Himself, unblemished to God, He can "cleanse" our consciences, not just cover them. If a guilty conscience is haunting you, Jesus Christ can wipe it clean - not just cover the sin - but take it away and clear your conscience. Our world needs to know what Jesus Christ has done for them and how they can be freed from the bondage of sin and the guilty conscience that follows. If you have experienced this cleansing yourself, why don't you be the one to tell them.

HEBREWS 9:14
...how much more will the blood of Christ, who through the eternal Spirit offered himself without blemish to God, purify our conscience from dead works to serve the living God.

MEANING OF FORGIVENESS

Today we learn that, what may be the most sought after commodity of mankind, is available to all. What is it? Forgiveness!! Today's reading tells us that we can truly be forgiven. It is true that we have all sinned and fallen short of God's standard. Some may feel that they have violated God to a greater degree than others, and that may be true. However, the opportunity for forgiveness is not based on the seriousness of the offense, but is based on the ability to forgive on the part of the one who has been violated. We learn that Jesus Christ paid the price for our sin and made it possible, by His death on the cross, for us to obtain forgiveness. According to verse seventeen, not only can we obtain forgiveness, but God remembers our sin no more. Verse eighteen further tells us that where there has been forgiveness, there is no longer a need for sacrifice for sin. There isn't anything else we need to do to take care of it. We can live free from guilt. We are forgiven and everything is made new. Our world needs to know that they can have their sins forgiven and be made new. How can you help them see that forgiveness is possible?

SAY WHAT?

How can today's reading help those who still suffer from guilt over past sin?

SO WHAT?

How can this passage help unsaved people who feel that their lives are too wicked to be forgiven?

NOW WHAT?

How can today's reading help you with your feelings of guilt?

THEN WHAT?

In light of this passage, what personal commitment can you make?

★ ★ ★ ★

HEBREWS 10:17

...then he adds, "I will remember their sins and their lawless deeds no more."

SAY WHAT?
Observation: What do I see?

SO WHAT?
Interpretation: What does it mean?

NOW WHAT?
Application: How does it apply to me?

THEN WHAT?
Implementation: What do I do?

How did you respond to the kind of truth we read yesterday? Is it just something you log in your memory bank? Or is there some kind of action we should be taking? The passage of Scripture that we read today answers that question. There are five challenges to us in this section all beginning with the words "let us." Number and then circle them in your Bible. First, we are to draw near to God. We do that by faithfully reading His Word every day and spending time with Him in prayer. Second, we are to hold unswervingly to the hope we have. God is faithful - we should not doubt Him or lose our confidence. Third, we are to consider how we can spur one another on toward love and good deeds. What can we do to challenge others to become more like Christ? Notice he used the word "spur." It may not be comfortable. Fourth, we need to make church attendance a priority. There isn't an option of whether or not to meet together. Finally, we are to encourage each other. We are to do things that boost others' spirits. We need to pray for others and ask how we can encourage them. How are you doing in these five areas?

HEBREWS 10:22
...let us draw near with a true heart in full assurance of faith, with our hearts sprinkled clean from an evil conscience and our bodies washed with pure water.

The book of Proverbs was designed to help us in "attaining wisdom and discipline; in understanding words of insight; in acquiring a disciplined and prudent life, doing what is right and just and fair; in giving prudence to the simple, knowledge and discretion to the young." As you read through this chapter, write down the verses that are most significant to you in your present circumstances.

| VERSE | WHAT TRUTH IT COMMUNICATES | HOW IT IMPACTS MY LIFE |

EVIDENCE OF FAITH

SAY WHAT?
Observation: What do I see?

SO WHAT?
Interpretation: What does it mean?

NOW WHAT?
Application: How does it apply to me?

THEN WHAT?
Implementation: What do I do?

How could Abraham do what he did in today's reading? How could he leave his home, family and career with an uncertain destination and future? Because he had faith! He was sure that God would reward those who seek Him. He was certain that God existed. Therefore, Abraham knew he could trust God in what He was asking him to do. Today it seems that we Christians want to know how everything is going to turn out before we step out for God. We may be willing to serve God, but we want to make sure we have something to fall back on in case it does not work out like we hope it will. We will take a stand for Christ if we know what the outcome will be. We don't want to get behind on work due to church activities for fear it may hurt our standing to gain rank. We are in desperate need of people today who have a totally committed faith - those who are sure and certain that God is real, and He will reward them for serving Him. This world needs to see those who will move out for Him without concern or fear. Are you a person with that kind of faith? What is keeping you from being a person of faith like those in this chapter?

★★★★

HEBREWS 11:6
And without faith it is impossible to please him, for whoever would draw near to God must believe that he exists and that he rewards those who seek him.

HEROES OF FAITH

Of all the men and women of faith listed in this chapter, which one leaves the greatest impression on you? As you read the list, did you identify with any one of them? While this list is amazing, there were so many others whose faith was remarkable, and, although their names weren't specifically mentioned, verses 33-38 lists the great things they did. How incredible it must have been to be able to accomplish what these people did for God. How amazing to be able to stand for Christ against all odds. Verse 38 is accurate by saying that the world was not worthy of them. Could your name ever be included in a chapter like this? Is it possible for us to have the kind of faith that would allow us to stand like they did? The answer is yes. In the passage we will read tomorrow, we will learn what is necessary to become men and women of faith. It may never be required of us to be stoned, sawn in two, or to be chained and put into prison for our faith, but we can take steps towards greater faith and standing strong for Christ in our worlds. Are you up to the demands this kind of faith will have on you? Are you this committed to Christ?

SAY WHAT?
Observation: What do I see?

SO WHAT?
Interpretation: What does it mean?

NOW WHAT?
Application: How does it apply to me?

THEN WHAT?
Implementation: What do I do?

HEBREWS 11:40
...since God had provided something better for us, that apart from us they should not be made perfect.

BECOMING PEOPLE OF FAITH

SAY WHAT?

List some examples of "things that hinder" in your life?

SO WHAT?

Which "things that hinder" need to be eliminated? How?

NOW WHAT?

What sins do you need to confess and forsake?

THEN WHAT?

In what ways can you "fix your eyes on Jesus" more consistently?

Today we learn what we must do to become men and women of faith. We see the role we need to play, and the role God plays in us in order to become people of faith. First, we must "throw off." We must do this in two important areas. In the first area, we must "throw off" everything that hinders. Those are the things which are not sin but slow us down and entangle us in our walks with God. Examples can be the TV, relationships, music, hobbies, videos, etc. In the second area, we must "throw off" any sin that is in our lives. We cannot tolerate any sin, large or small, and expect to become people of faith. Second, we must "run with perseverance." We must realize this is a long race and run it without slowing down, no matter what we may face. Third, we need to focus on Jesus Christ. He needs to be our priority and the only one we seek to please. It is a comfort to know that, while we seek to do these three things, God will also do His work to keep us on track. How? Through His loving discipline. Whenever we veer off track, He will discipline us to get us back where we need to be. We, however, must allow it to train us and not resist the discipline involved. Get started today.

★★★★

HEBREWS 12:5

And have you forgotten the exhortation that addresses you as sons? "My son, do not regard lightly the discipline of the Lord, nor be weary when reproved by him.

CONSUMING FIRE

What words would you use to describe God? If you stopped people on the street and asked them this question, what answers do you think you would get? Some see God as a big grandfather,someone who loves us and would never hurt us or send us to hell. He sits up in His rocking chair,pats us on the head and tells us how much He appreciates how hard we work on being good. When we stand before Him on that day, He will just overlook our sin. Today's reading however, gives us a much different picture of God. The writer of Hebrews tells us that God is a consuming fire (vs29). In light of that,we must worship Him with reverence and awe. A consuming fire is a long way from a grandfather in the sky, who will excuse us when we fail. While it is true that God loves us deeply, we must also keep in mind that God is to be feared. His holiness demands He punish sin and He will deal with the unrighteous. Those who die without Christ will spend eternity in hell. We must recognized who God is, serve Him faithfully, and share the gospel with those who don't know the truth about Him. It is our responsibility.

SAY WHAT?
Observation: What do I see?

SO WHAT?
Interpretation: What does it mean?

NOW WHAT?
Application: How does it apply to me?

THEN WHAT?
Implementation: What do I do?

HEB 12:28-29

Therefore let us be grateful for receiving a kingdom that cannot be shaken, and thus let us offer to God acceptable worship, with reverence and awe, for our God is a consuming fire.

KEY TO CONTENTMENT

SAY WHAT?
Observation: What do I see?

SO WHAT?
Interpretation: What does it mean?

NOW WHAT?
Application: How does it apply to me?

THEN WHAT?
Implementation: What do I do?

How would you describe your life? Would you say you are happy? If you had little in the way of possessions, would you still be happy? You would be if you truly believe what we are told in today's reading. In verse five, the writer of Hebrews makes a powerful statement. He tells us that we should be content with what we have, no matter how little that might be. Why? Because God has said He will never leave us or forsake us. In other words, even if we have nothing by the world's definition of something, we should still be happy because God is with us. Even if we are not as attractive as we might want to be, God is with us. Even if we are not as popular as we want to be, God is with us. Even if we do not have the clothes we might want, God is with us. Even if we are not as talented as we might want to be, God is with us. This fact alone ought to make us content no matter what we have or where we are. To be unhappy with who we are or what we have is a statement to God that He is not enough. To believe that to be happy and content, we need something besides Him is wrong. What does your life say to God?

★★★★

HEBREWS 13:5
Keep your life free from love of money, and be content with what you have, for he has said "I will never leave you nor forsake you."

PERSEVERENCE

What is so great about perseverance? James tells us that we should rejoice when trials come because they produce perseverance in our lives. The obvious question then is what is it about perseverance that makes trials something we should rejoice over? A word study in the New Testament on perseverance reveals that it means steadfast endurance toward aggression. It is the ability to stay put and stand our ground when opposition occurs. It is the strength needed to never give up and patiently wait for God to work. Why is this quality so important? Without it we can not successfully live the Christian life. It is the quality that leads to maturity and to ultimately be someone who lacks nothing (vs4). Without perseverance we will remain immature. Trials produce the quality we so desperately need in our lives,perseverance. Without trials we can not have perseverance,and without it,we would remain spiritual babies. We rejoice in trials because God is helping us develop what we need to live the Christian life. How are you responding to trials? Are you learning to preserver? God uses them to give you perseverance.

SAY WHAT?
What trials have you faced in the past?

SO WHAT?
How has God used them to help you mature in areas of your life?

NOW WHAT?
How can you apply this passage of Scripture in your life and then use it to help others as well?

THEN WHAT?
In light of this passage,what personal commitment can you make?

★★★★

JAMES 1:4
And let steadfastness have its full effect, that you may be perfect and complete, lacking in nothing.

MILITARYDEVOTIONAL.COM
@MILITARYDEVOS

The book of Proverbs was designed to help us in "attaining wisdom and discipline; in understanding words of insight; in acquiring a disciplined and prudent life, doing what is right and just and fair; in giving prudence to the simple, knowledge and discretion to the young." As you read through this chapter, write down the verses that are most significant to you in your present circumstances.

VERSE | WHAT TRUTH IT COMMUNICATES | HOW IT IMPACTS MY LIFE

TRUE SALVATION

If you were to make a list of three characteristics that demonstrate that one is truly saved, what three would you choose? You probably would not choose the three that James did in this passage. He lists three ways to be certain that one is truly saved. There are more people than you can imagine who sincerely feel that they are born again and, in reality, are not. The first test is that a true believer keeps a tight rein on his tongue (vs26). James uses this test because according to Christ, the mouth reveals the true condition of one's heart. Listen to yourself talk and you will know the true condition of your heart. Second, one who is truly saved looks after orphans and widows (vs27). The object of your charity reveals your motivation. Do you reach out to well liked people who can do something for you in return? Or do you reach out to the unlovely or unpopular? What then does your motivation reveal? Third, James says that true religion keeps itself from being polluted by the world (vs27). What we allow to influence us reveals the level of our commitment.

SAY WHAT?
Observation: What do I see?

SO WHAT?
Interpretation: What does it mean?

NOW WHAT?
Application: How does it apply to me?

THEN WHAT?
Implementation: What do I do?

★★★★

JAMES 1:27

Religion that is pure and undefiled before God, the Father, is this: to visit orphans and widows in their affliction, and to keep oneself unstained from the world.

MILITARYDEVOTIONAL.COM
@MILITARYDEVOS

FAVORITISM

SAY WHAT?
How do you see favoritism displayed in your unit or your church?

SO WHAT?
How do you demonstrate favoritism at church or unit?

NOW WHAT?
How can you stop showing favoritism and love others instead?

THEN WHAT?
In light of this passage, what personal commitment can you make?

How would you define favoritism? Does it exist at all in your church or unit? What can you do about it? The answers to all of these questions are found in today's reading. The word translated favoritism in verse one means "to show partiality based on outward appearance." Favoritism is being influenced by external qualities like appearance, possessions, education, popularity, etc. The example James gave illustrates what it looked like. This church treated people differently, not based on what was in their hearts, but on what others saw outwardly. The rich man got kindness and a seat of honor, the poor man did not. That is sin and shows that we judge people with evil thoughts. James then demonstrated that God does not show favoritism based on external appearances. In fact, the poor have a greater opportunity for spiritual growth than the rich. Do you show favoritism? Are there people at your church you do not sit with or talk to because of external qualities like appearance or how wealthy they are? We need to love people as God does. In what ways do you need to change?

★★★★

JAMES 2:1
My brothers, show no partiality as you hold the faith in our Lord Jesus Christ, the Lord of glory.

SAVING FAITH

James asks a very important question in verse fourteen. The question itself illustrates that it is possible to have a faith which will not save you. The answer one gives is vitally important. James asks whether or not a person's faith, which is not accompanied by action, can save him. In other words, if someone says he is saved, but he does not have actions that demonstrate it, is he really saved? As you read through this section, it becomes obvious that James' answer is no, this kind of faith does not save. Can a person who claims to be saved, really be saved if he does not reach out and meet others' needs when he becomes aware of them? Does just believing in your head and knowing factually that Jesus is God and that He died and rose again enough to get you to heaven? According to James, no it isn't (18-19). Is he saying then that we are saved by our works? No! He uses Abraham and Rahab to illustrate that works do not save you, but that if you really have saving faith, you will demonstrate it by the way you live. Faith is manifested by the way you act. What do your actions tell you about your faith?

SAY WHAT?
Observation: What do I see?

SO WHAT?
Interpretation: What does it mean?

NOW WHAT?
Application: How does it apply to me?

THEN WHAT?
Implementation: What do I do?

JAMES 2:14

What good is it, my brothers, if someone says he has faith but does not have works? Can that faith save him?

POWER OF A TONGUE

SAY WHAT?
Observation: What do I see?

SO WHAT?
Interpretation: What does it mean?

NOW WHAT?
Application: How does it apply to me?

THEN WHAT?
Implementation: What do I do?

There are four important principles in today's reading to illustrate the need to gain control of our tongues. Highlight or number them in your Bible. The first one is found in verses three and four. We see that although the tongue is small, it can do great damage. With a few small words we can cause someone great pain. The second principle is found in verse five. There we learn that the tongue can do irreparable damage. We can say things that hurt people in a way that permanently damages our relationship and ability to influence their lives positively. Third, we learn in verses seven and eight that if we are going to tame our tongues, we need the power of God. We cannot gain control of the tongue by using our own strength. Fourth, verses 9-12 tell us that the tongue has equal potential for good and evil. It can be used in great ways for God, or it can be a tool of Satan to do damage to the cause of Christ. So much damage in people's lives and in the life of the church is done with the tongue. How is your tongue being used? Have you allowed the Spirit of God to control your tongue so that everything you say please God?

★ ★ ★ ★

JAMES 3:2

For we all stumble in many ways. And if anyone does not stumble in what he says, he is a perfect man, able also to bridle his whole body.

GODLY WISDOM

What kind of wisdom are you using? Does your wisdom come from God or from this world? Is there a way for you to be able to tell which kind of wisdom you are using? You could use today's reading to help you find out. In this section, James defines two kinds of wisdom to help us avoid using the world's wisdom. First, he demonstrates the different motives between worldly wisdom and God's wisdom. The world's wisdom is motivated by envy and selfish ambition. God's wisdom is pure, peace-loving, considerate, submissive... (vs17). Second, these two kinds of wisdom also have different sources. Worldly wisdom's source is the depraved human mind, the world, and sometimes Satan himself. God's wisdom comes from God and His Word. He enables us to make wise choices and decisions. Third, James tells us that these two kinds of wisdom have different results. The world's wisdom results in disorder and every evil thing. God's wisdom results in a harvest of righteousness. If you want to know what wisdom you are living by, just examine your motives, your source and the results you are getting. It will be obvious if you are honest.

SAY WHAT?

How can you tell what your motives are when you make decisions?

SO WHAT?

How do you decide what your source of wisdome really is?

NOW WHAT?

What do the results of your decisions tell you about the type of wisdom you use?

THEN WHAT?

In light of this passage, what personal commitment can you make?

JAMES 3:17

But the wisdom from above is first pure, then peaceable, gentle, open to reason, full of mercy and good fruits, impartial and sincere.

FRIENDSHIP WITH THE WORLD

SAY WHAT?
Observation: What do I see?

SO WHAT?
Interpretation: What does it mean?

NOW WHAT?
Application: How does it apply to me?

THEN WHAT?
Implementation: What do I do?

What does it mean to have friendship with the world? Does it mean that we should not be friends with unsaved people at work? James gives us this important principle that we need to understand so that we do not violate it or apply it in error. The world James has in mind,is not the planet earth or the people in the world. He is talking about this world's system or society. He is not saying we should not be friends with people in the world. He is warning us however against being friendly with this world's views and positions. The world's philosophy says that money is number one. I am friends with the world when I believe it and make decisions based on it. The world says I should seek to be first,look out for #1. I am friends with the world when I make that my life's philosophy. We should never support or encourage that philosophy. If we do,we stand in direct opposition to God. Friendship with this world's system is enmity or separation from God. How friendly are you with the world? Do you allow its values to affect your decisions now and for the future? Have you adopted its goals for your own life?

JAMES 4:4
You adulterous people! Do you not know that friendship with the world is enmity with God? Therefore whoever wishes to be a friend of the world makes himself an enemy of God.

The book of Proverbs was designed to help us in "attaining wisdom and discipline; in understanding words of insight; in acquiring a disciplined and prudent life, doing what is right and just and fair; in giving prudence to the simple, knowledge and discretion to the young." As you read through this chapter, write down the verses that are most significant to you in your present circumstances.

VERSE | WHAT TRUTH IT COMMUNICATES | HOW IT IMPACTS MY LIFE

FUTURE PLANS

SAY WHAT?

Observation: What do I see?

SO WHAT?

Interpretation: What does it mean?

NOW WHAT?

Application: How does it apply to me?

THEN WHAT?

Implementation: What do I do?

Do verses thirteen through seventeen mean that we should not plan for the future? There are some who teach that these verses suggest that. A closer examination of this section, however, reveals a very different perspective. James' point is that there are many people who make plans for their future without ever considering God and what He might have planned for them. They have decided what to do after their contract ends, whether to join an activity, or pursue a certain girl/guy - without ever considering what God would have them do. James is making the point here that we do not know what will happen tomorrow, so how can we make plans without God? Instead of making our own plans, we should seek His direction for our lives. Verse seventeen takes it even a step further. To make plans without considering God is not only a bad idea; it is sin. Further, the one who knows that he ought to seek God's direction and doesn't do it, sins. Not to seek what God wants you to do in any decision you make is to sin. What plans are you considering? Have you sought God's direction? Why not ask Him about it!

JAMES 4:17

So whoever knows the right thing to do and fails to do it, for him it is sin.

NEVER GIVE UP!

Do you ever feel like giving up? You have tried your best to make it through, but nothing seems to be changing. There is no end in sight, and you just can't go on any more. If you could just be sure that God was going to move, you could hold on a little longer, but you just can't. Well, if that is how you feel today, or if you know someone who feels like this, this passage will bring comfort. James tells us to be patient. He reminds us that the Lord is coming and we need to keep holding on. His example is the farmer who plants his seed and then waits patiently for the crop to come. Rain comes and goes, sunshine comes and goes, and then the harvest arrives. James says likewise we need to stand firm and not give in to the trials we are facing. God's coming is near, and we must hold on. We must also remember the prophets who were before us. They set an example for us to follow. They faced great trials, but one day the end came. What are you now facing that makes you feel as though you can't go on? Be patient, God is at work, and He will always move on your behalf. Don't give up!! Do you know someone you can share this with?

SAY WHAT?
Why is it so hard to keep on going at times?

SO WHAT?
Who in Scripture faced trials similar to your current sitation?

NOW WHAT?
How can you use their examples to encourage you in your circumstances?

THEN WHAT?
In light of this passage, what personal commitment can you make?

★★★★

JAMES 5:8
You also, be patient. Establish your hearts, for the coming of the Lord is at hand.

MILITARYDEVOTIONAL.COM
@MILITARYDEVOS

SAY WHAT?
Observation: What do I see?

SO WHAT?
Interpretation: What does it mean?

NOW WHAT?
Application: How does it apply to me?

THEN WHAT?
Implementation: What do I do?

Of all the examples available in Scripture, why did James use Elijah as the example of a righteous man and what he could do through prayer? The reason is exciting. James lets us know that the prayer of a righteous man is powerful and effective. Would those two words describe your prayer life? It should encourage you to learn that all we have to do is to be righteous,and we can have a prayer life that is powerful and effective. Elijah is the example. In 1 Kings 18,he was a man who demonstrated boldness,courage, confidence,zeal,valiance,and was empowered by God. All these are characteristics we would expect from a righteous man. However, in chapter nineteen, we see that there were occasions when Elijah was scared, discouraged, lonely, and blind to what God was doing in his life. He doubted God's plan - doubts we would not normally associate with a righteous man. The point James is making is that He was a man,"just like us." James wants us to know that we can be righteous men and have powerful and effective prayers like Elijah. Underline "just like us" to remind you! Go to God and watch Him move on your behalf.

★★★★

JAMES 5:17
Elijah was a man with a nature like ours, and he prayed fervently that it might not rain,and for three years and six months it did not rain on the earth.

FINAL THOUGHTS

Take some time today to review your reading this past month,and reflect on what God has taught you or convicted you about. Use the questions below to help you reflect on what you read,and how it has impacted your life. Spend time praying,asking God to help you make the changes you have identified. Look forward to what God is going to do this next year as you spend time in His Word.

SAY WHAT?

What are some things you learned from this month's reading?

SO WHAT?

What sections in this month's reading had the greatest impact on you? Why?

NOW WHAT?

What surprised you as you read this past month?

THEN WHAT?

How do you want to be different in light of this month's reading?

JAMES 5:16

Therefore, confess your sins to one another and pray for one another, that you may be healed. The prayer of a righteous person has great power as it is working.

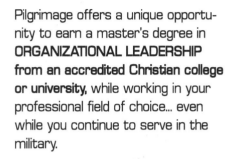

Made in the USA
Lexington, KY
29 August 2018